PIRKE AVOT

A Modern Commentary on Jewish Ethics

Edited and Translated by

LEONARD KRAVITZ and KERRY M. OLITZKY

Foreword by W. GUNTHER PLAUT

UAHC PRESS
NEW YORK, NEW YORK

Library of Congress Cataloging-in-Publication Data

Mishnah. Avot.
    Pirke Avot : a modern commentary on Jewish ethics/edited and
translated by Leonard Kravitz and Kerry M. Olitzky; foreword by
W. Gunther Plaut.
        p. cm.
    Text of Pirke Avot in Hebrew with English translation;
introduction and commentaries in English.
    Includes bibliographical references and index.
    ISBN 0-8074-0480-2 : $12.95
    1. Mishnah. Avot–Commentaries. 2. Judaism–Doctrines.
I. Kravitz, Leonard S. II. Olitzky, Kerry M. III. Mishnah. Avot.
English. 1993. IV. Title.
BM506.A2E5 1993   92-45802
296. 1'23–dc20   CIP

DESIGNER: JACK JAGET
Typesetting: El Ot Ltd.
This book is printed on acid-free paper
Copyright ©1993 by the UAHC Press
Manufactured in the United States of America

Feldman Library

THE FELDMAN LIBRARY FUND was created in 1974 through a gift from the Milton and Sally Feldman Foundation. The Feldman Library Fund, which provides for the publication by the UAHC of selected outstanding Jewish books and texts, memorializes Sally Feldman, who in her lifetime devoted herself to Jewish youth and Jewish learning. Herself an orphan and brought up in an orphanage, she dedicated her efforts to helping Jewish young people get the educational opportunities she had not enjoyed.

In loving memory of my beloved wife Sally
"She was my life, and she is gone;
She was my riches, and I am a pauper."

"Many daughters have done valiantly,
but thou excellest them all."

Milton E. Feldman

Contents

Foreword   *vii*

Acknowledgments   *ix*

Introduction   *xi*

CHAPTER ONE: *At Sinai Moses Received the Torah*   1

The Sadducees and the Pharisees ♦ A Fence around the Torah ♦
From Temple Service to Modern Worship ♦ The World to Come ♦
Judaism as a Missionary Religion ♦ The Jewish Court System

Gleanings: Torah: Reshaping Jewish Memory (Judith Plaskow) ♦
The Pharisaic Revolution (Ellis Rivkin) ♦
The Written and Oral Law (Solomon Freehof) ♦
The Image of Hillel (Abraham Geiger) ♦ The Bible and the Talmud (Leo Baeck)

CHAPTER TWO: *Which Is the Proper Path?*   18

Maimonides' Eight Levels of Charity ♦ Yochanan ben Zakkai and His Times ♦
Repentance ♦ The Evil Eye and the Evil Inclination ♦ Jewish Prayer: Keva and Kavanah

Gleanings: Mitzvot and Ethics (Maurice Eisendrath) ♦
Judaism as an Ethical Religion (Eugene B. Borowitz) ♦
Ethical and Social Commandments (Bernard Bamberger) ♦
The Problem of Evil (Joshua Loth Liebman) ♦ Moral Law (Alexander Guttmann)

CHAPTER THREE: *Know Where You Came From; Know Where You Are Going*   36

From Dust to Dust ♦ The Zohar ♦ God as the Place (Hamakom) ♦
The Yoke of the Torah ♦ Asceticism ♦ The Minyan ♦ Rabbi Akiva and His Time ♦
The Bar Kochba Revolt ♦ Judeo-Christians ♦ God's Omniscience and Free Will

Contents

Gleanings: Revelation and Silence (Lawrence Kushner) ♦
The Command to Study (Leo Baeck) ♦ The Torah of Israel (Judith Plaskow) ♦
Judaism and the Human Species (Abraham Geiger)

CHAPTER FOUR: *Who Is Wise?*   56

Transgression and Sin ♦ Pardes and Paradise ♦ The Rabbinate ♦ To Study to Do ♦
Rabbi Meir and Beruriah ♦ Students and Teachers ♦ Old Age and Learning

Gleanings: Development of Self (Joshua Loth Liebman) ♦
Novelty Seekers (Abba Hillel Silver) ♦ Between God and Man (Hugo Hahn) ♦
Can We Atone? (Abraham J. Feldman) ♦ Why I Believe in the Eternal (Adolph Moses)

CHAPTER FIVE: *The World Was Created by Ten Statements*   76

The Generations of Adam to Noah ♦ At the Twilight of Creation ♦
The Sword Came into the World ♦ Idolatry, Sexual Impropriety, and Bloodshed ♦
Gehinnom or Gan Eden? ♦ The Importance of Debate in Judaism

Gleanings: The Moral Gap (Robert I. Kahn) ♦
Seal the Torah in Their Hearts (Norman J. Cohen) ♦ My Faith (Lily Montagu) ♦
Ethics and Revelation (Isaac Mayer Wise) ♦
The Covenant: Its Purpose (Emil Fackenheim)

CHAPTER SIX: *Whoever Studies the Torah for Its Own Sake Merits Many Things*   97

Wisdom Literature ♦ The Divine Voice ♦ Mount Sinai

Gleanings: The Function of Education (Abba Hillel Silver) ♦ Memory (Anne Roiphe) ♦
The Spiritual Journey (Lawrence Kushner) ♦ The Repair of the World (Judith Plaskow)

Index   111

Authors of the Gleanings
General Subjects and Themes
The Sages of Pirke Avot

Foreword

All of us crave "how-to" books that promise to improve our lives, our skills, our fortunes. We want to know how to lose weight, cook, ski, fix the car and the TV, and–most important–how to be happy and how to relate to others and to ourselves. Some of these books enjoy a brief span of popularity; then they are forgotten. Others are more fortunate; but even these generally cannot hold the attention of their readers for very long. However, all of these volumes have some things in common: There is rarely a line that would adhere to anyone's memory, there is nothing quotable, there is nothing to be carried away as an idea. There are a few exceptions–very few.

This book, *Pirke Avot*, is one of these exceptions. Surprisingly, it has been around for more than fifty generations. Next to the Bible and the *haggadah*, *Pirke Avot* has been our favorite text. Jews used to read it regularly and knew much of it by heart. It is a small collection, which today we might call a mini-anthology for it is composed of pithy sayings of famous rabbis, men like Hillel and Shammai, Gamliel and Tarfon.

Since this is an old collection, it does not deal with modern technology, but it does deal with the essentials of today's life: with fixing broken relationships and–most important–it shows a Jew how to become a better person. In that sense, *Pirke Avot* belongs in the category of a "how-to" book, with quotable aphorisms and memorable metaphors. It teaches us the essentials of what life might be at its best. It is Jewish ethics in the broadest sense.

Originally *Pirke Avot* was part of regular Shabbat readings, and to this day it is reprinted, either whole or in part, in every prayer book. It is studied by Sephardim on Shabbat afternoons from Pesach to Shavuot and by Askenazim all the way to Rosh Hashanah. In the Reform prayer book excerpts of *Pirke Avot* are placed in the opening pages before all the prayers–a tribute to its abiding attraction.

The uninitiated are often surprised that even they are familiar with many or at least some of its sayings and phrases. Here are a few examples:

If not now, when?

Say little and do much.

Keep away from an evil neighbor.

Love work; hate tyranny.

Get yourself a teacher; acquire a friend to study with you.

The day is short.

Render to God what is God's.

Who are wise? Those who learn from other people.

Make a fence around the Torah.

Turn the Torah over and over again, for it contains everything.

The book you have opened will bring you scores of these pearls, and each is accompanied by a comment that will make it even more precious.

After each chapter the authors present us with brief essays and gleanings on a variety of subjects. These are written by eminent scholars and deal with such subjects as *mitzvah*, sin, paradise, study, and, of course, how to come closer to God.

What emerges is a fascinating guide to human and especially Jewish living, a basic compendium of what Jewish ethics is all about. Once you have begun to read the book it will captivate you for, while it is filled with the wisdom of our ancestors, it is as up to date as the latest newspaper or broadcast. Professors Kravitz and Olitzky have put us in their debt by bringing a new glow to this ancient gem. A biblical sage once complained gloomily that "of the making of books there is no end." He would have happily exempted this book from his critique.

If you will set a little time aside *now* and consider these sayings as urgently addressed to you, you will be heeding Hillel's observation: "Do not say I will study when I have leisure. You may never find that leisure." So do it now.

W. Gunther Plaut

Acknowledgments

While the writing of this book can be traced back to a specific point in time, it actually developed over a number of years. During the past eight years, the authors together took their thrice-weekly walks from the New York campus of Hebrew Union College-Jewish Institute of Religion in Greenwich Village to Penn Station and the Port Authority Bus Terminal where we would begin our separate journeys home. During these walks, we discussed many of the challenges of daily life, as reflected through the sayings of the rabbis in *Pirke Avot*. In this way, the hectic New York world was brought under control and the grind of commuting made more civilized. For us, these walks became a bond, epitomizing the instruction of the rabbis; we became colleague, teacher, and friend to each other. Thus, whatever we may offer in these pages is reflected by what *Pirke Avot* has given us in its most profound application.

We especially thank the rabbinic students at HUC-JIR who participated in the course on *Pirke Avot*, fall 1990-1991, taught by Leonard Kravitz. We also express our appreciation to the students in the course "Pirke Avot: Ethics for a New Age," spring 1991, that was part of the Institute for Jewish Studies at Washington Square. This cooperative venture between New York University and HUC-JIR allowed for much of the material to be used in the adult classroom. We also express our appreciation to Alfred Gottschalk, president of HUC-JIR, who continues to provide us with vision and inspiration–allowing us to do what we love most: teach Torah. Our thanks also to Paul Steinberg, vice-president of HUC-JIR, for his constant support and encouragement and to Norman Cohen, dean of the New York school, for being who he is and sharing his essential self with others. To work with these friends and colleagues in the vineyard of *Adonai* is indeed an unparalleled blessing.

Our thanks also go to David P. Kasakove, our editor at UAHC Press, for guiding this publication from its conception to the printed page. He will never know how much we appreciate his untiring labors on our behalf. We also thank those readers who offered valuable suggestions at various stages in the preparation of this manuscript: Robin Eisenberg, Lee J. Kubby, Elaine Merians, Kenneth A. Midlo, Evely Laser Shlensky, Jonathan A. Stein, Robert E. Tornberg, and Paul Yedwab. We also extend our gratitude to Annette Abramson for her sensitive copyediting and to Stuart Benick for overseeing the book's publication. A special word of thanks goes to Bernard M. Zlotowitz, who shared with us his scholarship and keen critical eye. This volume has been immeasurably enhanced by his contributions.

Acknowledgments

Finally, we thank our families. Words alone are inadequate to express our gratitude and love. Whatever words of Torah are contained in these pages are dedicated to them for they truly provide us with the source for them.

Leonard Kravitz
Kerry Olitzky
New York
5743

Introduction

PIRKE AVOT: HOW IT CAME TO BE

Pirke Avot is a Jewish literary classic. It is the most well known of all writings in rabbinic Judaism. *Pirke Avot* is so-named, according to the great commentator Rashi, because it contains the "sayings" of the first "fathers" of Judaism. Originally known simply as *Avot* (literally, "fathers" or "ancestors"), it is one of the sixty-three tractates found in the *Mishnah*, the code of Jewish law compiled in the early third century of the common era.

The word *mishnah* means "the teaching" (from the root שנ ה *shanah*, "to repeat," and then "to teach"). The *Mishnah* is the product of nearly five centuries of development from abut 300 B.C.E. to 200 C.E. It reflects the idea that God's revelation at Sinai included both the Written Law (the Torah) and the Oral Law. This notion of a twofold revelation made possible the development of subsequent forms of Judaism.

Originally, the elements of the Oral Law were developed and transmitted in the form of rabbinic commentaries on individual verses in the Torah. As this proved to be cumbersome, attempts were made to organize the material around specific categories. Using some of the earlier collections, Yehudah Ha-Nasi (Judah the Prince), 135-220 C.E., created the *Mishnah*, organizing the material into six main sections called *sedarim*, "orders," and sixty-three subsections called tractates. The tractates are further divided into chapters and individual statements, each one called a *mishnah*. (The term *mishnah* thus refers to the work as a whole or to its individual statements.)

The six orders of the *Mishnah* are: *Zeraim* ("Seeds"), *Moed* ("Holidays"), *Nashim* ("Women"), *Nezikin* ("Damages"), *Kodashim* ("Hallowed Things"), and *Toharot* ("Ritual Purity"). *Avot* is currently located toward the end of the fourth order of the *Mishnah*, *Nezikin*. Some scholars speculate that *Avot* was originally placed at the end of the sixth order, *Toharot*, as a kind of pinnacle to the entire *Mishnah*.

PIRKE AVOT AND RABBINIC JUDAISM

R. Judah said that in order to become a pious person [a Chasid], one must fulfill the words of [the entire section of the *Mishnah* called] *Nezikin*. Raba [and others say, Rabina] said, [the pious person must do] everything in the Tractate [*Pirke*] *Avot*; and [still] others say [that person has to fulfill all of the obligations in the Tractate] *Berachot*.

(B. Talmud, *Baba Kamma* 30a)

Unlike the other tractates in the *Mishnah*, *Avot* is made up of storylike material and maxims known as *aggadah*. It contains no *halachah*, binding legal material. Yet, it is supremely important because it justifies the authority of the rabbis, something the Bible could not do. It traces (in the first two chapters) the transmission of Jewish tradition from the revelation at Sinai through the leading rabbis of the generation that led the community following the destruction of the Second Temple. This unbroken chain of tradition provides a foundation for the *Mishnah* itself.

The claim of the divine origin of this Oral Law carried with it the claim of a divine sanction for those who taught that law and a justification, therefore, of the new religious figure, the rabbi, who would take over from the older figures of prophet and priest. That new role required an innovative link to the past.

The statements attributed to the rabbis in *Pirke Avot* express the basic concerns and central ideas that occupied the rabbis. Study becomes a religious act; the Torah becomes a text to be constantly studied; the reflections of past Torah study become an important link from one generation to the next; and Torah and its commentary become the literature that mirrors and shapes all Jewish experience.

The academies we read about were born out of Torah study. The hierarchy in society was based on learning: teacher, associate, and student. Those outside the academy were deemed ignorant. Any observances of the *mitzvah* system outside of the academy system had no efficacy. Bereft of the methods of rabbinic Judaism, only available in the academy, one cannot gain God's favor. Thus, according to rabbinic Judaism in *Pirke Avot*, the biblical text, standing alone, cannot provide salvation for the individual; only the interpretations and instructions of the rabbis give us eternal life.

In *Pirke Avot*, unlike most other literature of the period, the writers generally present their teachings without a proof-text from the Bible. These maxims or proverbs remind us of the Book of Proverbs, which the rabbis were probably trying to mimic as they created an entirely new literature. This confirms the importance of that new literature as an effort to wrestle away from the priests the mantle of leadership in the Jewish community.

Here we are presented with a paradox: While the maxims could stand alone without the biblical text (thereby disregarding the notion of revelation), the very beginning of *Pirke Avot* mentions Sinai where the revelation of the Torah was to have taken place. Ovadiah of Bartinoro, commentator to the *Mishnah*, seems to resolve that paradox by noting that other nations have written books of ethics that have their source in the human mind, but this book derives from Sinai and thus has its source in the Divine.

PIRKE AVOT AND JEWISH LIFE

Because of its popularity and central importance, *Avot* has been reprinted more often than any other rabbinic text. Both traditional and contemporary prayer books include *Avot* either in its entirety or with selected passages. *Avot* was first included with the talmudic tractate called *Berachot* ("Blessings") in *Seder Rav Amram*, the prayer book of Amram Gaon (ca. 875 C.E.); it has been included in the prayer book ever since. We first learn that *Pirke Avot* is to be studied on the Sabbath after the afternoon service in *Ha-Manhig* (ca. 1204), a book about synagogue practices by Abraham ben Nathan Ha-Yarchi. It became popular to read *Avot* in the Babylonian academies and synagogues on the Sabbath as a part of the liturgy, a custom that may even be pre-Gaonic. Throughout Jewish history, different communities adopted different practices for the reading and studying of *Pirke Avot*. Some communities studied *Pirke Avot* during the entire winter and summer; some studied it from Pesach to Sukot. Still others limited its study to the period when the Book of Exodus was read and only then from the Sabbath when *Parashat Yitro* (containing the Ten Commandments) was read to the Sabbath when the last portion of Exodus was read. Most Ashkenazic communities today read *Pirke Avot* chapter by chapter from the Sabbath after Pesach to the Sabbath before Shavuot; then they read two chapters each Sabbath from Shavuot to Rosh Hashanah. This allows time for the tractate to be read three times each year. The Sephardic tradition remains faithful to the early practices of reading it only from Pesach to Shavuot.

ABOUT THIS COMMENTARY

This new translation with traditional commentary, in essence, offers the reader an introduction to modern Judaism, as well as hands-on study of a classic Jewish text. The text is presented in its Hebrew original, based on the Vilna edition of the Talmud, alongside an inclusive translation that reflects the idioms of both rabbinic Hebrew and modern English. The rabbis are identified and the text is explored in the familiar traditional commentary format, using the insights of modern Jewish life. Each chapter concludes with brief essays, which focus on salient themes, followed by gleanings from liberal thinkers who offer insights into Jewish theology.

Although *Pirke Avot* lacks a traditional commentary, or *gemara*, a kind of commentary was developed between the eighth and ninth centuries that was known as *Avot de-Rabbi Natan*, "The Fathers According to Rabbi Nathan." [Hereafter this work will be cited as ARN.] ARN reflects scattered talmudic issues in a sermonic manner. One might consider ARN as a minor tractate of the Talmud that was not included in its final compilation. Thus, it is often printed at the end of *Nezikin* in order to approximate a *gemara* on *Avot*.

In addition to ARN, the traditional commentary is based on the works of the following scholars:

Rashi (1040-1105), who was born in Troyes, France, and lived in Worms, Germany, is considered a commentator par excellence. He elucidated the Bible and the Talmud and commented on *Pirke Avot*, as he did on all other talmudic tractates. Generally, his commentary is a straightforward exposition of the terms presented.

Maimonides (1135-1204), the great Jewish philosopher, who also wrote a commentary on the *Mishnah*, lived in Cordoba until 1148, wandering from place to place in Spain with his family for twelve years. He then lived in Fez (1160-1165) before moving to Cairo (then known as Fostat) where he spent the remainder of his life (1165-1204). For Maimonides, *Pirke Avot* is an ethical manual directed to those who were to be judges. Therefore, his commentary is a philosophical reading of the text.

Ovadiah ben Abraham Bartinoro, born in the second half of the fifteenth century in the town in Italy that gave him his name, is probably the most widely accepted commentator on the entire *Mishnah*. He wrote his commentary in Jerusalem where he was head of the community. His commentary is in essence a selection and clear exposition of the best of Rashi and Maimonides.

Yom Tov Lipman Heller (1579-1654) was a commentator whose work shows clear originality. Born in Wallerstein, Bavaria, Heller lived in Prague from 1597 to 1625, moved to Vienna (1625-1627), and returned to Prague (1627-1631). He spent the remainder of his life in Cracow, Poland (1631-1654). His commentary on the *Mishnah* is printed in editions that also contain Bartinoro's insights. He has a straightforward understanding of the text, brought to light in the context of his mastery of general and Jewish knowledge. Heller's commentaries on *Pirke Avot* reflect his involvement in controversies dealing with problems of the Jewish community in his day.

It is customary to begin the study of *Pirke Avot* with *Sanhedrin* 10:1.

> Every Israelite has a portion in the world to come, as it is stated [in Scripture]: "Your people shall be all righteous, they shall inherit the land forever; the branch of My planting, the work of My hands, wherein I glory." [Isa. 60:21]

This passage in *Sanhedrin*, which was used to establish the boundaries of heresy, continues further in the Talmud to indicate which Jew, as a result of personal beliefs, will *not* have a portion in the world to come.

> Rabbi Chananya, son of Akashya, said, "The Holy One of blessing wished to convey merit upon Israel; therefore God multiplied the Torah and commandments for them, as it is stated [in Scripture]: *Adonai* was pleased, for divine righteousness' sake, to make the teaching great and glorious." [Isa. 42:21]

The biblical proof-text is interpreted to support Rabbi Chananya's point: "*Adonai* wanted to make Israel righteous; so God magnified the Torah and made it glorious."

CHAPTER ONE

At Sinai Moses Received the Torah

1:1 At Sinai Moses received the Torah and handed it over to Joshua who handed it over to the elders who handed it over to the prophets who in turn handed it over to the men of the Great Assembly. The latter said three things: Be deliberate in judgment, raise up many disciples, and make a fence around the Torah.

א:א מֹשֶׁה קִבֵּל תּוֹרָה מִסִּינַי וּמְסָרָהּ לִיהוֹשֻׁעַ וִיהוֹשֻׁעַ לִזְקֵנִים וּזְקֵנִים לִנְבִיאִים וּנְבִיאִים מְסָרוּהָ לְאַנְשֵׁי כְנֶסֶת הַגְּדוֹלָה. הֵם אָמְרוּ שְׁלֹשָׁה דְבָרִים הֱווּ מְתוּנִים בַּדִּין וְהַעֲמִידוּ תַלְמִידִים הַרְבֵּה וַעֲשׂוּ סְיָג לַתּוֹרָה:

At Sinai Moses received the Torah. The origins of the Jewish people and Torah come from Sinai, where former slaves were given freedom by binding themselves to the Law. Moses is presented as the Lawgiver of that Torah in its broadest sense. Moses, however, is mortal and eventually dies. Therefore, before his death, Moses must hand over what he has received to his disciple Joshua who in turn will hand it over to a group of elders.

The foundation stone for rabbinic authority begins with this first מִשְׁנָה *mishnah* and describes the chain of tradition, which stretches from Moses to Judah the Prince (the rabbi who compiled the *Mishnah*). Thus the *Mishnah*, the product of the rabbis, those who argued that the Oral Law had been given at Sinai together with the Written Law, is inseparably linked to Moses who first received the Torah.

And handed it over to Joshua. Judaism depends on history, as played out through the life of the Jewish people. The very nature of history is a function of each generation passing on to the next generation what it has received from a prior generation. In rabbinic literature, Joshua is regarded as a faithful and humble man of great wisdom and discernment.

Elders. According to ARN and the four commentators under study (Rashi, Maimonides, Bartinoro, and Heller), the elders to whom Joshua transmitted the Torah were not the elders whom Moses had appointed in Numbers 11:16; rather, these elders lived in the time of Joshua.

Prophets. By suggesting in this *mishnah* that the initial revelation was eventually transmitted to the prophets, the rabbis who prepared this *mishnah* are claiming that whatever the later prophets were to discover was also given at Sinai.

Men of the Great Assembly. Not a great deal is known about the Great Assembly (or, alternatively, the Great Synagogue). ARN, Rashi, and Bartinoro suggest that the Great Assembly was so named because it returned the Torah to its original purity. It stems from the Persian period and represents for the rabbis the transition between the prophets and themselves. Ezra is identified by the rabbis as the leader of the men of the Great Assembly and is traditionally linked to Nehemiah 8-10. By including the men of the Great Assembly in the chain of tradition, the rabbis found a paradigm for their own work. Just as the men of the Great Assembly had to explain the meaning of Torah, the rabbis would also interpret what that Torah meant generation by generation. While they are credited with certain liturgical institutions, some modern scholars believe the entire institution is legendary.

Be deliberate in judgment. If Torah were to become the measuring rod of all life, as the rabbis wanted it to be, deliberate reflection on the demands of the past and the problems of the present would be required.

Raise up many disciples. Unlike the priesthood, which was generally dependent on ancestry, the rabbis needed many minds and therefore many disciples. Thus, they created a hierarchy of learning that any man (and, in modern times, any woman) could enter as long as one was willing to devote oneself to study. Never a mere professional body of knowledge, Torah study is open to every Jew.

Fence around the Torah. The rabbis used the metaphor of a fence around the Torah as a means of protecting the essence of Torah in the midst of a proliferation of new demands. The insights into the Law that they had already developed would need protection, even as they knew the Torah would continue to need to grow if the Jewish community was to survive.

1:2 Simon the Righteous was one of the last of the Great Assembly. His motto was: "The world stands on three things–the Torah, the [Temple] service, and loving acts of kindness."

אːב שִׁמְעוֹן הַצַּדִּיק הָיָה מִשְּׁיָרֵי כְנֶסֶת הַגְּדוֹלָה. הוּא הָיָה אוֹמֵר עַל שְׁלֹשָׁה דְבָרִים הָעוֹלָם עוֹמֵד עַל הַתּוֹרָה וְעַל הָעֲבוֹדָה וְעַל גְּמִילוּת חֲסָדִים:

Simon the Righteous [alternatively, Simeon the Just]. He was a High Priest, but his precise identity is not clear. He was either Simeon I (310-291 or 300-270 B.C.E.), son of Onias I, or Simeon II (219-199 B.C.E.), son of Onias II. He was termed "the Righteous" or "the Just" (the Hebrew term הַצַּדִּיק *hatzadik* allows for either translation) because of his piety, as well as the concern and kindness he showed to his people. Many stories are told about him, including one that does not conform to the dates assigned his life. It is said that he greeted Alexander the Great when he marched through Palestine in 333 B.C.E. Simon is the first in the chain of scholars, descending to Hillel and Shammai. He is also mentioned as one of the survivors of the Great Assembly–acting as a pivotal character for the transition of the authority from the priests to the rabbis. The reader finds in Simon's words the essential assumptions of Judaism.

His motto. The editor of *Pirke Avot* uses the formula "he used to say" to introduce the teachings of a particular teacher. Bartinoro translates it as "his motto" because the individual rabbi was known to have taught it often to his students.

The world stands on three things. Rashi and Maimonides differ on their understanding of the meaning of "the world stands." For Rashi, the world would not have come into being were it not for these three things. For Maimonides, proper human existence could not be maintained if it were not for these three things.

The Torah: The written *and* oral Torah is implied, with emphasis on the Oral Law.

The [Temple] service. In Simon's day, worship was centered in the Temple cult. From the basic elements of that worship, the synagogue and its liturgy developed. In turn, this model affected the religious development of Western society.

Loving acts of kindness. Religious commitment to God was to be manifested in one's behavior directed toward other persons. When an individual performed these acts of kindness, like giving to the poor, helping the widowed and the orphaned, and looking after the newcomer to a community, that person brought himself closer to God.

1:3 Antigonos of Socho received [the Tradition] from Simon the Righteous. His motto was: "Don't be like those who would serve a master on the condition that they would receive a reward. Rather, be like those who would serve without that condition. Even so, let the fear of Heaven be upon you."

א:ג אַנְטִיגְנוֹס אִישׁ סוֹכוֹ קִבֵּל מִשִּׁמְעוֹן הַצַּדִּיק. הוּא הָיָה אוֹמֵר אַל תִּהְיוּ כַּעֲבָדִים הַמְשַׁמְּשִׁין אֶת הָרַב עַל מְנָת לְקַבֵּל פְּרָס אֶלָּא הֱווּ כַּעֲבָדִים הַמְשַׁמְּשִׁין אֶת הָרַב שֶׁלֹּא עַל מְנָת לְקַבֵּל פְּרָס וִיהִי מוֹרָא שָׁמַיִם עֲלֵיכֶם:

Antigonos of Socho. Antigonos is a Greek name for a Jewish scholar who lived in the early part of the second century B.C.E. His name reflects the impact of Hellenism on the Jewish people. Even under Roman rule, Greek ideas and names formed part of the culture of the area. This is the only statement of Antigonos that has been preserved. For rabbinic Judaism, reward and punishment are part of the divine scheme. If one does not receive a reward for goodness in this life, then certainly that person can expect to receive it in the next life, in the world to come. Still, piety may come from a person's simple goodness and not in anticipation of a divine reward.

Fear of Heaven. The phrase "fear of Heaven" is understood as reverence for God. Although the calculation of gain and loss should not determine the ethical act, nevertheless, all human acts are played out before God.

1:4 Yose ben Yoezer of Zeredah and Yose ben Yochanan of Jerusalem received [the Tradition] from them. Yose ben Yoezer said, "Let your house be a meeting place for the wise; sit humbly at their feet; and, with thirst, drink in their words."

אַ:ד יוֹסֵי בֶּן יוֹעֶזֶר אִישׁ צְרֵדָה וְיוֹסֵי בֶּן יוֹחָנָן אִישׁ יְרוּשָׁלַיִם קִבְּלוּ מֵהֶם. יוֹסֵי בֶּן יוֹעֶזֶר אִישׁ צְרֵדָה אוֹמֵר יְהִי בֵיתְךָ בֵּית וַעַד לַחֲכָמִים וֶהֱוֵי מִתְאַבֵּק בַּעֲפַר רַגְלֵיהֶם וֶהֱוֵי שׁוֹתֶה בְצָמָא אֶת דִּבְרֵיהֶם:

Yose ben Yoezer and Yose ben Yochanan: Yose was probably a shortened form of the name Yosef, Joseph. The two Yoses are the first in the series of זוגות *zugot*, "pairs" of scholars, who headed the Sanhedrin for about 150 years until the beginning of the common era. The Sandhedrin was the central authority in Palestine during the Roman period. While it had political, religious, and judicial functions, it originated before the destruction of the Temple and existed until the patriarchate was abolished in approximately 425 C.E. Yose ben Yoezer was the נָשִׂיא *nasi*, the "head" of the Sanhedrin; Yose ben Yochanan was the אַב בֵּית דִּין *av bet din*, the "head of the court of law." It is not clear what was the functional difference between these two roles.

Zeredah. The town from whence Yose ben Yoezer came is mentioned in I Kings 11:26.

Let your house be a meeting place. Maimonides and Bartinoro suggest that having your house be a meeting place means that the scholars themselves will look at your house as the "perfect" place for study and discussion.

Sit humbly at their feet. Literally, "be covered by the dust of their feet." Rashi understands the phrase metaphorically, "serve them [the sages]." Bartinoro takes the phrase more literally: "walk after them [the sages]." He explains that, by walking after them, you will be covered by their dust. Bartinoro further explains that, in schools of old, a teacher sat on a bench while the students sat on the ground at his feet.

1:5 Yose ben Yochanan of Jerusalem said, "Let your house be open wide; let the poor be members of your household; and don't talk to your wife too much." They said that about his own wife, how much the more another man's wife. From this [statement] other sages said, "When a man talks too much to his wife, he causes evil to himself, disregards the words of the Torah, and in the end will inherit Gehinnom."

אַ:ה יוֹסֵי בֶּן יוֹחָנָן אִישׁ יְרוּשָׁלַיִם אוֹמֵר יְהִי בֵיתְךָ פָּתוּחַ לִרְוָחָה וְיִהְיוּ עֲנִיִּים בְּנֵי בֵיתֶךָ וְאַל תַּרְבֶּה שִׂיחָה עִם הָאִשָּׁה בְּאִשְׁתּוֹ אָמְרוּ קַל וָחֹמֶר בְּאֵשֶׁת חֲבֵרוֹ. מִכָּאן אָמְרוּ חֲכָמִים כָּל הַמַּרְבֶּה שִׂיחָה עִם הָאִשָּׁה גּוֹרֵם רָעָה לְעַצְמוֹ וּבוֹטֵל מִדִּבְרֵי תוֹרָה וְסוֹפוֹ יוֹרֵשׁ גֵּיהִנֹּם:

Let your house be open wide. In order to emulate Abraham's model, the *Mishnah* ordained hospitality on the part of each Jew. This was the way of dealing with the Jewish poor.

Don't talk to your wife too much. However we understand the phrase about talking to one's wife, we modern Jews reject the premise entirely. It seems to have been a problem for medieval Jewry as well. Rashi tries to limit this comment to the menstruant wife, thereby narrowing the category. The reader should remember that Rashi's own daughters were learned. Maimonides, on the other hand, follows his own past pattern of stressing reason over emotion and argues that conversation with women is a euphemism for sexual relations. Therefore, such urges should be controlled.

Gehinnom: Gehinnom is the rabbinic term for hell. It originally referred to a place near Jerusalem called "the valley of Hinnom" or "the valley of Ben Hinnom." (Josh. 15:8) There human sacrifices were offered to Molech. (II Kings 23:10)

1:6 Joshua ben Perachyah and Nittai of Arbel received [the Tradition] from them. Joshua ben Perachyah said, "Get yourself a teacher, find someone to study with, and judge everyone favorably."

א:ו יְהוֹשֻׁעַ בֶּן פְּרַחְיָה וְנִתַּאי הָאַרְבֵּלִי קִבְּלוּ מֵהֶם. יְהוֹשֻׁעַ בֶּן פְּרַחְיָה אוֹמֵר עֲשֵׂה לְךָ רַב וּקְנֵה לְךָ חָבֵר וֶהֱוֵי דָן אֶת כָּל הָאָדָם לְכַף זְכוּת:

Joshua [Yehoshua] ben Perachyah and Nittai of Arbel. One of the *zugot,* the "pairs" of scholars, they lived in the second century B.C.E. and were pupils of Yose ben Yoezer of Zeredah and Yose ben Yochanan of Jerusalem. Joshua served as *nasi* of the Sanhedrin while Nittai served as *av bet din.* Little is really known of Nittai's teaching.

Get yourself a teacher. Jewish study is both a sacred act and a religious obligation.

Find someone to study with. Maimonides quotes the rabbinic adage, "Either companionship or death" (B. Talmud, *Taanit* 23a) and speaks of the importance of friendship.

Judge everyone favorably. The last clause, literally, "judge everything in the pan of justice" presents the reader with the image of two scales of balance, a familiar image found in many cultures. The rabbi warns us against prejudging people.

1:7 Nittai of Arbel said, "Keep your distance from an evil neighbor; don't be the buddy of a wicked person; and don't give up on [the reality of] retribution."

א:ז נִתַּאי הָאַרְבֵּלִי אוֹמֵר הַרְחֵק מִשָּׁכֵן רָע וְאַל תִּתְחַבֵּר לְרָשָׁע וְאַל תִּתְיָאֵשׁ מִן הַפֻּרְעָנוּת:

Arbel. A town north of Tiberias in the Lower Galilee is mentioned in Hosea 10:14 as Bet Arbel.

Keep your distance. The commentators fear the contagion of evil; even good people may be affected by the acts of those who are bad. Bartinoro gives a homely example: A person who visits a tannery will be affected by the odors of the place. Likewise, those who come too close to evil will be ill-affected by it.

Don't be the buddy. Maimonides and Bartinoro see a connection between befriending a wicked person and retribution. When an individual becomes friendly with wicked people, the individual thinks that wicked people seem to get away with their crimes. Thus, that individual might want to emulate their actions. Such a person should be warned: The wicked will be punished in the end. If one follows their ways, that one, too, will be punished.

Don't give up on [the reality of] retribution: Retribution remains a problem in religious thinking. The rabbis try to convince us that a system of reward and punishment functions in this world and the next. However, we moderns generally reject such a notion. Rather, one should avoid evil for it is wrong and do good for it is right. By doing evil things, one degrades oneself and shames loved ones. By doing right, one enhances self and brings honor to loved ones.

1:8 Judah ben Tabbai and Shimon ben Shetach received [the Tradition] from them. Judah ben Tabbai said, "[When you are a judge] don't play the advocate's role. When the litigants stand before you, let them appear to you equally culpable. When they leave you, having accepted judgment, let them look equally blameless to you."

א:ח יְהוּדָה בֶן טַבַּאי וְשִׁמְעוֹן בֶּן שָׁטַח קִבְּלוּ מֵהֶם. יְהוּדָה בֶן טַבַּאי אוֹמֵר אַל תַּעַשׂ עַצְמְךָ כְּעוֹרְכֵי הַדַּיָּנִין וּכְשֶׁיִּהְיוּ בַּעֲלֵי הַדִּין עוֹמְדִים לְפָנֶיךָ יִהְיוּ בְּעֵינֶיךָ כִּרְשָׁעִים וּכְשֶׁנִּפְטָרִים מִלְּפָנֶיךָ יִהְיוּ בְעֵינֶיךָ כְּזַכָּאִין כְּשֶׁקִּבְּלוּ עֲלֵיהֶם אֶת הַדִּין:

Judah [Yehudah] ben Tabbai and Shimon ben Shetach. Judah ben Tabbai, one of the early *zugot*, the "pairs," lived in the first century B.C.E. In Jerusalem, he was a disciple of Joshua ben Perachyah and Nittai of Arbel. One tradition holds that he was *nasi* of the Sanhedrin and Shimon ben Shetach was *av bet din*. A second tradition reverses the roles. According to the Torah, Jethro, Moses' father-in-law, originated the Jewish court system. When Jethro saw Moses' attempt to be the only judge of the Israelite people, Jethro warned him of the danger of exhaustion and advised him to get help in judging from others among the people, who were capable, God-fearing, and trustworthy of spurning ill-gotten gains. (Exod. 18:21) Judah ben Tabbai's statement updates Jethro's advice in a rabbinic idiom.

1:9 Shimon ben Shetach said, "Ask many questions of the witnesses, but be very careful what you say [to them], lest from your words, they [the witnesses] learn to perjure [themselves]."

א:ט שִׁמְעוֹן בֶּן שָׁטַח אוֹמֵר הֱוֵי מַרְבֶּה לַחְקוֹר אֶת הָעֵדִים וֶהֱוֵי זָהִיר בִּדְבָרֶיךָ שֶׁמָּא מִתּוֹכָם יִלְמְדוּ לְשַׁקֵּר:

Shimon ben Shetach. Both Judah ben Tabbai and Shimon ben Shetach were caught up in the controversies between the Sadducees and the Pharisees. Judah fled to Alexandria when the Sadducees were dominant in the reign of King Alexander Yannai (103-76 B.C.E.). Shimon helped the Pharisees become dominant during the reign of Queen Salome Alexandra (76-63 B.C.E.), who was Yannai's widow and Shimon's sister.

It seems that Shimon acted as a judge in civil and criminal matters. The *Mishnah* (*Sanhedrin* 6:4) mentions him specifically in connection with the execution of witches.

Ask many questions. Rashi and Bartinoro understand Shimon's caution to refer to the kind of leading questions that will suggest to the witness the kind of answer one thinks the judge wants, rather than the true answer.

1:10 Shemayah and Avtalyon received [the Tradition] from them. Shemaya said, "Love labor, hate [the abuse of] power, and don't try to become the familiar friend of government."

א:י שְׁמַעְיָה וְאַבְטַלְיוֹן קִבְּלוּ מֵהֶם. שְׁמַעְיָה אוֹמֵר אֱהַב אֶת הַמְּלָאכָה וּשְׂנָא אֶת הָרַבָּנוּת וְאַל תִּתְוַדַּע לָרָשׁוּת:

Shemayah and Avtalyon: According to the Tradition, which Bartinoro reports, they were converts. Bartinoro also tells us about another tradition: According to the folk etymology of his name, Avtalyon reflected his role as protector of orphans since טַלְיָא *talya* means "young" in Aramaic and אָב *av* means "father" in both Hebrew and Aramaic.

Love labor. For both Rashi and Bartinoro (and the Tradition) any honest work is better than none. Rashi quotes the rabbinic adage that it is better to flay carcasses in the marketplace than to claim that even such labor is beneath one's dignity. (B. Talmud, *Pesachim* 113a) Quoting another rabbinic adage that idleness leads to stupidity, Bartinoro argues that, even if a person were wealthy, the person should work. (*Mishnah Ketubot* 5:5)

Hate [the abuse of] power. Rashi points out that the mantle of authority buries those covered by it. Maimonides warns against the temptations of power by quoting the rabbinic adage that, when one is appointed an official over a congregation on earth, that one may well be viewed as a sinner in Heaven! Even so, Maimonides served as the chief rabbi of his own community and his authority was accepted in much of his world.

The word רַבָּנוּת *rabbanut*, here translated as "[the abuse of] power," is in modern Hebrew the word for the "rabbinate"!

Don't try to become the familiar friend of government. From Roman times in Palestine to the beginning of the modern era, wherever Jews lived–in Europe, in Africa, or in Asia–the Jewish community regarded itself and was looked upon by others as a separate entity. That separate status was reinforced by both Jewish law and civil law, depending on the country in which the Jews lived. Although the two communities were separate, they did interact.

Therefore, it was necessary for the Jewish community to select a representative (later called the שְׁתַּדְלָן *shtadlan* in Eastern Europe) to deal directly with the non-Jewish authorities. The last clause of this *mishnah* is specifically directed to those representatives, urging them to be cautious in their dealings. Rashi quotes the statement of Rabban Gamliel (*Avot* 2:3) who urged caution in dealing with the government, saying that, when the government had dealings with the Jewish leaders, it was for the government's own benefit and not for the benefit of those Jewish leaders or the Jewish community.

1:11 Avtalyon said, "Sages, watch your words, lest you be punished by exile to a place of bad water, and lest your students, who follow after you, drink and die and, as a result, cause the name of Heaven to be profaned."

א:יא אַבְטַלְיוֹן אוֹמֵר חֲכָמִים הִזָּהֲרוּ בְּדִבְרֵיכֶם שֶׁמָּא תָחוּבוּ חוֹבַת גָּלוּת וְתִגְלוּ לִמְקוֹם מַיִם הָרָעִים וְיִשְׁתּוּ הַתַּלְמִידִים הַבָּאִים אַחֲרֵיכֶם וְיָמוּתוּ וְנִמְצָא שֵׁם שָׁמַיִם מִתְחַלֵּל:

Watch your words. According to Rashi, the sages should take special care when passing on traditions. Maimonides believes that the sages should exercise caution in speaking to the masses: Language that could be misinterpreted should not be used.

Bad water. Rashi believes that this metaphor refers to unfit students. For Maimonides, bad water is a euphemism for heresy. Bartinoro argues that the persistence of erroneous ideas is itself the profanation of God.

1:12 Hillel and Shammai received [the Tradition] from them. Hillel said, "Be one of Aaron's students, loving peace and pursuing it, loving people and bringing them to the Torah."

א:יב הִלֵּל וְשַׁמַּאי קִבְּלוּ מֵהֶם. הִלֵּל אוֹמֵר הֱוֵי מִתַּלְמִידָיו שֶׁל אַהֲרֹן אוֹהֵב שָׁלוֹם וְרוֹדֵף שָׁלוֹם אוֹהֵב אֶת הַבְּרִיּוֹת וּמְקָרְבָן לַתּוֹרָה:

Hillel and Shammai. They were the last of the *zugot,* the "pairs." Hillel was the president of the Sanhedrin; Shammai was the chief of the court of law. Hillel was probably the most eminent of all the sages. He was the very exemplar of the rabbinate. His life reflected the key values of rabbinic Judaism: study, devotion, and kindness. According to one tradition, Hillel, like Moses, lived for 120 years. It is also said that he came to Jerusalem from Babylonia when he was forty, spent the next forty years in study, and spent the following forty years as the leading scholar of his age. It may well be that his active period extended from 30 B.C.E. to 10 C.E. He was the first to establish a method of scriptural interpretation, which has come to be called the "seven rules of Hillel." Hillel's disciples became known as the house or school of Hillel. Their interpretations were opposed by the disciples of Shammai, the house or school of Shammai. Hillel's rulings tended to be more flexible than those of Shammai. The statement by Hillel in this *mishnah* follows his formulation of the Golden Rule: "What you would hate, don't do to someone else: that is the entire Torah, the rest is commentary, go and learn it." (B. Talmud, *Shabbat* 31a)

Be one of Aaron's students. Aaron's pursuit of peace was suggested in the story of the Golden Calf. In this incident Aaron actually went along with the people's desire for a concrete symbol of leadership and participated in its fabrication, hoping that the people would not do anything more blasphemous. He felt that in the interim Moses would return and restore order.

Loving peace...and people. Rashi gives two examples of Aaron's work as a peacemaker. In the first example, Aaron saw two men quarrel and depart. Aaron resolved the conflict by going first to the one and then to the other, saying to each that the other regretted the breach between them. As a result, the two would be brought together. In the second example, it seems that an irascible husband refused to provide his wife her conjugal rights until and unless she would spit in Aaron's eye. Hearing of it, Aaron went to the wife and claimed that he had an eye condition that required spittle to cure it. Thus the poor wife would be able to obey her husband's contemptible request!

Bringing them to the Torah. This comment raises the issue of conversion to Judaism. Although it may surprise some modern Jews, rabbinic Judaism was somewhat of a missionary religion. According to the rabbis, Abraham and Sarah were the first to bring non-Jews "beneath the shelter of the Divine Presence."

1:13 He used to say, "A name made great is a name destroyed; one who does not increase decreases; one who will not study deserves to die: one who makes [illicit] use of the crown will perish."

אי׳יג הוּא הָיָה אוֹמֵר נְגִיד שְׁמָא אֲבַד שְׁמֵהּ וּדְלָא מוֹסִיף יָסֵף וּדְלָא יַלִּיף קְטָלָא חַיָּב וּדְאִשְׁתַּמֵּשׁ בְּתַגָּא חֲלָף:

There is a stylistic difference in the sayings reported in the name of Hillel and those reported in the names of the other sages mentioned up until this point in the text. Three statements rather than the usual one per sage have been reported in his name. Other statements will be reported in Hillel's name in the next chapter as well. This may suggest some reworking of the material by the editor of *Pirke Avot*; it also emphasizes the preeminent status of Hillel.

He used to say. Since Hillel's statement was made in Aramaic, it seems to reflect that it was some kind of well-accepted proverb. Its proverbial quality suggests the possibility that Hillel adopted a well-established proverb as one of his own mottos.

One who does not increase. Rashi takes this phrase to refer to study time from the evening to the daytime. For Bartinoro, it is learning that is lost when it is not increased.

One who will not study. Rashi understands the third clause as "one who will not *teach* deserves to die." That drastic punishment is understood by Maimonides as applicable only to the one who will not study at all.

One who makes [illicit] use of the crown. The "crown" is taken by the commentators to refer to the crown of Torah. Maimonides contends that, if one makes a living by the teaching of the Torah, it is an illicit use of the crown. Such a comment reflects the ideal that Torah study and teaching should be unencumbered by financial gain or loss. Unlike those in the modern period, the rabbis who lived in the rabbinic period and the Middle Ages had vocations other than teaching. For example, Rashi was a vintner and Maimonides was a physician.

The word in Aramaic for "crown," תָּגָא *taga*, suggests another possibility. It may refer to the "toga," the Roman form of dress. If that was what was meant, then Hillel's words can be understood as a warning against mimicking Roman customs. For Jews in the past, as well as for some Jews in the present, the wearing of garments worn by those in the larger society were proscribed. The challenge that remains is a determination concerning appropriate "Jewish garments."

1.14   He used to say, "If I am not for myself, who will be for me? And, if I am for myself alone, then what am I? And, if not now, when?"

אי:יד   הוּא הָיָה אוֹמֵר אִם אֵין אֲנִי לִי מִי לִי וּכְשֶׁאֲנִי לְעַצְמִי מָה אֲנִי וְאִם לֹא עַכְשָׁו אֵימָתַי:

If I am not for myself. Rashi tells us that the first clause refers to the performance of מִצְוֹת *mitzvot*. Maimonides believes it refers to the direction of the soul to a higher reality. Bartinoro understands it to mean the general sense of acquiring virtue.

And, if I am for myself alone. This second clause is taken by Bartinoro as guidance for the individual, telling him that there is always more in life to be accomplished. And so, each day presents us with a new challenge. We also view this statement as an instruction to us not to restrict our concerns for social justice to members of the Jewish community. We are obligated to transcend our particularism and help all in our community who require assistance.

And, if not now, when? Rashi claims that this third clause refers to this world, the place for מִצְוָה *mitzvah* performance. Maimonides takes that clause to refer to the importance of establishing the proper patterns of living when one is young because, on self-reflection, he senses a resistance to change when one is old.

1:15   Shammai said, "Make your Torah [study] a habit; say little, but do much; and greet every person cheerfully."

אי:טו   שַׁמַּאי אוֹמֵר עֲשֵׂה תוֹרָתְךָ קֶבַע אֱמוֹר מְעַט וַעֲשֵׂה הַרְבֵּה וֶהֱוֵי מְקַבֵּל אֶת כָּל הָאָדָם בְּסֵבֶר פָּנִים יָפוֹת:

Make your Torah [study]. Since the first three Hebrew words in Shammai's statement, עֲשֵׂה תוֹרָתְךָ קֶבַע *aseh toratcha keva*, can be translated differently, they can also, therefore, be interpreted differently. קֶבַע *keva* is the key word; it means "fixed" or "set thing." For Rashi, the words mean "Set a fixed time for Torah study." For Maimonides, "Let the study of Torah be the one fixed thing [in your life; everything else should be secondary]." Bartinoro follows Maimonides and interprets it as "Make Torah your main occupation [and, only when you are exhausted from your studies, occupy yourself with something else]."

Say little. As an example of saying little but doing much, Bartinoro cites Genesis 18:4, 5 in which Abraham provided a lordly meal for the three angels that visited him when he had initially promised only a piece of bread.

Greet every person. While Shammai has a reputation as a difficult person, his statement seems to contradict this reputation. The Talmud even records the saying "one should always be as humble as Hillel rather than as overbearing as Shammai." (B. Talmud, *Shabbat* 30b)

1:16 Rabban Gamliel said, "Get yourself a teacher; avoid doubt; and don't guess when you tithe."

א:טז רַבָּן גַּמְלִיאֵל הָיָה אוֹמֵר עֲשֵׂה לְךָ רַב וְהִסְתַּלֵּק מִן הַסָּפֵק וְאַל תַּרְבֶּה לְעַשֵּׂר אֹמָדוֹת:

Rabban Gamliel. He lived in the first half of the first century C.E., was the grandson of Hillel, was the head of the Sanhedrin, and was the first to possess the honorific title רַבָּן *Rabban,* our Rabbi. It is he who is mentioned in the Christian Scriptures, Acts 5:34; 22:3: Paul is said to have sat at Gamliel's feet.

Avoid doubt. Rashi finds the importance of the teacher in the removal of doubt.

And don't guess. Bartinoro points out that guesswork in tithing may bring ruin to the individual should one give too little. Be precise; the minimum is 10 percent, no less.

1:17 His son Shimon said, "I have grown up among the sages all my days, yet I have never found anything better than silence. Study [of the Torah] is not the main thing; [the] doing [of Torah] is. All who talk too much bring sin."

א:יז שִׁמְעוֹן בְּנוֹ אוֹמֵר כָּל יָמַי גָּדַלְתִּי בֵּין הַחֲכָמִים וְלֹא מָצָאתִי לַגּוּף טוֹב מִשְּׁתִיקָה. וְלֹא הַמִּדְרָשׁ עִקָּר אֶלָּא הַמַּעֲשֶׂה. וְכָל הַמַּרְבֶּה דְבָרִים מֵבִיא חֵטְא:

Shimon [ben Gamliel]. He lived in the first century C.E., was the son of Rabban Gamliel the Elder whose teaching was given in *Pirke Avot* 1:16, and was the grandfather of Rabban Shimon ben Gamliel whose teaching follows in 1:18. This Shimon ben Gamliel was *nasi* ("head") of the Sanhedrin at the time of the first revolt against Rome. It is thought that he died before the revolt was put down in 70 C.E. The manner of his death is not clear. Some scholars maintain that he was executed by the Roman authorities; others hold that he was killed by the Zealots.

11

All who talk too much. According to Maimonides, most speech is without value. He notes that people are often so entranced with words that they pay little attention to their content. As an example, Maimonides tells us about people who reject Arabic poems no matter how exalted their content and accept Hebrew poems no matter how debased their content.

1:18 Rabban Shimon, the son of Gamliel, said, "The world stands on three things: on truth, on judgment, and on peace; as it is stated [in Scripture]: 'Execute the judgment of truth and peace in your gates.'" [Zech. 8:16]

אַ:יח רַבָּן שִׁמְעוֹן בֶּן גַּמְלִיאֵל אוֹמֵר עַל שְׁלֹשָׁה דְבָרִים הָעוֹלָם קַיָם עַל הָאֱמֶת וְעַל הַדִּין וְעַל הַשָּׁלוֹם שֶׁנֶּאֱמַר אֱמֶת וּמִשְׁפַּט שָׁלוֹם שִׁפְטוּ בְּשַׁעֲרֵיכֶם:

Truth. According to Maimonides, truth refers to the two kinds of human perfection: intellectual and ethical.

On judgment. Maimonides explains judgment in terms of a judicial system, the best institution to maintain order in society. Bartinoro understands judgment as justice—to acquit the innocent and condemn the guilty.

The Sadducees and the Pharisees

A sacred text is the result of revelation at a particular time in a particular place. It is difficult to apply that sacred text to another time and another place. The rabbis wanted to ensure that the Torah could be easily applied to the life of the Jewish people regardless of time and place. Thus, they developed the notion of a twofold law. It assumes that an Oral Law and Written Law were revealed at the same time. The Oral Law was revealed to interpret and expand the Written Law.

The group who conceived the Oral Law idea was called the Pharisees, or "separatists." They were opposed by the Sadducees, who took their name from Zadok, a priest in the time of Solomon. Since the Sadducees were priests, the institution of the Temple was the seat of their authority. They considered the Pharisees a threat to the primacy of the priesthood. The Pharisees created the institution of the synagogue and a new elite, the rabbis. The rabbis based their authority on the study of the written Torah and the elaboration of the Oral Law. While the Temple stood, the two elites, priests and rabbis, contended for power. When the Temple was destroyed, the Sadducees passed into history. From the Pharisees developed the institutions of rabbinic Judaism.

A Fence around the Torah

"A fence around the Torah," referred to by the men of the Great Assembly (1:1), was the means by which inadvertent transgression might be averted. This fence was really a set of expanded prohibitions established to protect the original law. Often, generations added to these prohibitions, further protecting the original precept. One might visualize a garden with two fences. Only one is really needed but the second fence prevents you from even reaching the first. For example, the Torah forbade the eating of leaven from the first day of the festival of Passover (Exod. 12:15);

rabbinic Judaism understood the "day" to begin at evening. Since it might seem that leaven could be eaten until the onset of nightfall, all eating was prohibited from the middle of the afternoon. (*Mishnah Pesachim* 10:1) To protect the original prohibition even further, the eating of leaven was prohibited from 10 A.M. on. (*Pesachim* 1:4)

From Temple Service to Modern Worship

Worship of God was transferred in Judaism from Temple sacrifice to synagogue service as the Israelites evolved into the Jewish people. The Bible records the movement of that people from the wilderness to the settled land to the city. The people developed from shepherds to farmers and later to merchants and artisans. The religious pattern of the Jewish people followed their early pattern of migration. In the wilderness as shepherds, they hearkened to prophets. On the land as farmers, they would come to the sanctuary and to the priest. In the city with its possibility of leisure, a new religious leader would emerge, the scribe, the one who mastered and taught the Book. Unlike the prophetic word, the teaching of this book did not depend on the presence of the prophet. Unlike the songs of the Levites and the

blessings of the priests, its words were available to all who could learn them.

Although it is clear (cf. *Mishnah Tamid* 5:1) that the sacrificial service that took place in the Temple contained texts proclaimed by prophets, as well as texts that had been developed by scribes, the new institution of the synagogue created by the scribes and their descendants (the rabbis) was devoted to the study, recitation, and use of texts as a means of reaching God. The texts that had been used in the sacrificial service became the core of the synagogue service, supplanting priestly authority by manipulating the very texts that gave them authority. In time, new texts would be added and some former texts removed. And again, the Jewish people create a new book: the prayer book.

The World to Come

That Judaism has had a belief in the world to come is attested by the liturgy. The traditional prayer text includes the phrase מְחַיֶּה מֵתִים בְּרַחֲמִים רַבִּים *mechayeh metim berachamim rabim*, "[God] revives the dead with great compassion." The Reform prayer book has changed it to נֹטֵעַ בְּתוֹכֵנוּ חַיֵּי עוֹלָם *notea betochenu chaye olam*, "[God] plants eternal life in our midst." The world to come, while subject to various inter-

pretations, generally refers to the period of time that begins with the end of earthly existence. Technically, the period ends with the Messianic Era. In it is implied divine retribution and resurrection.

A key element that distinguishes the difference between the Pharisees and the Sadducees was the concept of resurrection. Resurrection promised the individual Jew that somehow after death all wrongs would be righted, all sins would be punished, and, at the messianic advent, those who slept in the dust would arise and live on. The Pharisees found warrant for such a belief in the written Torah as they understood it. The Sadducees demurred and denied such a doctrine.

The persistence of liturgical statements about resurrection, even among modern Jewish movements, suggests the persistence of the hope among contemporary Jews. Obviously, such a hope cannot be "proven." Yet such a hope has existed from ancient times up to the present. Maimonides made it a cardinal principle. Since great latitude was given to the Jews in this area of belief throughout Jewish history, such openness to a variety of belief remains the norm.

Judaism as a Missionary Religion

It may seem strange to consider Judaism a missionary religion. Yet the Pharisees are described as "compass[ing] sea and land to make one proselyte." (Matthew 23:15) Rabbinic Judaism, the product of these Pharisees, saw in Abraham and Sarah the models for those who converted non-Jews to Judaism, speaking of them as "making souls." (Cf. Gen. 12:5.)

The proselyte was viewed with special favor. Unlike the Israelites at Sinai the proselyte had come under the wings of the Divine Presence without the impetus of thunder and lightning. Conversionary activity, however, diminished as Christianity gained power and proscribed conversion to Judaism. Even so, there were notable conversions to Judaism in the medieval period.

In the modern period with the advent of "Outreach" in the Reform Jewish community, there is renewed interest in presenting Judaism as an attractive option to those outside of Judaism who might be interested.

The Jewish Court System

The *bet din* (literally, "house of judgment") is the rabbinic term for a Jewish court of law. Today the same term is often used to refer to an ecclesiastical court (of arbitration) focusing on religious matters. (In modern Israel, the term refers to the rabbinic court.) Gaining its origin from the Bible when Moses sat as a magistrate among the people (cf. Exod. 18:13), the Jewish court system developed to meet the changing needs of time and place. Generally, courts of three judges sat in judgment over civil matters, as well as in the issues of divorce and conversion. Courts of twenty-three judges were assembled for criminal (and capital) cases. They also exercised jurisdiction in cases where animals were involved. A court of seventy-one judges, the Sanhedrin, exercised almost unlimited powers in judicial, legislative, and administrative matters. Certain individuals, such as the High Priest or the head of a tribe, and certain crimes, such as the uttering of false prophecy, could only be adjudicated by the court of seventy-one.

There was also a special court of priests, which was responsible for supervising the Temple ritual and the civil matters regarding the priests.

While no court could be composed of fewer than three judges, already in rabbinic times, single judges were established as experts in the law and could hold court (unless objected to by the defendant).

GLEANINGS

"Moses received the Torah" (1:1)

TORAH: RESHAPING JEWISH MEMORY

Entry into the covenant at Sinai is the root experience of Judaism, the central event that established the Jewish people. Given the importance of this event, there can be no verse in the Torah more disturbing to the feminist than Moses' warning to his people in Exodus 19:15, "Be ready for the third day: do not go near a woman." For here, at the very moment that the Jewish people stands at Sinai ready to receive the covenant–not now the covenant with individual patriarchs but with the people as a whole–at the very moment when Israel stands trembling waiting for God's presence to descend upon the mountain, Moses addresses the community only as men. The specific issue at stake is ritual impurity: an emission of semen renders both a man and his female partner temporarily unfit to approach the sacred. (Lev. 15:16-28) But Moses does not say, "Men and women, do not go near one another." At the central moment of Jewish history, women are invisible. Whether they too stood there trembling in fear and expectation, what they heard, when the men heard these words of Moses, we do not know. It was not their experience that interested the chronicler or that informed and shaped the Torah.

(Judith Plaskow, *Standing Again at Sinai*, New York: Harper and Row, 1990)

JUDITH PLASKOW. Contemporary feminist theologian and associate professor of Religious Studies at Manhattan College. She has presented a feminist reconstruction of Judaism.

"and handed it over" (1:1)

THE PHARISAIC REVOLUTION

A classic revolutionary situation was at hand, a crisis-laden opportunity for an audacious leadership to vault into power with a stirring proclamation of a constructive and creative solution. And such a revolutionary class did mount the barricades with a solution: the proclamation that God had revealed on Sinai to Moses not one law, but two. He had given him, not only the Pentateuch, but the Oral Law as well. This law promised eternal life and resurrection for the individual who remained loyal to the twofold law....

This doctrine was an ingenious innovation for it made the Pentateuch a handmaiden of the Oral Law even though it proclaimed the Pentateuch to be the word of God. The focus was shifted from a book to a scholar class. The Pharisees exercised authority; their teachings were not designed for congealment into some fixed and final corpus; their power was to be insulated against obsolescence; their broad mandate would enable them to respond quickly to new situations. To insure fresh and dynamic leadership, the hereditary principle of the Aaronides [priests] was abandoned, and proven competence in mastery of the twofold law became the measure for wielding authority.

(Ellis Rivkin, *The Shaping of Jewish History*, New York: Charles Scribner's Sons, 1971)

ELLIS RIVKIN (1918-   ). Historian and professor at HUC-JIR, Cincinnati, Ohio. He is best known for his reconstruction of the period of the Pharisees and his understanding of determinism in Jewish history.

"received [the Tradition]" (1:3)

THE WRITTEN AND ORAL LAW

The Written Law was recorded by Moses, but the Oral Law was handed down from pupil to pupil all through the ages. So when they discovered the laws in the written text, they said, "They are not new laws; they are the ancient oral laws given to Moses." This principle is illustrated in the following: A heathen came to Hillel and said, "I will accept Judaism on the basis of the Written Law. I believe that. But I will not accept the Oral Law; I cannot trust it, for maybe it is a mere invention." Hillel said, "Very well, I will begin with the Written Law. I will give you now your first lesson. Here are the first letters of the alphabet: *alef, bet, gimel, dalet.* Study these letters and then come back tomorrow and I will hear your lesson." The next day the Roman came back and Hillel said, "Recite," and the Roman said, *"Alef, bet, gimel, dalet."* Hillel said, "It should be *dalet, gimel, bet, alef."* The Roman said, "But yesterday you taught me *alef, bet, gimel, dalet."* And Hillel said, "You are recalling my oral teaching of yesterday. You believed me when I taught you. So I believed my own teacher and he believed his teacher." Thus the Oral Law has been transmitted from Moses to Joshua, Joshua to the elders, and so on to our day, based on the unbroken chain from one generation to the next and dependent on the reliability of the rabbis who transmitted it to revere their predecessors since they were the links of the chain in the tradition, and without tradition the Talmud would have no authority.

(Solomon Freehof, *Spoken and Heard*, Pittsburgh: Congregation Rodef Shalom, 1972)

SOLOMON FREEHOF (1892-1990). Rabbi and expert on Jewish legal responsa. He spent the majority of his career at Congregation Rodef Shalom in Pittsburgh, Pennsylvania. He was the architect behind the *Union Prayer Book* and is the author of several books on Reform responsa.

"If I am not for myself, who will be for me?" (1:14)

THE IMAGE OF HILLEL

Hillel conveys to us the image of–and this term will not degrade but ennoble his memory–a true reformer. He encountered all those difficulties that have been encountered at all times by efforts at revitalization and rejuvenation. Some may have asked him, "Why should you want to make changes?" "If I am not for myself," Hillel replied, "who will be for me?" If only that which the past has produced should have validity, if recognition should be accorded only to that which already exists without me, without my having created it–who else but I can create for me? To this, others may have countered: "So be it then. Keep it for yourself; you are free to see it so and to think and act accordingly. But why should you seek to come forth and make such changes for the entire community?" As if the idea were meant for the individual alone, as if it could be filed away in a drawer to be studied at some more opportune moment! As if it were not a living force that rules and impels man; even as the prophet put it, There is in my heart, as it were, a burning fire shut up in my bones; I cannot hold it in. "And, if I am only for myself," was Hillel's rejoinder, "what am I?" Do I seek anything for myself? Or is it the entire community that seeks new life? "Leave these things alone, my friend," still others may have warned him. "You are too rash." But, to this, Hillel replied, "If not now, when?"

Every age creates and must create, and, if we seek simply to crawl and drag ourselves through time, then our future will be nipped in the bud. Such a man was Hillel, and it will be clear to anyone who has ever taken even so much as a glance into the history of Judaism that Hillel was a man who dared openly to oppose those who sought to make the law more burdensome, and who was not at all afraid to be known as an advocate of leniency who sought to render the law less difficult.

(Abraham Geiger, "A Series of Thirty-four Lectures," in *Abraham Geiger and Liberal Judaism*, trans. Ernst J. Schlochauer, Philadelphia: Jewish Publication Society, 1962)

ABRAHAM GEIGER (1810-1874). A leader of the Reform movement in Germany and an outstanding scholar of *Wissenschaft des Judenthums*. He was a militant reformer who was active in several important Reform institutions in their incipient stages.

"Make your Torah [study] a habit" (1:15)

THE BIBLE AND THE TALMUD

The Bible is the most authoritative element of Judaism. But it is not the only one. Just as it had been preceded by tradition, so was it soon followed by tradition, the "Oral Law," which strives to penetrate into the essence of the Bible's written word. The Oral Law strives to apply the teachings of the Bible to all the events of existence; to provide religious and moral standards for all of life's activities; and to realize the Bible's teachings in the whole Jewish community. This tradition, which was ultimately established in the Talmud, had at first to fight for recognition; subsequently, it too became a conservative factor in Jewish religious life. It need scarcely be pointed out that, as regards religious influence, inner power, and effectiveness, the Talmud takes second place to the Bible. But the Talmud often proved to be an even more conservative factor. Its role was to put up a protective fence around Judaism. And as such it was particularly honored and cherished during the long ages of oppression. The Jews felt guarded by the Talmud, and so they in turn guarded it. For side by side with and second only to the Scriptures, the Talmud prevented the religion of Israel from going astray. The historical continuity and continued equilibrium of Judaism were largely the result of the canonical character acquired by the Bible and the decisive authority imparted to Talmud.

(Leo Baeck, *The Essence of Judaism*, New York: Schocken Books, 1948)

LEO BAECK (1873-1956). German-born rabbi who was a leader of Progressive Judaism in Europe. Instead of leaving Europe during the Nazi period, he dedicated himself to defending Jewish rights. Following his internment at Theresienstadt, he taught intermittently at HUC-JIR in Cincinnati as a historian and "witness of his faith."

CHAPTER TWO

Which Is the Proper Path?

2:1 Rabbi [Yehudah Ha-Nasi] was fond of saying: "Which is the proper path [of life] that one should select? The one that seems honorable for oneself and brings honor [bestowed by] others. Be as careful in the performance of [an ostensibly] minor commandment as [what seems to be] a major commandment, since you do not know the [potential] reward for [the performance of any of] the commandments. Compute the loss in doing a commandment against its reward and the benefit of a transgression against what will be lost. Think deeply about three things and you will never be gripped by the desire to commit a transgression. Know what is above you: an eye that sees, an ear that hears, and all your deeds are inscribed in a book.

בּ:א רַבִּי אוֹמֵר אֵיזוֹ הִיא דֶרֶךְ יְשָׁרָה שֶׁיָּבוֹר לוֹ הָאָדָם כָּל שֶׁהִיא תִפְאֶרֶת לְעֹשֶׂהָ וְתִפְאֶרֶת לוֹ מִן הָאָדָם. וֶהֱוֵי זָהִיר בְּמִצְוָה קַלָּה כְּבַחֲמוּרָה שֶׁאֵין אַתָּה יוֹדֵעַ מַתַּן שְׂכָרָן שֶׁל מִצְוֹת. וֶהֱוֵי מְחַשֵּׁב הֶפְסֵד מִצְוָה כְּנֶגֶד שְׂכָרָהּ וּשְׂכַר עֲבֵרָה כְּנֶגֶד הֶפְסֵדָהּ. הִסְתַּכֵּל בִּשְׁלֹשָׁה דְבָרִים וְאֵין אַתָּה בָא לִידֵי עֲבֵרָה. דַּע מַה לְמַעְלָה מִמְּךָ עַיִן רוֹאָה וְאֹזֶן שׁוֹמַעַת וְכָל מַעֲשֶׂיךָ בַּסֵּפֶר נִכְתָּבִים:

The sequence of these paragraphs follows the traditional layout of the *Mishnah*. However, it appears that 2:1-2:4 were added by a later editor and interrupt the themes established through 1:17 and continued in 2:5.

Rabbi [Yehudah Ha-Nasi]. Since he was the paradigmatic scholar of his generation, as well as the compiler of the entire *Mishnah*, Judah the Prince was known as "Rabbi," i.e., the rabbi par excellence. He lived from 135 to 219 C.E. and was a descendant of Hillel. Because he was said to have been born on the day that Rabbi Akiva died, *Kohelet Rabbah* applied to him the verse "The sun rises and the sun sets." By descent and by birth, Yehudah Ha-Nasi, the Tradition said, embodied the qualities of his great predecessors and thus received the appellation רַבֵּנוּ הַקָּדוֹשׁ *rabbenu hakadosh,* "our holy rabbi." Since he was head of the Sanhedrin, he was known as Yehudah Ha-Nasi, Judah the Prince.

Brings honor [bestowed by] others. Some texts substitute "to one's Maker" for the word "others," indicating that one should choose a course in life that brings divine approval.

Be as careful. For Maimonides, this advice manifests the philosophers' Golden Mean. Even so, for him, it warns the Jew to exercise diligence in the performance of all the commandments. As examples of minor commandments, Maimonides suggests the rejoicing at the festivals and the learning of Hebrew. As examples of major commandments, he offers circumcision; the wearing of צִיצִית *tzitzit*, "ritual fringes"; and the slaughtering of the pascal sacrifice.

Compute the loss. A loss can be either through self-denial or through a financial setback. Rashi also notes the lack of a clear formula anywhere in Jewish tradition or in sacred literature for computing the measure of reward and punishment. He compares it to a king who directed his servants to prune the trees in his garden, offering them some of the prunings as their reward. He argues that, were he to designate which trees were most valuable, the workers would abandon those that were least valuable. As a result, the king's garden would not receive proper care. Rashi also points out that what you lose by performing a *mitzvah*, like the income lost by working on Shabbat, or what you gain by transgressing a *mitzvah*, like money gained through stealing, is relevant only to this life. Real gains and losses will be computed in the world to come.

All your deeds. For Maimonides, this is simply the Torah's way of saying that God knows all human activities. Moses himself suggested it, in Exodus 32:32, by speaking of a divine book of records.

2:2 Rabban Gamliel, the son of Rabbi Yehudah Ha-Nasi, said, "It is good to join the study of Torah to some kind of work for the effort required by both robs sin of its power. Torah study without work will end up being useless and will cause sin. Let all who work with the congregation do so for the sake of Heaven; the merit of their ancestors will sustain them and, as a result, their righteousness will remain forever." As for you [God says], "I will credit you with a great reward, as if you had accomplished it all."

ב:ב רַבָּן גַּמְלִיאֵל בְּנוֹ שֶׁל רַבִּי יְהוּדָה הַנָּשִׂיא אוֹמֵר יָפֶה תַלְמוּד תּוֹרָה עִם דֶּרֶךְ אֶרֶץ שֶׁיְּגִיעַת שְׁנֵיהֶם מַשְׁכַּחַת עָוֹן. וְכָל תּוֹרָה שֶׁאֵין עִמָּהּ מְלָאכָה סוֹפָהּ בְּטֵלָה וְגוֹרֶרֶת עָוֹן. וְכָל הָעוֹסְקִים עִם הַצִּבּוּר יִהְיוּ עוֹסְקִים עִמָּהֶם לְשֵׁם שָׁמַיִם שֶׁזְּכוּת אֲבוֹתָם מְסַיַּעְתָּם וְצִדְקָתָם עוֹמֶדֶת לָעַד וְאַתֶּם מַעֲלֶה אֲנִי עֲלֵיכֶם שָׂכָר הַרְבֵּה כְּאִלּוּ עֲשִׂיתֶם:

Rabban Gamliel. He was the third to bear this name. The first was the grandson of Hillel. Hillel's son, Shimon, had a son named Gamliel (I). That first Gamliel had a son named Shimon whose son was named Gamliel (II); the second Gamliel had a son named Shimon whose son was Yehudah Ha-Nasi. Yehudah Ha-Nasi's son was the Gamliel (III) of this *mishnah.*

Robs sin of its power [literally, "makes sin forgotten"]. Rashi explains that one who is occupied with the study of Torah as well as with business will have no desire to steal the money of others. Rashi praises the work ethic and supports the pursuit of an occupation to help sustain the world.

Let all who work. Bartinoro instructs the individual to work with the congregation to move others to give charity or help redeem captives.

I will credit you. Maimonides and Rashi agree that this refers to the well-known problem of serving the community. People are often so occupied with the needs of the community that they are prevented from fulfilling a commandment. According to Maimonides, here the *mishnah* promises a reward for the performance of that commandment although it has not really been fulfilled.

2:3 Watch out for the government: They befriend a person to meet their own needs, appearing friendly when it is to their benefit; but they do not stand by a person when that person is in distress.

ב:ג הֱווּ זְהִירִין בָּרָשׁוּת שֶׁאֵין מְקָרְבִין לוֹ לָאָדָם אֶלָּא לְצֹרֶךְ עַצְמָן. נִרְאִין כְּאוֹהֲבִין בִּשְׁעַת הֲנָאָתָן וְאֵין עוֹמְדִין לוֹ לָאָדָם בִּשְׁעַת דָּחֳקוֹ:

Bartinoro sees this *mishnah* as a continuation of the injunctions in *Pirke Avot* 2:2 given to those who serve the community. It is they who must deal with the secular government (outside of the Jewish community). Thus, they must be warned that government deals only with them for its own purposes. (Cf. *Pirke Avot* 1:10.)

2:4 This was his motto: "Do God's will as if it were your own, so that God may do your will as God's own will. Adapt your will to God's will, so that God may change the will of others instead of yours." Hillel said, "Don't separate yourself from the community. Don't be overconfident until the day of your death. Don't judge your fellow human being until you have reached that person's place. Don't say anything that is unintelligible with the hope that it will be understood. And don't say, 'When I have leisure, I will study'–perhaps, you never will have that leisure."

ב:ד הוּא הָיָה אוֹמֵר עֲשֵׂה רְצוֹנוֹ כִּרְצוֹנְךָ כְּדֵי שֶׁיַּעֲשֶׂה רְצוֹנְךָ כִּרְצוֹנוֹ. בַּטֵּל רְצוֹנְךָ מִפְּנֵי רְצוֹנוֹ כְּדֵי שֶׁיְּבַטֵּל רְצוֹן אֲחֵרִים מִפְּנֵי רְצוֹנֶךָ. הִלֵּל אוֹמֵר אַל תִּפְרוֹשׁ מִן הַצִּבּוּר וְאַל תַּאֲמִין בְּעַצְמְךָ עַד יוֹם מוֹתְךָ וְאַל תָּדִין אֶת חֲבֵרָךְ עַד שֶׁתַּגִּיעַ לִמְקוֹמוֹ וְאַל תֹּאמַר דָּבָר שֶׁאִי אֶפְשָׁר לִשְׁמוֹעַ שֶׁסּוֹפוֹ לְהִשָּׁמַע וְאַל תֹּאמַר לִכְשֶׁאֶפָּנֶה אֶשְׁנֶה שֶׁמָּא לֹא תִפָּנֶה:

It would seem that Hillel's statement should begin a new *mishnah*. However, in the printed texts of the *mishnah* and the complete Talmud, Hillel's statement is included with Rabbi Gamliel's statement that begins this *mishnah*. The return to the statement of Hillel may indicate some original differences when the *mishnah* was redacted.

Do God's will. Since this does not suggest that one should turn over one's will to God, Rashi suggests that one can devote oneself to God while still taking care of one's own needs. Our challenge is to hear God's voice in the world and try to determine what God wants us to do.

Don't separate yourself. Rashi thinks that one should not separate from the community when it is experiencing difficulties so that one can be united with it when it experiences joy. Bartinoro adds that one who will not be with the community in time of sorrow will never be able to be with it at joyous times.

Don't judge your fellow human being. Bartinoro suggests that, if you see your neighbor ensnared by some temptation, do not judge your neighbor harshly until you have faced the same temptation and mastered it.

Don't say anything that is unintelligible. Maimonides suggests that one's statements should be easily understood.

Based on the Hebrew word לִשְׁמֹעַ *lishmoa*, which can mean either "to understand" or "to hear," Bartinoro suggests, "Don't say something you shouldn't just because you think no one can hear it; you never know who might indeed hear you!"

When I have leisure. For Maimonides, study should not be a function of leisure. Rather, study should be a fixed part of your daily routine.

2:5   Another of his [Hillel's] mottos: "The brute will not fear sin. The ignoramus will not be saintly. The inhibited will not learn. The irate cannot teach. Nor can one given over to business grow wise. In a place where there are no human beings, try to be one."

בּ:ה הוּא הָיָה אוֹמֵר אֵין בּוּר יְרֵא חַטְא וְלֹא עַם הָאָרֶץ חָסִיד וְלֹא הַבַּיְשָׁן לָמֵד וְלֹא כָּל הַקַּפְּדָן מְלַמֵּד וְלֹא כָּל הַמַּרְבֶּה בִסְחוֹרָה מַחְכִּים וּבִמָקוֹם שֶׁאֵין אֲנָשִׁים הִשְׁתַּדֵּל לִהְיוֹת אִישׁ:

The brute will not fear. Rashi explains בּוּר *bur*, here translated as "brute," as one bereft of any qualities. For Maimonides, such a person lacks only wisdom or ethical qualities.

The ignoramus will not be saintly. The Hebrew term for "ignoramus," עַם הָאָרֶץ *am haaretz*, has an interesting history. The Hebrew phrase literally means "people of the land." In the Bible, those words had an honorific meaning. For example, Abraham was to plead his case for a burial plot before the *am haaretz* (Gen. 23:7, 13), the notables of the area. In the rabbinic period, perhaps reflecting the viewpoint of the city, the term had come to mean "ignoramus." The English word "boor" shows a similar historical development, emerging from the Dutch word *boer*, "farmer."

Rashi and Maimonides agree that the ignoramus is better than the brute, having, at the very least, one ethical quality: the ignoramus *does* fear sin. Throughout most of Jewish history, ignorant piety has not been a value; virtue without wisdom has not been thought possible. Learning coupled with observance has been expected of every Jew.

The inhibited will not learn. In the question-and-answer method of traditional Jewish study, it was incumbent upon students to ask what they did not know. Were they too bashful to ask, they would not be able to learn. Were teachers to inhibit students from asking, then the students could not learn and the teachers could not teach.

Nor can one given over to business. Reflecting the modes of commerce of their times, Rashi and Bartinoro apply the verse "It is not over the sea" (Deut. 30:13) as the explanation for why one overly engaged in commerce would not be wise. Those who go overseas on business will not have the opportunity to study Torah.

In a place where there are no human beings. In his explanation, Rashi continues the theme of study. He suggests that, if there are no other persons available to respond to the needs of the community, then you must do it. If there are indeed others, then devote yourself to study.

The modern reader may make a broader application. In a place where true humanity is not apparent, it is incumbent on the religious individual to make it manifest.

2:6 He once saw a skull floating on the surface of the water. He said to it, "Because you drowned people, others drowned you. They in turn will be drowned by others."

בו אַף הוּא רָאָה גֻלְגֹּלֶת אַחַת שֶׁצָּפָה עַל פְּנֵי הַמָּיִם אָמַר לָהּ עַל דְּאַטֵּפְתְּ אַטְפוּךְ וְסוֹף מְטַיְּפָיִךְ יְטוּפוּן׃

He once saw a skull. Hillel's lament on the legacy of violence was given in Aramaic. The skull was the visible part of a floating corpse. Hillel probably knew the identity of the deceased.

Because you drowned people. Rashi, Maimonides, and Bartinoro all see this statement as an example of measure for measure.

2:7 He used to say, "The more flesh, the more worms; the more possessions, the more worry; the more wives, the more witchcraft; the more maidservants, the more lewdness; the more menservants, the more theft; the more Torah, the more life; the more schooling, the more wisdom; the more counsel, the more understanding; the more righteous charity, the more peace. One who has acquired a good name has acquired it for oneself. One who has acquired the words of Torah has acquired for oneself a place in the world to come.

בז הוּא הָיָה אוֹמֵר מַרְבֶּה בָשָׂר מַרְבֶּה רִמָּה מַרְבֶּה נְכָסִים מַרְבֶּה דְאָגָה מַרְבֶּה נָשִׁים מַרְבֶּה כְשָׁפִים מַרְבֶּה שְׁפָחוֹת מַרְבֶּה זִמָּה מַרְבֶּה עֲבָדִים מַרְבֶּה גָזֵל׃ מַרְבֶּה תוֹרָה מַרְבֶּה חַיִּים מַרְבֶּה יְשִׁיבָה מַרְבֶּה חָכְמָה מַרְבֶּה עֵצָה מַרְבֶּה תְבוּנָה מַרְבֶּה צְדָקָה מַרְבֶּה שָׁלוֹם קָנָה שֵׁם טוֹב קָנָה לְעַצְמוֹ קָנָה לוֹ דִבְרֵי תוֹרָה קָנָה לוֹ חַיֵּי הָעוֹלָם הַבָּא׃

Bartinoro sees a progression in Hillel's warnings, a kind of catalogue of the dangers of success. The first success is having too much to eat and eating too well, thus becoming a glutton. A higher level of success is having so many possessions that one must worry that they will be stolen, misplaced, or uncared for. After that level, one may feel rich enough to afford marriage, not only once, but several times. Even in the modern world, serial polygamy may be looked upon as an indication of status. Moreover, each spouse will need a servant, providing temptation to the other spouse. To support a successful household, one will need an estate with fields and vineyards. Such an estate requires a staff of servants, presumably menservants. The *mishnah* warns that these servants may take advantage of and steal from this *nouveau riche* householder.

The more wives, the more witchcraft. The modern reader may have difficulty perceiving the connection between wives and witchcraft. Hillel's statement suggests that many wives made for many rivals who might use witchcraft (or worse) to compete for the attention of their husband. Polygamy existed for Western Jews until Rabbenu Gershom (ca. 1000 C.E.) prohibited it. It was not until the establishment of the State of Israel in 1948 that Sephardic Jews were included in that prohibition as well.

The more Torah. Turning from financial success and its luxuries to a life of Torah will save an individual's soul. A life of Torah suggests a world entirely different from the previous lifestyle of spending.

The more righteous charity. For the rabbis, charity is not a freewill offering; it is a religious obligation. One's righteousness is determined by the fulfillment of the commandment. Such giving will bring peace.

One who has acquired a good name. Hillel understands the acquisition of a good name for oneself as merely an acquisition for this life. On the other hand, he argues, words of Torah are acquired for this world and for the world to come.

2:8 Rabban Yochanan ben Zakkai received [the Tradition] from Hillel and from Shammai. He would say, "If you have learned much Torah, don't take the credit, for it was for that purpose that you were created." Rabban Yochanan ben Zakkai had five students. They were Rabbi Eliezer ben Horkenos, Rabbi Yehoshua ben Chananya, Rabbi Yose Ha-Kohen, Rabbi Shimon ben Netanel, and Rabbi Elazar ben Arach. He would [often] recount their merits [as follows]: "Rabbi Eliezer ben Horkenos is like a cemented cistern that does not lose a drop; as for Rabbi Yehoshua, 'Happy is she who

ב:ח רַבָּן יוֹחָנָן בֶּן זַכַּאי קִבֵּל מֵהִלֵּל וּמִשַּׁמַּאי. הוּא הָיָה אוֹמֵר אִם לָמַדְתָּ תּוֹרָה הַרְבֵּה אַל תַּחֲזִיק טוֹבָה לְעַצְמְךָ כִּי לְכָךְ נוֹצָרְתָּ. חֲמִשָּׁה תַלְמִידִים הָיוּ לוֹ לְרַבָּן יוֹחָנָן בֶּן זַכַּאי וְאֵלּוּ הֵן רַבִּי אֱלִיעֶזֶר בֶּן הוֹרְקָנוֹס רַבִּי יְהוֹשֻׁעַ בֶּן חֲנַנְיָא רַבִּי יוֹסֵי הַכֹּהֵן רַבִּי שִׁמְעוֹן בֶּן נְתַנְאֵל וְרַבִּי אֶלְעָזָר בֶּן עֲרָךְ. הוּא הָיָה מוֹנֶה שְׁבָחָם רַבִּי אֱלִיעֶזֶר בֶּן הוֹרְקָנוֹס בּוֹר סוּד שֶׁאֵינוֹ מְאַבֵּד טִפָּה רַבִּי יְהוֹשֻׁעַ בֶּן חֲנַנְיָה אַשְׁרֵי יוֹלַדְתּוֹ רַבִּי יוֹסֵי הַכֹּהֵן חָסִיד רַבִּי שִׁמְעוֹן בֶּן נְתַנְאֵל יְרֵא חֵטְא רַבִּי אֶלְעָזָר בֶּן עֲרָךְ כְּמַעְיָן הַמִּתְגַּבֵּר. הוּא הָיָה אוֹמֵר אִם יִהְיוּ כָּל חַכְמֵי יִשְׂרָאֵל בְּכַף מֹאזְנַיִם וֶאֱלִיעֶזֶר בֶּן הוֹרְקָנוֹס בְּכַף שְׁנִיָּה מַכְרִיעַ אֶת כֻּלָּם:

bore him!'; Rabbi Yose is a pious man; Rabbi Shimon ben Netanel is one who fears sin; Rabbi Elazar ben Arach is [like] an ever-gushing spring." He [Rabbi Yochanan] would often say, "Were all the sages of Israel in one balance pan of a scale and Rabbi Eliezer ben Horkenos in the other, he [Rabbi Eliezer] would outweigh them all." Abba Shaul [remembered the teaching differently and] quoted him, "If all the sages of Israel including Rabbi Eliezer ben Horkenos were in one balance pan of a scale and Rabbi Elazar ben Arach in the other, he [Rabbi Elazar] would outweigh them all."

אַבָּא שָׁאוּל אוֹמֵר מִשְּׁמוֹ אִם יִהְיוּ כָּל חַכְמֵי יִשְׂרָאֵל בְּכַף מֹאזְנַיִם וֶאֱלִיעֶזֶר בֶּן הוֹרְקְנוֹס אַף עִמָּהֶם וְאֶלְעָזָר בֶּן עֲרָךְ בְּכַף שְׁנִיָּה מַכְרִיעַ אֶת כֻּלָּם:

Yochanan ben Zakkai. Yochanan ben Zakkai, who lived in the first century C.E., was the leading rabbinic sage toward the end of the Second Temple period and during the years following the destruction of the Temple. While what we know of his life is a mix of fact and legend, he is credited with establishing the school at Yavneh when, following the destruction of the Temple, Jerusalem could no longer be the national religious center of the Jewish people.

If you have learned much Torah. Rashi explained that one might wish to credit oneself for having learned Torah in order to receive undeserved honor from other people.

Eliezer ben Horkenos. Eliezer ben Horkenos lived during the end of the first and the beginning of the second century C.E. He was sometimes called Eliezer the Great or referred to without reference to his father. A student of Yochanan ben Zakkai, he and his colleague Yehoshua ben Chananya smuggled Yochanan out of Jerusalem in a coffin when the city was under siege. (Cf. B. Talmud, *Gittin* 56a.)

Yehoshua ben Chananya. Yehoshua ben Chananya lived during the end of the first and the beginning of the second century C.E. He was well known for the logical foundation behind his *halachah*, as well as for his worldly wisdom. After he and Eliezer ben Horkenos carried ben Zakkai out of Jerusalem, Yehoshua returned to help bring out Rabbi Zadok. Following the destruction of the Temple, he settled in Peki'in, a small town near Yavneh.

Yose ha-Kohen. Yose ha-Kohen lived in the end of the first century C.E., was a pupil of Yochanan ben Zakkai, and was known for his piety. He was engaged in the study of mysticism and is sometimes identified with Yose Kittunta. (Cf. *Sotah* 9:15.)

Shimon ben Netanel. Shimon ben Netanel lived in the second half of the first century C.E. He was one of Yochanan ben Zakkai's five most outstanding students. A priest, he married the daughter of Gamliel I. While not much of what he taught is preserved, his sayings reflect great piety.

Elazar ben Arach. Elazar ben Arach lived in the second half of the first century C.E. and was considered the most outstanding of Yochanan ben Zakkai's inner circle of outstanding students. Like Yose Ha-Kohen, he, too, was engaged in mystical speculation.

He would [often] recount their merits. Maimonides explains the various praises given by Rabbi Yochanan: Rabbi Eliezer has a good memory. Rabbi Yehoshua's ethical qualities endear him to all. Rabbi Yose possesses intellectual ability and is an ethical individual. Rabbi Shimon pursues good with utter diligence and avoids evil. Rabbi Elazar is praised for his profound understanding.

Regarding the rivalry between Rabbi Eliezer and Rabbi Elazar, Bartinoro suggests that, as far as memory is concerned, none could compare to Rabbi Eliezer. However, as far as understanding is concerned, none could compare to Rabbi Elazar.

2:9 He [Rabbi Yochanan] said to them: "Go and see which way one should follow." Rabbi Eliezer said, "[One should have] a good eye." Rabbi Yehoshua said, "[One should be] a good friend." Rabbi Yose said, "[One should be] a good neighbor." Rabbi Shimon said, "[One should] anticipate the future." Rabbi Elazar said, "[One should have] a good heart." Rabbi Yochanan responded, "I prefer Rabbi Elazar's answer to all of the other answers because it contains all of the others." [Rabbi Yochanan] then said, "Go out and see from what should one flee?" Rabbi Eliezer said, "[Having] an evil eye." Rabbi Yehoshua said, "[Being] a bad neighbor." Rabbi Shimon said, "[Being] one who borrows and does not repay. Whether one borrows from a neighbor or from God, it is the same, as it is written, 'The wicked borrow and do not repay, while the righteous graciously give.'" [Ps. 37:21] Rabbi Elazar said, "[Having] an evil heart." Rabbi Yochanan responded, "I prefer Rabbi Elazar's answer. All of your answers are included in his statement."

ב:ט אָמַר לָהֶם צְאוּ וּרְאוּ אֵיזוֹ הִיא דֶרֶךְ טוֹבָה שֶׁיִּדְבַּק בָּהּ הָאָדָם. רַבִּי אֱלִיעֶזֶר אוֹמֵר עַיִן טוֹבָה רַבִּי יְהוֹשֻׁעַ אוֹמֵר חָבֵר טוֹב רַבִּי יוֹסֵי אוֹמֵר שָׁכֵן טוֹב רַבִּי שִׁמְעוֹן אוֹמֵר הָרוֹאֶה אֶת הַנּוֹלָד רַבִּי אֶלְעָזָר אוֹמֵר לֵב טוֹב. אָמַר לָהֶם רוֹאֶה אֲנִי אֶת דִּבְרֵי אֶלְעָזָר בֶּן עֲרָךְ מִדִּבְרֵיכֶם שֶׁבִּכְלַל דְּבָרָיו דִּבְרֵיכֶם. אָמַר לָהֶם צְאוּ וּרְאוּ אֵיזוֹ הִיא דֶרֶךְ רָעָה שֶׁיִּתְרַחֵק מִמֶּנָּה הָאָדָם. רַבִּי אֱלִיעֶזֶר אוֹמֵר עַיִן רָעָה רַבִּי יְהוֹשֻׁעַ אוֹמֵר חָבֵר רָע רַבִּי יוֹסֵי אוֹמֵר שָׁכֵן רָע רַבִּי שִׁמְעוֹן אוֹמֵר הַלֹּוֶה וְאֵינוֹ מְשַׁלֵּם אֶחָד הַלֹּוֶה מִן הָאָדָם כְּלֹוֶה מִן הַמָּקוֹם שֶׁנֶּאֱמַר לֹוֶה רָשָׁע וְלֹא יְשַׁלֵּם וְצַדִּיק חוֹנֵן וְנוֹתֵן רַבִּי אֶלְעָזָר אוֹמֵר לֵב רָע. אָמַר לָהֶם רוֹאֶה אֲנִי אֶת דִּבְרֵי אֶלְעָזָר בֶּן עֲרָךְ מִדִּבְרֵיכֶם שֶׁבִּכְלַל דְּבָרָיו דִּבְרֵיכֶם:

A good eye. Maimonides explains that a good eye means that one should be content with what one has. For Maimonides, such contentment implies an important ethical quality. Bartinoro adds that contentment is not affected by another having more.

A good friend. For Bartinoro, a good friend is the one who, when it is necessary, will reprove his friend. For both Bartinoro and for Rashi, to be a good neighbor is more important than to be a good friend. Because of the way we live, we are more likely to see our neighbors more frequently than we might see our friends.

Anticipate the future. Maimonides, arguing in a philosophical mode, explains that the anticipation of the future is simply the deduction of what will be from what is.

A good heart. Maimonides reports the then current view of both philosopher and physician that the seat of the responsible aspect of the soul is the heart. All good actions, all ethical qualities, all love of the good emerge from this aspect of the soul.

From what should one flee. Bartinoro observes that it is necessary to list specifically all those elements of the evil way of life. Evil is not simply the antithesis of good. For example, חֲסִידוּת *chasidut,* "piety," according to Bartinoro, is acting beyond what is required by the Law. The opposite to such action, simply following the law as written, obviously cannot be considered evil. Thus, it is necessary for the list to include specific items.

An evil eye. For both Maimonides and Bartinoro, the evil eye is the pursuit of excess.

2:10 **They each said three things. Rabbi Eliezer said, "Let your friend's honor be as precious to you as your own. Be difficult to provoke. And repent one day before your death." [He also said], "Warm yourself by the fire of the sages, but take care that you don't get burned by their coals. Their bite is the bite of a fox; their sting is a scorpion stinging; and their hiss is a viper hiss. Indeed, all their words are like coals of fire."**

ב:י הֵם אָמְרוּ שְׁלֹשָׁה דְבָרִים. רַבִּי אֱלִיעֶזֶר יְהִי כְבוֹד חֲבֵרְךָ חָבִיב עָלֶיךָ כְּשֶׁלָּךְ וְאַל תְּהִי נוֹחַ לִכְעוֹס וְשׁוּב יוֹם אֶחָד לִפְנֵי מִיתָתְךָ וֶהֱוֵי מִתְחַמֵּם כְּנֶגֶד אוּרָן שֶׁל חֲכָמִים וֶהֱוֵי זָהִיר בְּגַחַלְתָּן שֶׁלֹּא תִכָּוֶה שֶׁנְּשִׁיכָתָן נְשִׁיכַת שׁוּעָל וַעֲקִיצָתָן עֲקִיצַת עַקְרָב וּלְחִישָׁתָן לְחִישַׁת שָׂרָף וְכָל דִּבְרֵיהֶם כְּגַחֲלֵי אֵשׁ:

Let your friend's honor. ARN adds, "Even as one looks out for one's personal honor so should that person look after a friend's honor. Likewise, one should make sure that one's friend's honor is not held in disrepute as one would his own." The sages strongly warn us not to injure anyone's honor or reputation nor expose anyone to disgrace or ridicule. It is part of the biblical injunction "Love your neighbor as yourself" (Lev. 19:18), which the rabbis considered to be the essence of Torah. (*Bereshit Rabbah* 24:7)

Be difficult to provoke. Maimonides relates this to the rabbinic notion that one who gives in to anger is the same as one who gives in to idolatry. (B. Talmud, *Shabbat* 105b) The *mishnah* is suggesting, "Don't be quick to lose your temper, especially since so many matters are inconsequential." The rabbis spoke out against anger. In the Talmud (*Shabbat* 105b), they went as far as to say that one who allows oneself to be carried away in one's own anger is considered to be like one who worships idols. There is an oft-quoted idiom that puns the Hebrew: One's character can be determined by his כּוֹסוֹ *koso* ["cup when drinking"], כִּיסוֹ *kiso* ["money bag"], and כַּעֲסוֹ *ka'aso* ["anger"]. (B. Talmud, *Eruvin* 65b)

26

Repent one day. Both Rashi and Maimonides understand this to mean that you should repent each day of your life since you cannot be sure when you will die.

The fire of the sages. Maimonides reminds us that fire warms at a distance but is dangerous up close. This is a warning to the student not to trouble the sages nor to overextend one's welcome in their presence. The bite, the sting, and the hiss are understood by Maimonides as metaphors for the various verbal rebukes scholars may direct toward unworthy students. Bartinoro adds that, once one provokes a scholar, it may be difficult to appease that scholar.

2:11 Rabbi Yehoshua said, "The evil eye, the evil urge, and hatred of [one's fellow] creatures take one out of the world."

בּ:יא רַבִּי יְהוֹשֻׁעַ אוֹמֵר עַיִן הָרָע וְיֵצֶר הָרָע וְשִׂנְאַת הַבְּרִיּוֹת מוֹצִיאִין אֶת הָאָדָם מִן הָעוֹלָם:

The evil eye. Although the commentators do not make a distinction between *an* evil eye and *the* evil eye, it is necessary to do so. *An* evil eye is simply the dissatisfaction with what one has, envious of the possessions of others. *The* evil eye carries a much more sinister meaning. It connotes envy tinged with malevolence, an envy that not only begrudges the other the possessions but also wishes evil upon that individual for having them.

The evil urge. יֵצֶר הָרָע *yetzer hara,* the "evil urge," is that aspect of human nature, found in us all, that, when uncontrolled, leads us to sin. Yet it is a necessary part of creation: "For were it not for the *yetzer hara,* no one would build a house, marry, start a business." (*Bereshit Rabbah* 9:7)

Hatred of [one's fellow] creatures. Rashi and Bartinoro agree that Rabbi Yehoshua is implying a kind of hatred without reason.

Take one out of the world. Maimonides, a physician and philosopher, explains that the frenzied pursuit of money and the mad craving for pleasure will have deleterious effects upon the soul. They will led to melancholy. The afflicted person will reject normal experience and will be unable to live with other human beings, preferring to live in desolate places amidst wide animals. Such a pattern of life will cause one to die before one's time.

2:12 Rabbi Yose would say, "Let your friend's property be as dear to you as your own. Since you cannot inherit the Torah, you must prepare yourself to study it. Let all that you do be for the sake of Heaven."

בּ:יב רַבִּי יוֹסִי אוֹמֵר יְהִי מָמוֹן חֲבֵרְךָ חָבִיב עָלֶיךָ כְּשֶׁלָּךְ וְהַתְקֵן עַצְמְךָ לִלְמוֹד תּוֹרָה שֶׁאֵינָהּ יְרֻשָּׁה לָךְ וְכָל מַעֲשֶׂיךָ יִהְיוּ לְשֵׁם שָׁמָיִם:

Let your friend's property. A mutuality of interest was assumed in the Jewish community. The Talmud teaches: "All Israel is responsible for one another." (B. Talmud, *Shevuot* 39a)

We have translated מָמוֹן *mamon* as "property"; in most places, *mamon* means "money." It may well have been in a mercantile community that most property was in the form of some sort of liquid assets.

You cannot inherit the Torah. Rashi explains: "Let no one say that, since my parents and my grandparents were scholars, I need not exert myself to learn the Torah." The opposite also is true: Let no one say that, "since my parents were not scholars, I need not study either."

Let all that you do. Bartinoro suggests that every aspect of human life, including eating, drinking, and even sexual relations between husband and wife, should transcend bodily pleasure in order to fulfill a divine purpose.

2:13 Rabbi Shimon said, "Be very careful in reciting the *Shema* and the *Tefilah*. When you pray, don't make your prayer a fixed form, but rather [infuse it with] a plea for mercy and grace before God, as Scripture teaches, 'For God is a compassionate and gracious God, long suffering and abounding in steadfast love and relenting of evil.' [Joel 2:13] [Moreover] don't be wicked in your own mind."

ב:יג רַבִּי שִׁמְעוֹן אוֹמֵר הֱוֵי זָהִיר בִּקְרִיאַת שְׁמַע וּבִתְפִלָּה וּכְשֶׁאַתָּה מִתְפַּלֵּל אַל תַּעַשׂ תְּפִלָּתְךָ קֶבַע אֶלָּא רַחֲמִים וְתַחֲנוּנִים לִפְנֵי הַמָּקוֹם שֶׁנֶּאֱמַר כִּי חַנּוּן וְרַחוּם הוּא אֶרֶךְ אַפַּיִם וְרַב חֶסֶד וְנִחָם עַל הָרָעָה. וְאַל תְּהִי רָשָׁע בִּפְנֵי עַצְמֶךָ:

Be very careful. The שְׁמַע *Shema* (Deut. 6:4-9) takes its name from the first word, *Shema*, of the first verse of the passage "Hear, O Israel: *Adonai* is our God, *Adonai* is One." It became the central affirmation of Judaism from a very early time. Recited in the Temple (cf. *Mishnah Tamid* 5:1), it soon became the basis of the developing prayer book. In addition, two passages from the Torah (Deut. 11:13ff. and Num. 15:37ff.) follow the basic *Shema*. To the morning recital of the *Shema* were added two preceding benedictions and one following benediction; in the evening two benedictions preceded the *Shema* and two benedictions followed it.

While the *Shema* has its origin in the Bible, הַתְּפִלָּה *Ha-Tefilah* (literally, "The Prayer"), also known as the *Shemoneh Esreh* or *Amidah*, dates to the rabbinic period. This presents us with the basic prayer pattern of Judaism. According to the Babylonian Talmud (B. Talmud, *Berachot* 28b), *Ha-Tefilah* was composed by Shimon Ha-Pikoli in Yavneh in the presence of Rabban Gamliel. However, according to *Mishnah Berachot* 4:3, there was a disagreement as to how many of the Eighteen Benedictions of *Ha-Tefilah* had to be said. According to Rabban Gamliel, one should say all of them. According to Rabbi Yehoshua, only an abstract of the Eighteen Benedictions needed to be recited. According to Rabbi Akiva, the amount to be read was dependent on the ability of the one reciting the text.

Don't make your prayer a fixed form. The preceding disagreement regarding *Ha-Tefilah* leads us to the question: Is it the text of the prayer or the recitation of the prayer that is to be fixed?

Rabbi Eliezer says, "Regarding the one who makes the prayer fixed, the prayer is not a plea for grace." Rabbi Yehoshua says, "One who goes about in a place of danger, let that one pray a short prayer. Let that one say, 'Save, O *Adonai*, Your people, the remnant of Israel; at every crossroads, may their needs be before You. Blessed are You who hears prayer.'" (*Mishnah Berachot* 4:4) By context, we determine that it is the text that is to be fixed.

While this may well have been the meaning in *Pirke Avot*, the commentators come to this passage accustomed to the recitation of all the benedictions. They, therefore, understand the *mishnah* to imply a fixed recitation. Hence, Rashi explains that one should not treat prayer as if it were a heavy burden thrust upon a person that one is eager to throw off. Our hearts should lead us in prayer. We should become holy vessels through which the Divine Spirit can flow.

Don't be wicked in your own mind. Rashi takes this as a warning to be careful to prevent guilt and become wicked. Maimonides, however, sees the matter in psychological terms. He suggests that one who sees oneself as wicked will not be motivated to change for the better and may even become worse. Low self-esteem may lead to unfortunate behavior.

2:14 Rabbi Elazar would say, "Study the Torah diligently. Know how to answer the nonbeliever. And know in whose presence you work and how dependable your Employer is to pay your wage."

בּ:יד רַבִּי אֶלְעָזָר אוֹמֵר הֱוֵי שָׁקוּד לִלְמוֹד תּוֹרָה וְדַע מַה שֶׁתָּשִׁיב לְאֶפִּיקוֹרוֹס וְדַע לִפְנֵי מִי אַתָּה עָמֵל וּמִי הוּא בַּעַל מְלַאכְתְּךָ שֶׁיְּשַׁלֶּם לְךָ שְׂכַר פְּעֻלָּתֶךָ:

Know how to answer the nonbeliever. In Hebrew, the word for "nonbeliever," אֶפִּיקוֹרוֹס *apikoros*, is a form of the name of the Greek philosopher Epicurus (341-270 B.C.E.). In the rabbinic mind all manner of heresy was attributed to him. The nonbeliever's notion that human beings have neither creator nor destiny was particularly abhorrent to the rabbis. As a result, the rabbis stressed the reward for the "work" of Jewish observance. Bartinoro argues that such a nonbeliever condemns the Torah as meaningless.

2:15 Rabbi Tarfon used to say, "The day is short; there is much work [to be done]; [yet,] the laborers are lazy, [even though] the wages are great and the Householder is insistent."

בּ:טו רַבִּי טַרְפוֹן אוֹמֵר הַיּוֹם קָצָר וְהַמְּלָאכָה מְרֻבָּה וְהַפּוֹעֲלִים עֲצֵלִים וְהַשָּׂכָר הַרְבֵּה וּבַעַל הַבַּיִת דּוֹחֵק:

Rabbi Tarfon was a contemporary of the students of Rabbi Yochanan. He lived in Lydda (Lod).

The day is short. Rashi takes the shortness of the day to refer to this life; in the next life, the wages for the service of God will be paid. Maimonides takes the shortness of day to indicate how few are the years and how many are the sciences that one should study.

There is much work. For Bartinoro, the "work" to be accomplished is the study of the Torah.

The laborers are lazy. We tend to waste so much of our time on trivial matters that we are too tired to spend time on what really counts: the study of Torah.

The wages are great. The study of Torah itself produces joy and happiness. Not only do we acquire wisdom through the study of Torah, but it also secures us a place in the world to come, say the rabbis.

The Householder is insistent. God encourages us to study Torah, to draw near to God. We are taught in the *Tanach*: "This book of the law shall not depart from your mouth. You shall dwell on it day and night." (Josh. 1:8)

2:16 He would say, "It is not up to you to finish the work, yet you are not free to avoid it. If you have studied much Torah, then you will receive much in wages for your Employer is dependable to pay the wage for your work. Know that the giving of the wages for the righteous is in the time to come."

בּ:טז הוּא הָיָה אוֹמֵר לֹא עָלֶיךָ הַמְּלָאכָה לִגְמוֹר וְלֹא אַתָּה בֶן חוֹרִין לְהִבָּטֵל מִמֶּנָּה אִם לָמַדְתָּ תּוֹרָה הַרְבֵּה נוֹתְנִין לְךָ שָׂכָר הַרְבֵּה וְנֶאֱמָן הוּא בַּעַל מְלַאכְתְּךָ שֶׁיְּשַׁלֶּם לְךָ שְׂכַר פְּעֻלָּתֶךָ וְדַע שֶׁמַּתַּן שְׂכָרָן שֶׁל צַדִּיקִים לֶעָתִיד לָבֹא:

Rabbi Tarfon continues the metaphor of God as Employer and the individual Jew as employee. Bartinoro reminds us that as Jews the yoke of Torah has been placed upon us, whether we like it or not. Maimonides notes that the term "the time to come" is also known as "the world to come," הָעוֹלָם הַבָּא *haolam haba*, an unspecified future.

Maimonides' Eight Levels of Charity

Maimonides in his *Yad, Mattenot Aniyyim* (10:7-12) lists eight ways or levels of giving *tzedakah*, "righteous acts of charity." Each level is progressively more virtuous.

1. One gives but reluctantly.
2. One gives less than is appropriate, but with a giving heart.
3. One gives after being asked.
4. One gives before being asked.
5. One gives in such a way that the donor does not know the identity of the recipient.
6. One gives in such a way that the recipient does not know the identity of the donor.
7. One gives in such a way that neither the donor nor the recipient knows the identity of the other.
8. The highest form is not a *gift* of funds. Rather, it is when one helps another rehabilitate himself/herself by lending money, taking the person as a business partner, employing that person, or setting the person up in business. In this way, no one loses self-respect.

Yochanan ben Zakkai and His Times

Yochanan ben Zakkai was the leading sage in the period following the destruction of the Second Temple. While much of what we know about him is a blend of fact and legend, the focus of his life was teaching Torah. Generally, he encouraged dialogue as a method of instruction, teaching primarily *halachah*, *aggadah*, ethics, the reasons behind the various *mitzvot*, and mysticism. After the destruction of the Second Temple, he was not satisfied merely with consoling the people. He worked to renew the Israelite nation's religious and national leadership through the *bet din* at Yavneh, laboring to reestablish the position of *nasi*. The Jerusalem Talmud (*Sotah* 9:15) summed up his life best: "When R. Yochanan ben Zakkai died, the luster of wisdom ceased."

Repentance

While repentance (*teshuvah*) is usually associated with the Ten Days of Repentance that begin on Rosh Hashanah and end on Yom Kippur, repentance (literally, returning to God) is an act Jews should undertake throughout their lives. According to Jewish tradition, it is a prerequisite for divine forgiveness. If one does not repent, divine pardon, which is always there waiting, will not be proffered. Rabbi Eliezer said, "Repent one day before your death. Since no one knows when death will come, spend all your days in repentance." (B. Talmud, *Shabbat* 153a)

The Evil Eye and the Evil Inclination

The evil eye (*ayin hara*) appears in early Jewish literature as a matter of fact. It was a widespread belief that some people could cause evil for others by looking at them. Such magical powers were not limited to those intent on doing evil. Folk heroes who worked as sacred wonderworkers exercised these powers, according to folk legend, to transform evil people.

According to this same tradition, one can either prevent or counteract the evil eye by the avoidance of any expression of praise or by "qualifying" any praise with an expression like the Yiddish *kein ayen hore*, "may there be no evil eye," sometimes shortened to *keinahora*. The rabbis have taught that every person is endowed with a *yetzer hatov* and a *yetzer hara*, loosely translated as an instinctive inclination to do good and an inclination to do evil. The creative tension between these two forces prods us forward in life. These are major features in rabbinic psychology and anthropology. The *yetzer hara* is not intrinsically evil. Rather, it is raw, untamed energy that manifests itself in the form of drives, especially sexual. Nevertheless, without it, according to the rabbis, one would not be driven to marry, have children, build a home, or engage in business. (Cf. *Bereshit Rabbah* 9:7.) Of course, the rabbis teach that the most effective antidote is the study of Torah. (Cf. B. Talmud, *Kiddushin* 30b.)

Jewish Prayer: Keva and Kavanah

Fixed and spontaneous prayer, the two forms that operate in a sort of creative tension throughout Jewish liturgy, are set as parameters by the rabbis to direct our communication with the Deity. The best example of this tension can be seen in the *Amidah* (also called the *Shemoneh Esreh* or *Ha-Tefilah*). Originally this prayer, which was established as the core for Jewish worship, merely established themes to direct our prayers. The formula for blessing "*Baruch Atah Adonai...*" that begins each section establishes the theme, and the prayer is concluded by a reiteration of the theme called *chatimah*, "seal." Later, texts were developed (as favorites of individual rabbis) that fixed the prayer and pushed the spontaneous aspect of prayer for the worshiper to the end of the entire prayer. This became known as the silent meditation. And, even there, the favorite prayers of individual rabbis were offered to direct the worshiper once again.

GLEANINGS

"Which is the proper path [of life] that one should select?" (2:1)

MITZVOT AND ETHICS

...man, by his very nature, struggles to understand the Divine...for us as Jews the most important record of that struggle is the Bible and our religious literature. As a result of this search, a number of incandescent ideas have flashed into the mind–or spirit–of man, not exclusively in Judaism, but preponderantly there. Such concepts as one God, one mankind [*sic*], a Messianic Age are more than the fruit of man's ratiocination. To me, they are the consequences of what may well be designed as inspiration, illumination, or, if you will, revelation. Above all, they cannot be neatly or scientifically delineated or systematized. I am led to believe, therefore, that the source of this revelation is that force, power, or being-beyond-all-else, the concept of which–or whom–we only grow to grasp from generation to generation. This concept and its concomitant demands vary from age to age. As our rabbis long ago pointed out, realization and revelation of the God of Abraham, Isaac, and Jacob differed (since each came to God through his own experience) and advanced (since each added something new).

Besides, I do not believe that the question of the identical value of the 613 commandments is really a relevant question for our time. Not only did Saadia distinguish between the rational and dogmatic commandments, but he definitely claimed superiority for the rational. The Talmud, too, indicates a scale of values in terms of the dominant consideration of the saving of life. It also demonstrates under what conditions one should sanctify God's name. So I am within solid Jewish tradition, not only Reform, but even Orthodox, in distinguishing among the commandments.

It is incumbent upon us to observe those commandments that adumbrate the essence of Judaism or that can be related to such an essence. Obviously, one cannot in such a brief exposition define what that essence is. One can, however, assert that all the commandments that are corollary to Judaism's ethical monotheism–however that unity is currently interpreted–and to its consequent moral imperatives should be obeyed.

(Maurice Eisendrath, "The State of Jewish Belief," *Commentary*, August 1966)

MAURICE EISENDRATH (1902-1973). An outspoken community leader who addressed many social and political issues. He served the UAHC as president from 1943 until his death.

"the more Torah, the more life" (2:7)

JUDAISM AS AN ETHICAL RELIGION

This entire argument rests on a deep-lying assumption that should be faced; namely, that modern Jewish obligation, ethics, though apparently different from the Judaism of earlier ages, has always been the essence of Judaism. Neither the Bible nor the Talmud know the word "ethics," and one can argue that they do not have an abstract concept analogous to it. Instead they tell how God gave the Torah, Written and Oral, to the people of Israel, and they take it for granted, therefore, that the Jews are obligated to follow it. Jewish duty has classically meant fulfilling the commandments God gave in the Torah, and these cover a whole range of activities, a significant number of which we cannot reasonably call ethics.

The founders of Reform rejected [this] idea of Torah, and this constituted their major break with Jewish tradition. They did not believe all of Jewish law as they received it was God's commandment. They differed as to the content of what God wanted done, but they did not reject the root Jewish religious intuition, one shared by few other of the world's religions, that God revealed commands and that religion was living in response to them. They largely limited their sense of what was commanded to moral law, but they did not differ with the basic Jewish experience of what God asked of them. They transformed Oral Law into moral law, but they remained believers in law.

(Eugene B. Borowitz, *Reform Judaism Today*, New York: Behrman House, 1978)

EUGENE B. BOROWITZ (1924-   ). Scholar and rabbi who is regarded as one of the leading liberal Jewish theologians in the United States. Formerly the director of education at the UAHC, he has been a member of the HUC-JIR faculty in New York for over thirty years.

"Go and see which way one should follow" (2:9)

ETHICAL AND SOCIAL COMMANDMENTS

The commandments of Scripture and tradition, ethical and social, as well as ceremonial, are not to be adopted blindly. They must be considered thoughtfully and reverently. Only on the basis of genuine understanding can the individual make the decision as to which of the commandments he can and should obey, which should be modified, and which he may (or even should) discard. In arriving at such judgments, he may well be guided by the opinion of informed and committed members of his own religious community, and he will not lightly disregard the consensus. But, as a free person, he must assume the responsibility of the ultimate choice.

(Bernard Bamberger, "The State of Jewish Belief," *Commentary*, August 1966)

BERNARD BAMBERGER (1904-1980). A scholar who spent most of his rabbinate in Temple Shaaray Tefila in New York City. He was a classic liberal who was convinced that Reform Judaism held the key to the meaningful continuation of Jewish existence.

"hatred of [one's fellow] creatures take[s] one out of the world" (2:11)

THE PROBLEM OF EVIL

This is the most naive and magical of all ideas, perhaps–to assert that moral values are real in a totally accidental world, that they have miraculously sprung up like trees in a waterless, seedless, sunless wasteland and at the same time to maintain that there can be no God at work in the world. The ethical atheists do not realize their own inconsistencies. They find it impossible to believe in God creating the world out of nothing, but, strangely enough, find it easy to believe that values emerge out of nothing.

God, in fact, is indicated both by order in the physical universe and by morality in the human world. The resolute atheist will, however, be unconvinced by this empirical approach to the universe. He may admit the existence of a certain amount of order, design, and purpose in the universe, but he might well say to the religionist, "You ignore the bloody and brutal disharmonies of the world. Before me, however, stretches the landscape of bombed cities and blighted fields. In a world of earthquakes and flood, strife and war, disease and death, can you still speak of a Providential Divinity?"

This problem of evil is for us, as it was for our ancestors, the crux of the matter. We have to arrive at some understanding of its presence in the world before we can come to any conclusions about Providence....

Moral evils have their source in man's free choice. Appalled at the colossal iniquity for which some men are responsible, there are moments when sensitive spirits in despair dream of a world in which the human race would be ethically sterilized, made impotent as far as decisive action is concerned. "Why," we ask, "did not God fashion man incapable of doing wrong?" Speaking symbolically, we may say that God was logically faced with two alternatives. He could make man either all-good–therefore a replica of Himself and therefore superfluous–or He could make man not God but man and therefore partly good and partly evil. Man is not a duplicate of God. If he were, he would be redundant. We may take from Plato the idea of limitation, but, instead of considering this limitation, namely, the possibility of evil in the world, as a defeat, we would rather ascribe it to the generosity of God. He tolerates the possibility of evil in order to give man the opportunity of building a moral world.

Morality, then, cannot be created by God. It is never a divine gift. It is a human achievement. It is not the child of grace but of effort. Now, as a matter of fact, even though moral evil originates in the very fact of human freedom, we would not cast our ballot for an ethically neutral world, a world without tasks, without challenge. We would not desire a petrified moral forest of a world. We could not enjoy the sun, love friends, write books, fashion governments, or pursue justice were we but emotionless puppets.

We resent coercion and force. We wish to be responsible agents, compelled neither by man nor by God, but persuaded to action by our own insight and counsel. We have to pay the price of pain and sorrow if we wish to achieve worth and dignity. No personality is possible in a tyranny, whether it be man-built or God-ruled. Man is a thing, an It, in a dictatorship, whether human or divine. The deepest yearning of many, however, is always to be a subject, not an object; a person, not a thing.

(Joshua Loth Liebman, "God and the World Crisis–Can We Still Believe in Providence?" *Central Conference of American Rabbis Yearbook* LI, Philadelphia, 1941)

JOSHUA LOTH LIEBMAN (1907-1948). Reform rabbi, widely known as a radio preacher. His book *Peace of Mind* was phenomenally successful. It made an important contribution to the fields of religion and psychology, which were growing together at the time.

"Let your friend's property be as dear to you as your own" (2:12)

MORAL LAW

The major part of the moral obligations that were developed into laws has a negative character. Their purpose is to protect the society and the individual, primarily the weak, thus preventing anarchy and chaos. The positive moral obligations, while often emphasized in most lofty pronouncements, were less frequently transformed into laws. There are two obvious reasons for this: their infraction would not lead to chaos–the primary concern of society–and, in some instances, the moral precept, if converted into a law, would lose its original value or would be unenforceable by its nature. How, for example, could love, love of fellowmen, of God, of the Torah, etc., be enforced?

However, some of the positive moral obligations actually had been converted into laws. The Bible has numerous noble pronouncements demanding support of the poor. On the whole, however, helping the poor particularly in the Diaspora remained a moral obligation. The rabbis developed the *mitzvah*–here meaning moral obligation–of helping the poor into a full system of legal (halachic) obligations that are enforceable as any other legal obligation.

(Alexander Guttmann, "The Moral Law as Halachah in Reform Judaism," *Central Conference of American Rabbis Yearbook* LXVIII, Chicago, 1959)

ALEXANDER GUTTMANN (1901-   ). Professor of Talmud at HUC-JIR, Cincinnati. He trained at the *Hochschule fuer die Wissenschaft des Judentums* in Berlin, where he became the ordaining rabbi, and was among the leading Jewish scholars whose escape from Nazi Germany was facilitated by HUC-JIR.

CHAPTER THREE

Know Where You Came From;
Know Where You Are Going

3:1 Akavya ben Mahalalel used to say, "Reflect on three things and you will not come into the grasp of sin: know where you came from; know where you are going; and [know] in whose presence you will have to make an accounting." Where do you come from? From a disgusting drop. Where are you going? To a place of dust, of worms, and of maggots. In whose presence will you have to make an accounting: the most Sovereign of sovereigns, the Holy One of Blessing.

ג:א עֲקַבְיָא בֶּן מַהֲלַלְאֵל אוֹמֵר הִסְתַּכֵּל בִּשְׁלֹשָׁה דְבָרִים וְאֵין אַתָּה בָא לִידֵי עֲבֵרָה. דַּע מֵאַיִן בָּאתָ וּלְאָן אַתָּה הוֹלֵךְ וְלִפְנֵי מִי אַתָּה עָתִיד לִתֵּן דִּין וְחֶשְׁבּוֹן. מֵאַיִן בָּאתָ מִטִּפָּה סְרוּחָה וּלְאָן אַתָּה הוֹלֵךְ לִמְקוֹם עָפָר רִמָּה וְתוֹלֵעָה וְלִפְנֵי מִי אַתָּה עָתִיד לִתֵּן דִּין וְחֶשְׁבּוֹן לִפְנֵי מֶלֶךְ מַלְכֵי הַמְּלָכִים הַקָּדוֹשׁ בָּרוּךְ הוּא.

Unlike other chapters in *Avot*, this chapter lacks a chronological order.

Akavya ben Mahalalel. Akavya ben Mahalalel, who lived in the first century C.E. and was a contemporary of Hillel, was a member of the Sanhedrin. Known for his disagreement with the majority, he was labeled the "rebellious scholar" and was eventually excommunicated because of an unusual legal decision.

Bartinoro explains that the one who reflects on his origin will be saved from pride; the one who reflects on his destined place will be saved from lust and the desire for money; and the one who reflects on his ultimate future will be saved from sin.

3:2 Rabbi Chanina, the deputy of the priests, would often say, "Pray for the welfare of the government, for were it not for the fear of it, people would swallow each other alive." Rabbi Chananya ben Teradyon said, "If two sit together and exchange no words of Torah, then they are like an assembly of

ג:ב רַבִּי חֲנִינָא סְגַן הַכֹּהֲנִים אוֹמֵר הֱוֵי מִתְפַּלֵּל בִּשְׁלוֹמָהּ שֶׁל מַלְכוּת שֶׁאִלְמָלֵא מוֹרָאָהּ אִישׁ אֶת רֵעֵהוּ חַיִּים בְּלָעוֹ. רַבִּי חֲנִינָא בֶּן תְּרַדְיוֹן אוֹמֵר שְׁנַיִם שֶׁיּוֹשְׁבִין וְאֵין בֵּינֵיהֶם דִּבְרֵי תוֹרָה הֲרֵי זֶה מוֹשַׁב לֵצִים שֶׁנֶּאֱמַר וּבְמוֹשַׁב לֵצִים לֹא יָשָׁב. אֲבָל שְׁנַיִם שֶׁיּוֹשְׁבִין וְיֵשׁ בֵּינֵיהֶם דִּבְרֵי תוֹרָה שְׁכִינָה שְׁרוּיָה

scoffers, for it is written, 'Nor did he sit in the assembly of the scoffers.' [Ps. 1:1] However, [when] two sit together and do exchange words of Torah, then, the Divine Presence dwells with them, even as it is written, 'Then those who feared *Adonai* spoke the one to the other, and *Adonai* listened and heard and for those who feared *Adonai* and who thought of God, a book of remembrance was inscribed.' [Mal. 3:16] This verse applies to two [people]. How may I learn from Scripture that were one person to sit and study Torah, the Holy One would grant a proper reward? From the verse that states, 'Though one sit alone and be still, yet will he receive [the reward].'" [Lam. 3:28]

בֵּינֵיהֶם שֶׁנֶּאֱמַר אָז נִדְבְּרוּ יִרְאֵי יְהֹוָה אִישׁ אֶל רֵעֵהוּ וַיַּקְשֵׁב יְהֹוָה וַיִּשְׁמָע וַיִּכָּתֵב סֵפֶר זִכָּרוֹן לְפָנָיו לְיִרְאֵי יְהֹוָה וּלְחֹשְׁבֵי שְׁמוֹ. אֵין לִי אֶלָּא שְׁנַיִם מִנַּיִן אֲפִלּוּ אֶחָד שֶׁיּוֹשֵׁב וְעוֹסֵק בַּתּוֹרָה שֶׁהַקָּדוֹשׁ בָּרוּךְ הוּא קוֹבֵעַ לוֹ שָׂכָר שֶׁנֶּאֱמַר יֵשֵׁב בָּדָד וְיִדֹּם כִּי נָטַל עָלָיו:

Rabbi Chanina. He was always known as סְגַן הַכֹּהֲנִים *segan hakohanim,* the "deputy of the priests" (rather than by his father's name). While his name is not listed among the rabbis executed by the Romans and thus considered martyrs, he probably was executed along with Shimon ben Gamliel and Rabbi Yishmael ben Elisha. He lived in the first century of the common era and was among the great scholars during the last year of the Second Temple.

Pray for the welfare of the government. Rabbi Chanina anticipates the view of the social philosopher Thomas Hobbes (1588-1679) who wrote that "...except they be restrained through fear of some coercive power, every man will dread and distrust each other." Both Hobbes and Rabbi Chanina assume that society can only operate through fear. When Rabbi Chanina penned these words, he was considering the Roman government. Throughout history, readers responded to his words positively or negatively, depending on the circumstances in which they found themselves.

Rashi sees Rabbi Chanina's statement in the light of Jeremiah's call to "...seek the peace of the city whither I have caused you to be carried away captive." (Jer. 29:7)

Chananya ben Teradyon. He lived in the second century C.E. during the era of Yavneh. He was the head of the yeshivah of Sichnin in the Galilee. He was martyred by the Romans (for teaching Torah) by being wrapped in a Torah scroll and set afire. Only a few of his sayings have been preserved. He was the father of Beruriah, the well-known wife of Rabbi Meir.

3:3 Rabbi Shimon would say, "If three have eaten at one table and have not spoken words of Torah, it is as if they had eaten sacri-

ג:ג רַבִּי שִׁמְעוֹן אוֹמֵר שְׁלֹשָׁה שֶׁאָכְלוּ עַל שֻׁלְחָן אֶחָד וְלֹא אָמְרוּ עָלָיו דִּבְרֵי תוֹרָה כְּאִלּוּ אָכְלוּ מִזִּבְחֵי מֵתִים שֶׁנֶּאֱמַר כִּי כָּל שֻׁלְחָנוֹת מָלְאוּ קִיא צוֹאָה בְּלִי

fices offered to the dead. [Cf. Ps. 106:28.] Even Scripture says, 'All their tables are filled with filth and vomit without the Divine Presence.' [Isa. 28:8] However, three who have eaten at one table and have spoken words of Torah, Scripture states, 'He said to me, this table is in the presence of God.'" [Ezek. 41:22]

מָקוֹם. אֲבָל שְׁלֹשָׁה שֶׁאָכְלוּ עַל שֻׁלְחָן אֶחָד וְאָמְרוּ עָלָיו דִּבְרֵי תוֹרָה כְּאִלּוּ אָכְלוּ מִשֻּׁלְחָנוֹ שֶׁל מָקוֹם. שֶׁנֶּאֱמַר וַיְדַבֵּר אֵלַי זֶה הַשֻּׁלְחָן אֲשֶׁר לִפְנֵי יְהוָֹה:

Rabbi Shimon. Rabbi Shimon (bar Yochai) lived in the middle of the second century C.E. He is almost always referred to as Rabbi Shimon. A student of Akiva, he studied under him even while Akiva was in prison; he was one of Akiva's five students who survived the Bar Kochba revolt. Tradition attributes these students with the arrangement of the Oral Tradition. Rabbi Shimon was forced to remain in hiding after the defeat of Bar Kochba. Associated with mystical doctrines, he is considered the author of the *Zohar*.

If three have eaten at one table. This incremental pattern of one, two, and three people eating, which appears both in this *mishnah* and in the one preceding, refers to some kind of table-fellowship, a kind of religious act, not merely the act of eating. The connection of food and worship is ancient and is found in many cultures. The rabbis introduced *Hamotzi* (the blessing of bread), which is recited before the meal, and *Birkat Hamazon* (grace after meals), which is recited after the meal, as a practical method of insuring that words of Torah would be uttered at the meal table. The source for the grace after meals is Deuteronomy 8:10, "You shall eat and be satisfied and bless *Adonai* your God for the good land that God has given you."

All their tables are filled with filth and vomit. The passage from Isaiah 28:8 has been translated with midrashic (poetic) license to make Rabbi Shimon's point. In the context of the Bible, the verse means, "For all tables are filled with filthy vomit and no place (*makom*) is clean." (The Hebrew word מָקוֹם *makom*, "place," was understood by the rabbis to mean God.) This may be taken figuratively to refer to the low state of morality and religion in Jerusalem or it may refer to a literal scene witnessed by the prophet. It is suggested that a banquet was being held by the Judean aristocracy to celebrate the break away from Assyria and that Isaiah, surprising the revelers, came upon the scene described in these verses.

3:4 Rabbi Chanina ben Chachinai would say, "One who spends the night awake or who goes on a journey alone or who turns one's mind to useless thoughts sins against one's own soul."

ג:ד רַבִּי חֲנִינָא בֶּן חֲכִינַאי אוֹמֵר הַנֵּעוֹר בַּלַּיְלָה וְהַמְהַלֵּךְ בַּדֶּרֶךְ יְחִידִי וּמְפַנֶּה לִבּוֹ לְבַטָּלָה הֲרֵי זֶה מִתְחַיֵּב בְּנַפְשׁוֹ:

Rabbi Chanina ben Chachinai. Sometimes called simply ben Chachinai, he lived in *Eretz Yisrael* in the middle of the second century C.E. A distinguished disciple of Rabbi Akiva, he was martyred with him.

One who spends the night awake. Rashi and Bartinoro contend that the first clause specifically refers to one who spends the night hours thinking the wrong kinds of thoughts.

Who goes on a journey alone. Bartinoro connects the last two clauses in our *mishnah*. Since the night is a dangerous time, the lone traveler dare not distract his mind from Torah, which would be his only real defense against brigands or deadly accidents.

3:5 Rabbi Nechunya ben Hakanah would often say, "Anyone who will accept the yoke of the Torah, from that one will be removed the yoke of the government and the yoke of worldly care. But anyone who spurns the yoke of the Torah, upon that one will be placed the yoke of the government and the yoke of worldly care."

ג:ה רַבִּי נְחוּנְיָא בֶּן הַקָּנָה אוֹמֵר כָּל הַמְקַבֵּל עָלָיו עוֹל תּוֹרָה מַעֲבִירִין מִמֶּנּוּ עוֹל מַלְכוּת וְעוֹל דֶּרֶךְ אֶרֶץ וְכָל הַפּוֹרֵק מִמֶּנּוּ עוֹל תּוֹרָה נוֹתְנִין עָלָיו עוֹל מַלְכוּת וְעוֹל דֶּרֶךְ אֶרֶץ:

Rabbi Nechunya ben Hakanah. Rabbi Nechunya, a student of Rabbi Yochanan ben Zakkai, lived in the second half of the first century and was a teacher of Rabbi Yishmael. Rabbi Nechunya was noble in character and known for his benevolent acts and his good relations with colleagues.

The yoke of the Torah. For Maimonides, the yoke of the Torah refers to its continual study. If one takes on the yoke of the Torah, Maimonides teaches, God will deliver one and lessen one's daily troubles. Bartinoro thinks that the struggle to make a living will be lessened for the one who accepts the yoke of the Torah.

The yoke of the government. Both Maimonides and Bartinoro believe that the yoke of the government (מַלְכוּת *malchut*, literally, "kingdom") indicates all the impositions of the king and his retinue.

The yoke of worldly care. Maimonides contends that the yoke of worldly care implies the difficulties of any time.

Anyone who spurns the yoke of the Torah. For Maimonides, this spurning פּוֹרֵק *porek* (literally, "breaking") of the yoke of the Torah refers to one who will not abide by the Torah, denying its divine source. For Bartinoro, the image symbolizes the individual's simple unwillingness to fulfill the Torah regardless of reason or intent.

3:6 Rabbi Chalafta ben Dosa, who lived in Kefar Chananya, used to say, "If ten sit and engage in Torah study, the Divine Presence abides among them, as it is said, '*Adonai* stands in the congregation of God.' [Ps. 82:1]

ג:ו רַבִּי חֲלַפְתָּא בֶּן דּוֹסָא אִישׁ כְּפַר חֲנַנְיָא אוֹמֵר עֲשָׂרָה שֶׁיּוֹשְׁבִין וְעוֹסְקִין בַּתּוֹרָה שְׁכִינָה שְׁרוּיָה בֵּינֵיהֶם שֶׁנֶּאֱמַר אֱלֹהִים נִצָּב בַּעֲדַת אֵל. וּמִנַּיִן אֲפִלּוּ חֲמִשָּׁה שֶׁנֶּאֱמַר וַאֲגֻדָּתוֹ עַל אֶרֶץ יְסָדָהּ. וּמִנַּיִן אֲפִלּוּ שְׁלֹשָׁה

How do we know that it applies to five? Because of the verse 'He has founded his bunch on the earth.' [Amos 9:6] How do we know that it applies even to three? Because of the verse 'He will judge in the midst of judges.' [Ps. 82:1] How do we know that it applies even to two? The verse teaches, 'Then they who feared *Adonai* spoke one to the other and *Adonai* listened and heard.' [Mal. 3:16] It applies even to one, since it is said, 'In every place where I cause My name to be mentioned, I will come and bless you.'" [Exod. 20:24]

שֶׁנֶּאֱמַר בְּקֶרֶב אֱלֹהִים יִשְׁפֹּט. וּמִנַּיִן אֲפִלּוּ שְׁנַיִם שֶׁנֶּאֱמַר אָז נִדְבְּרוּ יִרְאֵי יְהוָה אִישׁ אֶל רֵעֵהוּ וַיַּקְשֵׁב יְהוָה וַיִּשְׁמָע. וּמִנַּיִן אֲפִלּוּ אֶחָד שֶׁנֶּאֱמַר בְּכָל הַמָּקוֹם אֲשֶׁר אַזְכִּיר אֶת שְׁמִי אָבֹא אֵלֶיךָ וּבֵרַכְתִּיךָ:

Rabbi Chalafta. Rabbi Chalafta ben Dosa lived in the early part of the second century in Seforis (located in Israel in the Galil region) as leader of the community. He was the father of Rabbi Yose and a disciple of Rabbi Meir. His charming use of proof-texts includes certain assumptions about the Jewish community. For example, the minimum number of a congregation, מִנְיָן *minyan*, "quorum," is ten. While it is not clear why a bunch has a minimum number of five, it seems related to what can be grasped in one hand (five fingers). And, according to *Mishnah Sanhedrin* 1:1, the minimum number for a court is three.

This passage argues that the sense of God's presence is available to any Jew who studies the Torah, whether alone or in a group.

3:7   Rabbi Elazar who lived in Bartota would say, "Give God what is God's, since you and all that you have are God's. Thus, David said, 'Since all things come from You, that which we give You is Yours.'" [I Chron. 29:14] Rabbi Yaakov said, "Were one to be walking on the road while studying and then stop one's studies to say, 'How beautiful is this tree!' or 'How nice is that field!' such a person would be considered by the Torah to have sinned against one's own soul."

ג:ז רַבִּי אֶלְעָזָר אִישׁ בַּרְתּוֹתָא אוֹמֵר תֶּן לוֹ מִשֶּׁלּוֹ שֶׁאַתָּה וְשֶׁלְּךָ שֶׁלּוֹ וְכֵן בְּדָוִד הוּא אוֹמֵר כִּי מִמְּךָ הַכֹּל וּמִיָּדְךָ נָתַנּוּ לָךְ. רַבִּי יַעֲקֹב אוֹמֵר הַמְהַלֵּךְ בַּדֶּרֶךְ וְשׁוֹנֶה וּמַפְסִיק מִמִּשְׁנָתוֹ וְאוֹמֵר מַה נָּאֶה אִילָן זֶה מַה נָּאֶה נִיר זֶה מַעֲלֶה עָלָיו הַכָּתוּב כְּאִלּוּ מִתְחַיֵּב בְּנַפְשׁוֹ:

Rabbi Elazar [ben Yehudah]. Rabbi Elazar, who lived in the first half of the second century of the common era, was a disciple of Rabbi Yehoshua ben Chananya and a contemporary of Rabbi Akiva, whom he challenged. Bartota was a city in the Galilee, whose precise location is unknown.

Give God what is God's. Bartinoro understands the first part of our *mishnah* as an exhortation to be involved with divine purposes whether the cost requires the giving of self or the giving of substance.

Were one to be walking on the road while studying. According to Rashi, the study of Torah will protect the individual from the dangers of travel. To break off from such study puts one's life at risk.

How nice is that field. Bartinoro notes that the field spoken of in this second part of the *mishnah* is a plowed field. Thus, it might then be said that Rabbi Yaakov is denouncing the admiration of the work of human hands in place of the admiration of the Torah, the work of God.

3:8 Rabbi Dostai, the son of Rabbi Yannai, in the name of Rabbi Meir, said, "One who forgets anything one has learned, Scripture accounts it as if one had sinned against one's soul, for it says, 'Only be careful and diligently watch your soul so that you do not forget anything your eyes have seen.' [Deut. 4:9] One might think that [this caution] might apply even in the case where the studies were too difficult for the one engaged in them. Therefore, the verse continues, 'Lest they [the words of Torah] depart from your heart all the days of your life.' Thus one would sin against one's soul only if one intended to remove them from one's heart."

ג:ח רַבִּי דוֹסְתָּאי בַּר יַנַּאי מִשּׁוּם רַבִּי מֵאִיר אוֹמֵר כָּל הַשּׁוֹכֵחַ דָּבָר אֶחָד מִמִּשְׁנָתוֹ מַעֲלֶה עָלָיו הַכָּתוּב כְּאִלּוּ מִתְחַיֵּב בְּנַפְשׁוֹ שֶׁנֶּאֱמַר רַק הִשָּׁמֶר לְךָ וּשְׁמֹר נַפְשְׁךָ מְאֹד פֶּן תִּשְׁכַּח אֶת הַדְּבָרִים אֲשֶׁר רָאוּ עֵינֶיךָ. יָכוֹל אֲפִלּוּ תָּקְפָה עָלָיו מִשְׁנָתוֹ תַּלְמוּד לוֹמַר וּפֶן יָסוּרוּ מִלְּבָבְךָ כֹּל יְמֵי חַיֶּיךָ הָא אֵינוֹ מִתְחַיֵּב בְּנַפְשׁוֹ עַד שֶׁיֵּשֵׁב וִיסִירֵם מִלִּבּוֹ:

Rabbi Dostai [bar Yannai]. An older contemporary of Rabbi Yehudah Ha-Nasi and a disciple of Rabbi Meir, he lived in the second half of the second century. His sayings often reflect a sharp wit. This statement, like the previous *mishnah* of Rabbi Yaakov, stresses the importance of the careful retention of Torah, particularly important in the transmission of an oral tradition.

Rabbi Meir. He lived in the second century of the common era and was one of the outstanding leaders of the generation that followed the failed Bar Kochba revolt. Since he was mostly concerned with *halachah*, he played an important role in the development of the *Mishnah*. Tradition holds that he was a descendant of proselytes and that his name was really Nehorai, but he was called Meir because his teachings enlightened (in Hebrew, מֵאִיר *meir*) the sages in regard to the *halachah*. While he studied under Rabbi Yishmael and Elisha ben Abuyah, he was primarily a student of Rabbi Akiva.

So that you do not forget anything your eyes have seen. For Bartinoro, the individual who forgets is culpable because memory loss can be avoided by the constant reviewing of what one has learned. Forgetting puts one's soul at risk because it may lead to allowing what is prohibited.

Lest they [the words of Torah] depart from your heart. Yom Tov Lipman Heller goes beyond the simple meaning of the text, which implies inaction may be dangerous for we may forget the words of Torah, and claims that, when you concentrate on something else, words of Torah may also leave your heart.

3:9 Rabbi Chanina ben Dosa often said, "One whose fear of sin precedes one's wisdom, one's wisdom will last. One whose wisdom precedes one's fear of sin, one's wisdom will not last." He [also] would say, "One whose deeds exceed one's wisdom, one's wisdom will last. One whose wisdom exceeds one's deeds, one's wisdom will not last."

ג:ט רַבִּי חֲנִינָא בֶּן דּוֹסָא אוֹמֵר כֹּל שֶׁיִּרְאַת חֶטְאוֹ קוֹדֶמֶת לְחָכְמָתוֹ חָכְמָתוֹ מִתְקַיֶּמֶת. וְכֹל שֶׁחָכְמָתוֹ קוֹדֶמֶת לְיִרְאַת חֶטְאוֹ אֵין חָכְמָתוֹ מִתְקַיֶּמֶת. הוּא הָיָה אוֹמֵר כֹּל שֶׁמַּעֲשָׂיו מְרֻבִּין מֵחָכְמָתוֹ חָכְמָתוֹ מִתְקַיֶּמֶת. וְכֹל שֶׁחָכְמָתוֹ מְרֻבָּה מִמַּעֲשָׂיו אֵין חָכְמָתוֹ מִתְקַיֶּמֶת:

Rabbi Chanina ben Dosa. A wonder worker and mystic, he was a student and colleague of Rabbi Yochanan ben Zakkai. He lived in the first century of the common era in Arav (located in the lower Galilee). Distinguished by his extreme piety, he was zealous in observing *mitzvot*.

One whose fear of sin precedes one's wisdom. Wisdom is based on a response to the relationship of the individual with God. Proverbs 1:7 says it best: "The beginning of wisdom is reverence for God." The Talmud summarizes the position in a metaphor: The one who is learned in Torah but does not revere God is like the gatekeeper who has been given keys to the inner doors but not the outer ones. How is that person able to enter? (B. Talmud, *Shabbat* 31a-b)

3:10 He would often say, "Whomever people like, God likes. Whomever people do not like, God does not like." Rabbi Dosa ben Harkinas used to say, "Morning sleep, mid-day wine, children's talk, and attendance at the meeting places of the ignorant–all will take a person out of this world."

ג:י הוּא הָיָה אוֹמֵר כֹּל שֶׁרוּחַ הַבְּרִיּוֹת נוֹחָה הֵימֶנּוּ רוּחַ הַמָּקוֹם נוֹחָה הֵימֶנּוּ וְכֹל שֶׁאֵין רוּחַ הַבְּרִיּוֹת נוֹחָה הֵימֶנּוּ אֵין רוּחַ הַמָּקוֹם נוֹחָה הֵימֶנּוּ. רַבִּי דּוֹסָא בֶּן הַרְכִּינַס אוֹמֵר שֵׁנָה שֶׁל שַׁחֲרִית וְיַיִן שֶׁל צָהֳרַיִם וְשִׂיחַת הַיְלָדִים וִישִׁיבַת בָּתֵּי כְנֵסִיּוֹת שֶׁל עַמֵּי הָאָרֶץ מוֹצִיאִין אֶת הָאָדָם מִן הָעוֹלָם:

The three teachers listed in the previous מִשְׁנָיוֹת *mishnayot* (*Avot* 3:8, 9, and 10), Rabbi Dostai, Rabbi Chanina ben Dosa, and Rabbi Dosa ben Harkinas, are not contemporaries. Their sayings were probably included one after another due to the similarity in their names.

Whomever people like, God likes. Yom Tov Lipman Heller finds that the first part of this *mishnah* explicates the verse from Proverbs 3:4: "So shall you find grace and good favor in the sight of God and people."

Rabbi Dosa ben Harkinas. Rabbi Dosa was a contemporary of Rabbi Joshua and lived about the year 100 C.E. A man of wealth, he was a younger contemporary of Rabbi Yochanan ben Zakkai. His name often appears without his father's name. He lived to see the Second Temple and survive its destruction. He died during the second decade of the second century.

Morning sleep, midday wine, children's talk, and attendance at the meeting places of the ignorant. Rashi understands the last part of this *mishnah* to refer to the one who oversleeps the time for the recital of the morning *Shema*, to one who chances drunkenness by drinking at noon, to one who spends his time listening to idle talk from young people, and to one who spends his time among those who are occupied with vain matters and are thereby ignorant.

3:11 Rabbi Elazar of Modin used to say, "One who desecrates holy things, and one who condemns the festivals, and one who publicly shames a fellow human being, and one who breaks the covenant [Berit Milah] of Abraham our ancestor, and one who misinterprets the Torah–even if that person were to possess [great knowledge of] Torah and [were a great doer of] good deeds, that person would have no portion in the world to come."

ג:יא רַבִּי אֶלְעָזָר הַמּוֹדָעִי אוֹמֵר הַמְחַלֵּל אֶת הַקֳּדָשִׁים וְהַמְבַזֶּה אֶת הַמּוֹעֲדוֹת וְהַמַּלְבִּין פְּנֵי חֲבֵרוֹ בָּרַבִּים וְהַמֵּפֵר בְּרִיתוֹ שֶׁל אַבְרָהָם אָבִינוּ וְהַמְגַלֶּה פָנִים בַּתּוֹרָה שֶׁלֹּא כַהֲלָכָה אַף עַל פִּי שֶׁיֵּשׁ בְּיָדוֹ תּוֹרָה וּמַעֲשִׂים טוֹבִים אֵין לוֹ חֵלֶק לָעוֹלָם הַבָּא:

Rabbi Elazar of Modin. Rabbi Elazar lived toward the end of the first century and the beginning of the second century C.E. Although he supported Bar Kochba, his nephew, in his revolt against Rome (132-135 C.E.), Rabbi Elazar was suspected of treason against his people and was executed by Bar Kochba. Modin is the well-known home of the Maccabees.

One who desecrates holy things. It may well be that the person to whom Rabbi Elazar refers was a Judeo-Christian since that new religious notion was said to free the individual from the requirements of some Jewish rituals and the observance of Jewish festivals. Circumcision was not conside. Circumcision wasred necessary for Christianity. (Cf. Romans 4:9ff.)

Rashi takes the person to whom Rabbi Elazar is referring to be an *apikoros*, in the rabbinical context, a "nonbeliever." By definition, such a person will be cut off in this world and in the next world.

Who misinterprets the Torah. For Maimonides, the misinterpretation of the Torah relates to one who acts in a manner that differs from the understanding established by *halachah*. Bartinoro adds that such a person acts with presumption and lack of shame. He adds, however, that the power of repentance is so great that, should one repent before one's death, that person will have a portion in the life to come.

3:12 Rabbi Yishmael would say, "Be speedy to obey a superior; be dignified before the young; and cheerfully greet every person."

רַבִּי יִשְׁמָעֵאל אוֹמֵר הֱוֵי קַל לְרֹאשׁ וְנֽוֹחַ לְתִשְׁחֽוֹרֶת וֶהֱוֵי מְקַבֵּל אֶת כָּל הָאָדָם בְּשִׂמְחָה:

Rabbi Yishmael [ben Elisha]. He lived in the first half of the second century and was the grandson of a High Priest. Having been taken to Rome as a captive after the fall of Jerusalem, his release was affected through the efforts of Rabbi Yehoshua ben Chananya. He was among the few sages whose personality as a teacher as well as his teachings left a stamp on the literature and Judaism of the period of the rabbis called the *tannaim*. He was among the chief spokesmen at Yavneh. Yishmael argued that "the Torah speaks in the language of human beings" and should be interpreted according to its plain meaning. An intimate colleague of Rabbi Akiva, he argued with him about most matters. Like Akiva, Yishmael died as a martyr.

Be speedy to obey a superior; be dignified before the young. Rashi takes רֹאשׁ *rosh* to refer to God and understands תִשְׁחֽוֹרֶת *tishchoret* as "old age." Thus, it is Yishmael's advice that one should be swift to obey God in one's youth so that such obedience will be נֽוֹחַ *noach*, "easy," in one's old age.

Cheerfully greet every person. For Bartinoro, one should be especially swift to serve the head of the academy, but one should greet with joy any person, whatever the rank.

3:13 Rabbi Akiva often said, "Laughter and frivolity lead to lewdness. Tradition is a fence around the Torah. Tithes are a fence around wealth. Vows are a fence around abstinence. And silence is a fence around wisdom."

רַבִּי עֲקִיבָא אוֹמֵר שְׂחוֹק וְקַלּוּת רֹאשׁ מַרְגִּילִין אֶת הָאָדָם לְעֶרְוָה. מָסֹרֶת סְיָג לַתּוֹרָה מַעְשְׂרוֹת סְיָג לָעֽשֶׁר נְדָרִים סְיָג לִפְרִישׁוּת סְיָג לַחָכְמָה שְׁתִיקָה:

Rabbi Akiva. One of the best-known teachers in Israel, Akiva lived from 60 to 135. Legends abound regarding his life. He was a shepherd who began his study at age forty (a student of Yehoshua ben Chananya) and married his wealthy employer's daughter. He joined Bar Kochba in the revolt against Rome and was put to death in 135. Rabbi Akiva was one of the great heroes of rabbinic Judaism. Because of his method of interpretation, it is said that he could deduce "mountains of law" from parts of each letter of the Written Law.

Tradition is a fence around the Torah. The oral tradition, מָסֹרָה *masorah*, handed down from one generation to the other, was a fence around the Torah. This *masorah* preserved the correct text.

Tithes are a fence around wealth. Bartinoro explains how tithes are a fence around wealth by quoting the rabbinic *midrash* on the commandment to tithe (Deut. 14:22). The biblical text reads עַשֵּׂר תְּעַשֵּׂר *aser te'aser*, "you will certainly tithe"; the *midrash* reads עַשֵּׂר תְּעַשֵּׁר *aser te'asher*, "you will certainly become wealthy."

Vows are a fence around abstinence. Maimonides explains that, if one vows and fulfills the vow, that individual will gain self-control. That self-control will lead to the habit of abstinence.

Silence is a fence around wisdom. Bartinoro points out that the kind of silence requested here is from useless chatter. He then quotes, "Even a fool, when he holds his peace, is counted wise." (Prov. 17:28)

3:14 He used to say, "Human beings are loved because they were made in God's image. That they were created in God's image was made known by a special love, as it is said, 'For God made human beings in the divine image.' [Gen. 9:6] Israel is loved for they are called children of God. That they were called children of God was made known to them by a special love, as it is said, 'You are children of *Adonai* your God.' [Deut. 14:1] Israel is [even more] loved because to them was given a precious instrument. That such a precious instrument was given to them was made known to them by a special love, as it is said, 'For I have given you a good doctrine, do not forsake my Torah.'" [Prov. 4:2]

ג:יד הוּא הָיָה אוֹמֵר חָבִיב אָדָם שֶׁנִּבְרָא בְּצֶלֶם. חִבָּה יְתֵרָה נוֹדַעַת לוֹ שֶׁנִּבְרָא בְּצֶלֶם שֶׁנֶּאֱמַר כִּי בְּצֶלֶם אֱלֹהִים עָשָׂה אֶת הָאָדָם. חֲבִיבִין יִשְׂרָאֵל שֶׁנִּקְרְאוּ בָנִים לַמָּקוֹם. חִבָּה יְתֵרָה נוֹדַעַת לָהֶם שֶׁנִּקְרְאוּ בָנִים לַמָּקוֹם שֶׁנֶּאֱמַר בָּנִים אַתֶּם לַיהֹוָה אֱלֹהֵיכֶם. חֲבִיבִין יִשְׂרָאֵל שֶׁנִּתַּן לָהֶם כְּלִי חֶמְדָּה חִבָּה יְתֵרָה נוֹדַעַת לָהֶם שֶׁנִּתַּן לָהֶם כְּלִי חֶמְדָּה שֶׁנֶּאֱמַר כִּי לֶקַח טוֹב נָתַתִּי לָכֶם תּוֹרָתִי אַל תַּעֲזֹבוּ:

Human beings are loved. Rabbi Akiva's stress on love may serve to soften those views of Judaism that see it merely as a religion of law. For Akiva, the human awareness of the divine source of our life should be the source of our own sense of love. More than that, if our bond to God is one of love, it is incumbent upon us to relate lovingly to one another, as human beings, as fellow images of God.

Rashi sees our being created in God's image as the basis for obedience to God. Maimonides states in his *Guide* (I:1) that it is intellectual comprehension that indicates that human beings were created in the divine image.

Israel...was given a precious instrument. The כְּלִי חֶמְדָּה *keli chemdah*, here translated as "precious instrument," is so called because, for the rabbis, the Torah was the plan of the universe. *Bereshit Rabbah* points out that, when a builder builds, the builder requires a set of plans.

Thus, when God was about to create the world, God, too, required a set of plans, namely the Torah. Through Torah, the world came into being. Thus, it was subsequently given to Israel to study and to keep.

For I have given you a good doctrine. Bartinoro connects the word לֶקַח *lekach,* "doctrine," in Proverbs 4:2 with the same word in Deuteronomy 32:2, "My doctrine shall drop as the dew."

3:15 All is foreseen, yet [free] choice is given. By [God's] goodness is the world judged. Yet all things follow the larger portion of [human] acts.

ג:טו הַכֹּל צָפוּי וְהָרְשׁוּת נְתוּנָה וּבְטוּב הָעוֹלָם נָדוֹן וְהַכֹּל לְפִי רוֹב הַמַּעֲשֶׂה:

All is foreseen. This *mishnah* is often cited to point to a paradox: God's foreknowledge of events versus human freedom. If God knows about all events, then how can human activity really be free from God's control? Were the individual not free, however, it might be argued that human beings are not responsible for their actions. The rabbis argue that, since God is perfect, such a paradox can function effectively in this world.

Rashi understands the word צָפוּי *tzafui,* here translated as "foreseen," to mean "seen," i.e., all human acts whether in public or in private are seen by God. Even so, it is up to the individual to do good or bad.

Maimonides points to the importance of the notion that each individual has the ability to choose. Thus nothing and no one, not even God, can impair that choice.

By [God's] goodness is the world judged. The notion of God carries with it the notion of divine goodness. Why else would God be worthy of devotion or emulation? For Rashi, there is a relationship between the acts of human beings and God's goodness. God does not judge human beings according to their deeds, but rather God judges the human species with compassion.

All things follow the larger portion of [human] acts. As human beings we are not required to be perfect. That's why we are so dependent on God's goodness. However, we are required to work in the world so that our good deeds outweigh our sins. The path of repentance is always available to us. Together we must work as partners with God to repair the broken world. In a sense, therefore, the future of the world is in our hands.

Maimonides takes רוֹב הַמַּעֲשֶׂה *rov hamaaseh,* here translated as the "larger portion of [human] acts," to indicate that the inculcation of the moral virtues depends on the repetition of conditioning acts. Only in this manner can the soul be affected.

3:16 He used to say, "Everything is given on pledge and a net is spread out for all that lives. The shop is open; the shopkeeper

ג:טז הוּא הָיָה אוֹמֵר הַכֹּל נָתוּן בָּעֵרָבוֹן וּמְצוּדָה פְרוּסָה עַל כָּל הַחַיִּים הֶחָנוּת פְּתוּחָה וְהַחֶנְוָנִי מַקִּיף וְהַפִּנְקָס פָּתוּחַ וְהַיָּד כּוֹתֶבֶת וְכָל הָרוֹצֶה לִלְוֹות יָבֹא וְיִלְוֶה

extends credit; the ledger is open; and the hand writes. One may come and borrow, but the collectors make their rounds each and every day; and they collect whether one wants it or not; what they have got, they can depend on, for the judgment is a true one, and everything is prepared for the banquet."

וְהַגַּבָּאִים מַחֲזִירִין תָּדִיר בְּכָל יוֹם וְנִפְרָעִין מִן הָאָדָם מִדַּעְתּוֹ וְשֶׁלֹּא מִדַּעְתּוֹ וְיֵשׁ לָהֶם עַל מַה שֶׁיִּסְמֹכוּ וְהַדִּין דִּין אֱמֶת וְהַכֹּל מְתֻקָּן לַסְּעוּדָה:

Rabbi Akiva's parable reflects the business practices of his time, as well as the business practices of other generations.

The shop is open. Rashi, perhaps reflecting the business in which he was engaged, initially describes the shop as one that sells wine. He then applies the parable. The shop is the world, and God is the shopkeeper. The ledger contains a record of our deeds and misdeeds. The collectors are the acts of Heaven. The banquet is prepared for the world to come. Rashi also offers an alternative reading that "all is prepared for the Day of Judgment." We are all accountable for our actions, good and bad, and God will judge us mercifully but with specific regard to how we have led our lives in this world. The world and its things are solely in the possession of God. God merely lends us things to use. Nothing is given to humankind outright; it is given only on condition that the individual follows the laws of God. The individual who does not follow the divine path of life will fall into the net of wrongdoing. It is easy to access the darkness of things in life. Nothing is under lock and key. One is free to use whatever one takes for good or bad. Though God does not demand immediate payment, the Eternal One records what the individual does with the goods borrowed. The soul goes to heaven each night for this recording. Sometimes the individual is not even aware of this recording and to where it will lead.

3:17 Rabbi Elazar ben Azaryah said, "Where there is no Torah, there will be no good conduct; where there is no good conduct, there will be no Torah. Where there is no wisdom, there will be no reverence; where there is no reverence, there will be no wisdom. Where there is no understanding, there will be no knowledge; where there is no knowledge, there will be no understanding. Where there is no bread [literally, flour], there will be no Torah; where there is no Torah, there will be no bread." He would often say, "To what shall be compared one whose wisdom is greater than one's deeds? To a tree whose branches are

ג:יז רַבִּי אֶלְעָזָר בֶּן עֲזַרְיָה אוֹמֵר אִם אֵין תּוֹרָה אֵין דֶּרֶךְ אֶרֶץ אִם אֵין דֶּרֶךְ אֶרֶץ אֵין תּוֹרָה אִם אֵין חָכְמָה אֵין יִרְאָה אִם אֵין יִרְאָה אֵין חָכְמָה אִם אֵין דַּעַת אֵין בִּינָה אִם אֵין בִּינָה אֵין דַּעַת אִם אֵין קֶמַח אֵין תּוֹרָה אִם אֵין תּוֹרָה אֵין קֶמַח. הוּא הָיָה אוֹמֵר כֹּל שֶׁחָכְמָתוֹ מְרֻבָּה מִמַּעֲשָׂיו לְמָה הוּא דוֹמֶה לְאִילָן שֶׁעֲנָפָיו מְרֻבִּין וְשָׁרָשָׁיו מוּעָטִין וְהָרוּחַ בָּאָה וְעוֹקַרְתּוּ וְהוֹפַכְתּוּ עַל פָּנָיו שֶׁנֶּאֱמַר וְהָיָה כְּעַרְעָר בָּעֲרָבָה וְלֹא יִרְאֶה כִּי יָבֹא טוֹב וְשָׁכַן חֲרֵרִים בַּמִּדְבָּר אֶרֶץ מְלֵחָה וְלֹא תֵשֵׁב. אֲבָל כֹּל שֶׁמַּעֲשָׂיו מְרֻבִּין מֵחָכְמָתוֹ לְמָה הוּא דוֹמֶה לְאִילָן שֶׁעֲנָפָיו מוּעָטִין וְשָׁרָשָׁיו מְרֻבִּין שֶׁאֲפִלּוּ כָּל הָרוּחוֹת שֶׁבָּעוֹלָם בָּאוֹת וְנוֹשְׁבוֹת בּוֹ אֵין מְזִיזִין אוֹתוֹ מִמְּקוֹמוֹ שֶׁנֶּאֱמַר וְהָיָה כְּעֵץ שָׁתוּל עַל

many, but whose roots are few, so that, when the wind comes, it will uproot it and overturn it, as it says, 'One shall be like a tamerisk in the desert and shall not see when good comes; but shall inhabit the parched places in the wilderness.' [Jer. 17:6] To what shall be compared one whose works are more numerous than one's wisdom? To a tree whose branches are few, but whose roots are many, so that, even if all the winds of the world were to come and blow upon it, they could not move it from its place, even as it says, 'For one shall be as a tree planted by the water, that spreads out its roots by the river. It shall not fear when heat comes, for its leaf shall be green. It shall not worry in a year of drought, for it shall never cease yielding fruit.'" [Jer. 17:8]

מַיִם וְעַל יוּבַל יְשַׁלַּח שָׁרָשָׁיו וְלֹא יִרְאֶה כִּי יָבֹא חֹם וְהָיָה עָלֵהוּ רַעֲנָן וּבִשְׁנַת בַּצֹּרֶת לֹא יִדְאָג וְלֹא יָמִישׁ מֵעֲשׂוֹת פֶּרִי:

Rabbi Elazar ben Azaryah. Rabbi Elazar ben Azaryah of Yavneh lived from 50 to 120. He was president (*nasi*) of the Sanhedrin for a brief time following the deposition of Rabban Gamliel II. After the restoration of Rabban Gamliel II to that position, Rabbi Elazar became the *av bet din*, the vice-president. A man of great wealth, he was also devoted to the welfare of the Jewish community.

Where there is no knowledge, there will be no understanding. Bartinoro suggests that knowledge is the finding of reasons for things. Understanding, on the other hand, is the finding of the relationship between things.

Where there is no bread [literally, flour], there will be no Torah. Rashi comments most directly: If one does not eat, how can one learn?

3:18 Rabbi Elazar ben Chisma would say, "[Laws concerning] the offering of birds and the onset of menstruation are the main elements of the laws, while astronomy and geometry are but the appetizers of wisdom."

ג:יח רַבִּי אֶלְעָזָר (בֶּן) חִסְמָא אוֹמֵר קִנִּין וּפִתְחֵי נִדָּה הֵן הֵן גּוּפֵי הֲלָכוֹת. תְּקוּפוֹת וְגִמַּטְרִיָּאוֹת פַּרְפְּרָאוֹת לַחָכְמָה:

Rabbi Elazar ben Chisma. A renowned astronomer, he was a student of Rabbi Yehoshua ben Chananya. He lived in the first half of the second century C.E. and was one of the sages at Yavneh. While not rejecting his own avocation of astronomy, perhaps he meant to suggest that, at a time when Jewish life was under great stress, the study of science should be put aside in order to encourage only the study of Torah.

Offering of birds. This refers to the sacrificial system (cf. Lev. 5:7-10; 12:8; 14:22; 30ff.; 15:14ff. and Num. 6:9ff.) and is discussed at length elsewhere in *Mishnah*, Tractate *Kinnim* ("Birds' Nests").

Menstruation. These laws are fully described in Leviticus 15:19-24 and elsewhere in *Mishnah*, Tractate *Niddah* ("Menstruation").

The main elements of the laws. While these items (birds and menstruation) seem trivial, they should receive attention because they are divine commandments. Bartinoro suggests that the גוּפֵי הֲלָכוֹת *gufei halachot* refer to the main elements of the Oral Law. A reward will be granted to those who follow its dictates.

From Dust to Dust

In Genesis 3:19, the Torah teaches, "You are dust and to dust shall you return." From this statement and others, we learn that the expedient burial of the deceased is required in Judaism. While cremation is forbidden in traditional Judaism and is not encouraged, although permitted, in Reform Judaism, such a practice was not unknown to the early Hebrews. Tradition considered cremation to be an idolatrous practice–also maintaining that cremation denied the possibility of bodily resurrection (at the end of days) and was an affront to human dignity.

The Zohar

The *Zohar*, the "Book of Splendor," is attributed to Rabbi Shimon bar Yochai. It is said that he wrote it when living in a cave where he was hiding from the Romans. The *Zohar*, the chief text of the mystical movement in Judaism, is a collection of books (five volumes) or sections, which include homilies, *midrashim*, and discussion on a wide array of topics. Most are supposed to be the teachings of Rabbi Shimon, but others appear anonymously. The main part of the book is arranged according to the weekly Torah portion and forms a kabbalistic *midrash* on the Torah. The entire volume is probably the work of a Spanish Kabbalist, Moses b. Shem Tov de Leon (who died in 1308).

God as the Place (Hamakom)

To avoid using the name of God, the rabbis were predisposed to using euphemisms such as "Heaven" or the "Holy Blessed One" or "the One who spoke and the world came to be." Among the earliest of such euphemisms was the word *Makom*, "place," for God. It is first attested in a *baraita*, one of the earliest strata of tannaitic literature. The term was used in the *Mishnah* and in the *Tosephta*. In the tannaitic literature, the term is used in an unselfconscious manner with no attempt to explain its meaning. In the amoraic literature, the question is put, "Why is God called *Hamakom*, the Place?" To which the answer is given, "Because God is the place of the world." Since human beings live in spatial divisions, *Hamakom* is also used to denote the Divine Presence in the midst of people. God is not only here in "this place" but God is "the place."

The Yoke of the Torah

An implement taken from the pastoral life served as a metaphor in rabbinic literature, itself the product of city life. That implement was the yoke, which in linking animals to the plow and to one another made farming possible. For the rabbis, there were two yokes. The first was the yoke of Heaven: the acceptance of the existence of God as one and unique and the proclamation that there was no other. The second was the yoke of commandments: the acceptance by the Jew that the same God had enjoined the people to follow a particular path and to live a particular kind of life. The commandments were both ceremonial and ethical; their specificity grew out of a specific concept of God. Thus the yoke of Heaven created a particular kind of yoke of commandments.

Asceticism

The rigorous abstention from worldly pleasures of any kind–in an effort to reach a higher spiritual state–never occupied a central place in Judaism. The sages considered personal privation of any sort to be an affront against God. Personal care and bathing of the body were religious obligations. (*Vayikra Rabbah* 34:3)

Nonetheless, throughout Jewish history individuals did practice asceticism, and it gained more widespread acceptance following the destruction of the Second Temple. Yet, even in this context, typical acts of asceticism such as self-denial in the form of sexual deprivation, celibacy, were seldom practical. Even the Dead Sea sect, the Essenes, did not value asceticism in its own right; rather, they taught that asceticism was a prerequisite for justice and purity. In all cases, historical circumstances motivated individuals or groups to engage in ascetic behavior. Since it is not considered a religious way to worship God, asceticism never emanated from Judaism itself.

The Minyan

According to tradition, a quorum of ten adults over thirteen years of age is necessary for public worship and other religious ceremonies. The Talmud derives the original concept of *minyan* from the word *edah*, "community" (B. Talmud, *Berachot* 21b; *Megillah* 23b), as applied to ten of the spies (Num. 14:27) sent by Moses to scout the Promised Land. "How long shall I bear with this evil congregation that keeps murmuring against Me?" Thus, these ten constitute a congregation. In *Ketubot* 7b, there is also mention of Ruth 4:2, "And he took ten men of the elders of the city," and Psalms 68:27, "In full assemblies bless God, *Adonai*, you who are from the fountain of Israel." Some authorities even relate the numerical definition to Abraham's plea to

God to save Sodom if ten righteous people could be found there. (Gen. 18:32) On this basis, the Talmud records (*Berachot* 6a) that the Divine Presence is with ten who pray together. While the Reform movement has rejected this specific numerical requirement, it should be noted that the aspect of community in the context of worship and ceremony should not be disregarded. While we may pray individually, we worship, celebrate, and mourn together as a community. Not only does community provide us with support, but as a community we share a collective memory and responsibility.

Rabbi Akiva and His Time

Akiva, living in the first and second centuries of the common era, was probably the most outstanding scholar of his time. He greatly influenced the development of *halachah* and died as a martyr, teaching Torah in spite of Roman edicts prohibiting such activity. He is credited with systematizing the *Midrash halachot* and *aggadot*. Akiva's guiding principle was that there is no redundancy in Torah since it emanates from God. In 132 C.E., during Akiva's lifetime, the great revolt against Rome broke out. It is often called the Bar Kochba revolt in honor of its leader. Akiva supported the revolt and regarded Bar Kochba in messianic terms, recognizing in him the possibility of the liberation of Israel from its oppressors.

The Bar Kochba Revolt

Bar Kochba was known also as Bar Kosiba. The name Bar Kochba is an epithet derived from Rabbi Akiva's application of the verse from Numbers 24:17: "There shall come a star [כּוֹכָב *kochav*] out of Jacob who shall smite the corners of Moab and destroy all the children of Seth." Unlike previous battles, such as in the Jewish Wars (66-70), this revolt was united under a single commander-in-chief. The people accepted Bar Kochba's leadership–perhaps because they yearned for liberation so fiercely, remembering their recent defeat. The revolt itself occurred during the reign of Roman Emperor Publius Aelius Hadrian (117-138).

At first, the Jewish people were hopeful that Hadrian would bring about positive change. There were rumors that Hadrian would rebuild the Temple. Instead, a temple to Jupiter was built in Jerusalem, and the city was renamed Aelia Capitolina. It is not clear whether Hadrian issued anti-Jewish decrees before the Bar Kochba revolt but, once the rebellion took place, anti-Jewish decrees were set into motion. These decrees restricted the study of Torah and the practice of Judaism (most notably of circumcision), making such a practice a capital offence.

To prepare for battle, the Jews had seized towns with fortified walls and subterranean passages before actually engaging Hadrian and his forces. Although Bar Kochba had succeeded in taking Jerusalem, he was ultimately defeated in 135, making his final stand at Bethar in the Judean Hills.

Judeo-Christians

Generally referred to as Ebionites, these early Judeo-Christians (born as Jews but accepting of Jesus) have characteristics that are best described in two general areas: (1) their basic adherence to Jewish practices and (2) their understanding of the nature and mission of Jesus and the early history of Christianity. They were even verbally attacked for their stalwart adherence to the Torah and the Jewish festivals and rituals. They were vegetarians, taking literally Genesis 9:4, "Only flesh with the life thereof, which is the blood thereof, shall you not eat." They faced Jerusalem when praying. But they disagreed among themselves regarding sacrifices, often opting for baptism in its stead. While they conflated both traditions, they were Gnostic in character and tended to be considered heretics by both Jews and the Church.

God's Omniscience and Free Will

According to biblical and rabbinic theology, God is omniscient. Such wisdom is God's alone. "God understands the way and God knows the place." (Job 28:23) "God reveals the deep and secret things; God knows what is in the darkness, and the light dwells with God." (Dan. 2:22) Furthermore, only God envisions and reveals the future. "All the nations are gathered together, / And the peoples are assembled; / Who among them can declare this, / And announce to us former things? / Let them bring their witnesses, that they may be justified; / And let them hear, and say: 'It is truth.'" (Isa. 43:9)

The belief in God's omniscience is in dynamic tension with the concept of free will, which posits that individual human beings are free to choose their own course of action among numerous choices. Some say that there is only the appearance of free will; God (or nature) is the compelling force behind such action. In Judaism, the majority of thinkers do not argue in favor of such determinism. In this way, one is able to account for the moral responsibility for one's individual actions.

Yet, this leads to the philosophical/ theological problem: If there is free will, then God does not know all. This doctrine of God's omniscience coupled with free human will posed the essential Pharisaic outlook and characterized the difference between the Pharisees and the Sadducees. The Sadducees rejected this notion. They consigned everything to chance and denied providential guidance of any sort. Philosophers like Saadyah and Yehudah Ha-Levi have resolved this by suggesting that, while the individual has free choice, God knows in advance what choice the individual will make. Some modern philosophers like Hermann Cohen argued that free will, in the sense of being totally unaffected by other causes, does not exist. It does exist, however, even for Cohen in the ethical realm. Martin Buber, on the other hand, suggested that there is no free will in "I-It" relationships. However, in the world of "I-Thou," real decisions can and must take place.

GLEANINGS

"[when] two sit together...the Divine Presence dwells with them" (3:2)

REVELATION AND SILENCE

At the time of teaching, it is the teacher who–by some word or deed, a question, a blow, or simply through silence–forces the student to hear a voice that comes from within. All genuine learning is thus the self's disclosure to itself. The voice issues with such clarity that the ones who learn refuse to believe that it is their own, insisting instead that it has come from the teacher who is across the room. All the great teachers share this alert passivity–a willingness to draw out of the novice an innermost self. [A great teacher] will remain long enough for a student to step back and discover what he or she has thought all along, or said, or done.

This student/teacher transaction is re-created by a therapist. Through transference, the patient comes to discover the archetypal relationships that have predetermined all relationships, have contaminated all conversations, sealed off each past word of address. The patient is able to hear what he or she has been saying all along. And, in so doing, the experience of insight is initiated.

How odd and yet how universal the misconception, on the part of all who would learn, that the knowledge they seek is outside them. To what lengths we go geographically, financially, and spiritually to find someone who will enable us to hear our own inner voice. And, of course, our culture's finest example of "the great learning" is what it calls theophany, the self-disclosure of God. At Sinai everyone is a student. According to our myth, all hear the voice of the Teacher. But not only is it a clear, publicly audible, external voice, it is also a voice that is the sound of our own breathing, a very precious, alert silence.

(Lawrence Kushner, *The River of Light: Spirituality, Judaism, and Consciousness*, Woodstock, Vermont: Jewish Lights Publishing, 1990)

LAWRENCE KUSHNER (1943-   ). Reform rabbi at Temple Beth El in Sudbury, Massachusetts. He is a driving force behind mystical spiritual renewal in Reform Judaism.

"were one person to sit and study Torah (3:2)

THE COMMAND TO STUDY

Since the ancient Scriptures carried with them the command for constant study, they could not become a dead weight; they implied the adaptation of the materials of the past to the present. Even the forces of authority in Jewish religious life had to acknowledge and accept the tendency of constant reinterpretation. Thus authority did not lead to dogmatism. The mental struggle to discover the true idea, the true command, the true law (a hundred-sided question without a final answer) always began anew. The Bible remained the Bible, the Talmud came after it, and after the Talmud came religious philosophy, and after that came mysticism, and so it went on and on. Judaism never became a completed entity; no period of its development could become its totality. The old revelation ever becomes a new revelation: Judaism experiences a continuous renaissance.

(Leo Baeck, *The Essence of Judaism*, New York: Schocken Books, 1948)

LEO BAECK (1873-1956). German-born rabbi who was a leader of Progressive Judaism in Europe. Instead of leaving Europe during the Nazi period, he dedicated himself to defending Jewish rights. Following his internment at Theresienstadt, he taught intermittently at HUC-JIR in Cincinnati as a historian and "witness of his faith."

"they were made in God's image" (3:14)

THE TORAH OF ISRAEL

According to many ancient Jewish sources, the Torah preexisted the creation of the world. It was the first of God's works, identified with the divine wisdom in Proverbs 8: 22ff. "*Adonai* made me at the beginning, the first of God's work of old." It was written with black fire on white fire and rested on the knee of God. It was the architectural plan God consulted in creating the universe. For the Kabbalists, this preexistent or primordial Torah is God's wisdom and essence; it expresses the immensity of God's being and power. Our Torah of ink and parchment is only the "outer garment," a limited interpretation of what lies hidden, a document that the initiate must penetrate more and more deeply to gain momentary glimpses of what lies behind. A later development of the idea of a secret Torah asserted that each of the 600,000 souls that stood at Sinai had its own special portion of Torah that only that soul could understand. Obviously, no account of revelatory experience by men or women can describe or exhaust the depths of divine reality. But this image of the relation between hidden and manifest Torah reminds us that half the souls of Israel have not left for us the Torah they have seen. Insofar as we can begin to recover women's experience of God, insofar as we can restore a part of their history and vision, we have more of the primordial Torah, the divine fullness, of which the present Torah of Israel is only a fragment and sign.

(Judith Plaskow, *Standing Again at Sinai*, New York: Harper and Row, 1990)

JUDITH PLASKOW. Contemporary feminist theologian and associate professor of Religious Studies at Manhattan College. She has presented a feminist reconstruction of Judaism.

"where there is no knowledge, there will be no understanding" (3:17)

JUDAISM AND THE HUMAN SPECIES

How the time will develop farther, how mankind will form itself in that wrestling, is not in doubt for the presentient eye, spying into the distance. The mind of mankind is striving upward, the nations altogether as individual members of one great body of humanity will be illuminated by the real, divine spirit, all mutually promoting, strengthening, and purifying each other, and religion will appear as the energy of life, rejuvenated as the noblest flower of wisdom in the minds....

Animated by the breath of complete liberty, constantly more and more imbued with the spirit of science and widening and deepening the view, Judaism of the present will steadily become more and more conscious of its task and strive for its accomplishment, a task that corresponds as much to all deeper endeavor of the present as it is deeply rooted in its own basic essence: to become the religion of mankind. Only that religion that is reconciled with free thought has the justification but, at the same time, also the guarantee of its continuance. On the contrary, every religion that makes battle against the right of the mind will be crushed under the wheels of time. Only that religion that carries the guarantee of its future within itself, that considers that its task is to send its blessings to all mankind [will survive]. [On the contrary,] one that confines itself to a narrow circle, withdraws into a cell, bars itself from the rest of mankind as if that were a soulless or alien body and is absorbed by preference into its own petty interest [will not]. Judaism will always bear in mind that it is called to strive for the goal, even if that cannot be brought about by us alone, that God will be acknowledged as one and [God's] name as one.

(Abraham Geiger, *Judaism and Its History*, trans. Maurice Mayer, New York: Thelmessing and Cahn, 1866)

ABRAHAM GEIGER (1810-1874). A leader of the Reform movement in Germany and an outstanding scholar of *Wissenschaft des Judenthums*. He was a militant reformer who was active in several important Reform institutions in their incipient stages.

CHAPTER FOUR

Who Is Wise?

4:1 Ben Zoma said, "Who is wise? The one who learns from everyone, as it is said, 'From all who would teach me, have I gained understanding.' [Ps. 119:99] Who is mighty? One who controls one's [natural] urges, as it is said, 'One who is slow to anger is better than the mighty and one who rules one's spirit than one who conquers a city.' [Prov. 16:32] Who is rich? One who is happy with what one has, as it says, 'When you eat what your hands have provided, you shall be happy and good will be yours.' [Ps. 128:2] You shall be happy in this world; and good will be yours in the world to come. Who is honored? One who honors others, as it says, 'Those who honor Me, will I honor, and those who despise Me will be lightly esteemed.'" [I Sam. 2:30]

ד:א בֶּן זוֹמָא אוֹמֵר אֵיזֶהוּ חָכָם הַלוֹמֵד מִכָּל אָדָם שֶׁנֶּאֱמַר מִכָּל מְלַמְּדַי הִשְׂכַּלְתִּי כִּי עֵדְוֹתֶיךָ שִׂיחָה לִי. אֵיזֶהוּ גִבּוֹר הַכּוֹבֵשׁ אֶת יִצְרוֹ שֶׁנֶּאֱמַר טוֹב אֶרֶךְ אַפַּיִם מִגִּבּוֹר וּמוֹשֵׁל בְּרוּחוֹ מִלֹּכֵד עִיר. אֵיזֶהוּ עָשִׁיר הַשָּׂמֵחַ בְּחֶלְקוֹ שֶׁנֶּאֱמַר כִּי תֹאכַל אַשְׁרֶיךָ וְטוֹב לָךְ אַשְׁרֶיךָ בָּעוֹלָם הַזֶּה וְטוֹב לָךְ לָעוֹלָם הַבָּא. אֵיזֶהוּ מְכֻבָּד הַמְכַבֵּד אֶת הַבְּרִיּוֹת שֶׁנֶּאֱמַר כִּי מְכַבְּדַי אֲכַבֵּד וּבֹזַי יֵקָלּוּ:

Ben Zoma. Shimon ben Zoma lived in the second century and studied under Yehoshua ben Chananyah. An outstanding scholar, he was regarded as "a disciple of the sages." (B. Talmud, *Kiddushin* 49b) Yet, he was never ordained as a rabbi. In *Berachot* 57b, it is written, "Whoever sees Ben Zoma in a dream may hope for wisdom." Shimon ben Zoma and Shimon ben Azzai (whose statement follows in *Avot* 4:2) were both colleagues of Rabbi Akiva. The three of them, along with Elisha ben Abuyah, entered Paradise. According to the Talmud (B. Talmud, *Hagigah* 14b), they were engaged in mystical and theosophical speculation. Only Rabbi Akiva "entered in peace and left in peace." Elisha ben Abuyah became a heretic; ben Zoma went mad; and ben Azzai died as a young man.

The one who learns from everyone. Rashi's view is that one fit to be called a scholar is one who is not too conceited to learn from even those who may be less learned.

One's [natural] urges. The *yetzer hara* is the human drive or the propensity to do evil. This drive is always in conflict with the *yetzer hatov*, the propensity to do good. Both inclinations are found in every human being.

One who honors others. Rashi explains: If God will honor those who honor God, how much more fitting is it that we who are merely flesh and blood should honor those who honor us.

4:2 Ben Azzai would say, "Run to do the least of the commandments as you would to do the most important. Run away from a transgression, for a commandment pulls along a commandment and a transgression pulls along a transgression. The reward of a commandment is a commandment and the reward of a transgression is a transgression."

ד:ב בֶּן עַזַּאי אוֹמֵר הֱוֵי רָץ לְמִצְוָה קַלָּה וּבוֹרֵחַ מִן הָעֲבֵרָה שֶׁמִּצְוָה גוֹרֶרֶת מִצְוָה וַעֲבֵרָה גוֹרֶרֶת עֲבֵרָה שֶׁשְּׂכַר מִצְוָה מִצְוָה וּשְׂכַר עֲבֵרָה עֲבֵרָה:

Ben Azzai. Like his colleague ben Zoma, Shimon ben Azzai was held in high esteem for his learning, but he was never ordained as a rabbi. He lived in the early second century of the common era in Tiberias. According to one legend, he was engaged (but never married) to Akiva's daughter. (*Ketubot* 63a) "With the death of ben Azzai, diligent scholarship passed from the earth." (Cf. *Sotah* 9:15.)

The least of the commandments: Rashi notes that the distinction between the "least" important and the "most" important commandments is made in the human and not in the divine mind.

4:3 He used to say, "Treat no one lightly and think nothing is useless, for everyone has one's moment and everything has its place."

ד:ג הוּא הָיָה אוֹמֵר אַל תְּהִי בָז לְכָל אָדָם וְאַל תְּהִי מַפְלִיג לְכָל דָּבָר שֶׁאֵין לְךָ אָדָם שֶׁאֵין לוֹ שָׁעָה וְאֵין לְךָ דָּבָר שֶׁאֵין לוֹ מָקוֹם:

Treat no one lightly. Maimonides explains that every person has the possibility to aid or to hurt at any given time.

Everything has its place. Rashi offers the reader two views, both based on the alternative meanings of the Hebrew word דָּבָר *davar* as either "thing" or "word." He says, if you think that something can't happen now, be aware that it might happen in the future. Hence, one should exercise care, facing its future possibility. Taking *davar* to mean "word," Rashi suggests that one should neither reject nor postpone the opportunity to acquire any word of wisdom.

4:4 Rabbi Levitas, a man of Yavneh, used to say, "Be exceedingly humble of spirit, for the human hope is only the worm." Rabbi Yochanan ben Beroka would say, "Whoever would profane the name of God in secret will be punished in public. It makes no difference whether such profanation was intended or not."

ד:ד רַבִּי לְוִיטַס אִישׁ יַבְנֶה אוֹמֵר מְאֹד מְאֹד הֱוֵי שְׁפַל רוּחַ שֶׁתִּקְוַת אֱנוֹשׁ רִמָּה. רַבִּי יוֹחָנָן בֶּן בְּרוֹקָא אוֹמֵר כָּל הַמְחַלֵּל שֵׁם שָׁמַיִם בַּסֵּתֶר נִפְרָעִין מִמֶּנּוּ בַּגָּלוּי אֶחָד שׁוֹגֵג וְאֶחָד מֵזִיד בְּחִלּוּל הַשֵּׁם:

Rabbi Levitas. Mentioned in no other place, he was a contemporary of Rabban Gamliel II.

The human hope is only the worm. The Hebrew word תִּקְוָה *tikvah* generally means "hope" but in some contexts may mean "end" or "limit." Some, therefore, would translate, "Everyone's end is the worm."

Rashi sees the statement of Rabbi Levitas as an injunction against any form of pride. For Maimonides, humility is the midpoint between pride and self-debasement. Maimonides quotes the rabbinic dictum (B. Talmud, *Megillah* 31a) that, wherever one finds evidence of God's power, one finds evidence of God's humility. Humility is one of God's attributes. (B. Talmud, *Megillah* 31a) Because of the humility of Moses (as described in Num. 12:3), Moses was worthy of reaching the status of master of wisdom and master of Torah.

Bartinoro notes that, in all other ethical qualities, moderation is the best, except in the case of humility.

Rabbi Yochanan ben Beroka. He was a contemporary of Rabbi Akiva who lived in the beginning of the second century of the common era. While he was a student of Yehoshua ben Chananyah, he was chiefly influenced by Yochanan ben Nuri.

Whoever would profane the name of God. Rashi finds support for Rabbi Yochanan's statement in Proverbs 26:26, "Though one's hatred is concealed with deceit, one's wickedness shall be revealed before the congregation." Rashi suggests that, when a scholar sins, the Torah is demeaned. This bad example drives others from Torah study. For Rashi, such profanation of God is worse than idolatry.

4:5 Rabbi Yishmael, his son, was accustomed to saying, "The one who studies in order to teach will be enabled to study and to teach. The one who studies in order to practice will be enabled to study and to teach, to observe and to practice." Rabbi Tzadok said, "Do not separate yourself from the community. Don't be like those who try to influence judges. Don't use [the words of the

ד:ה רַבִּי יִשְׁמָעֵאל בְּנוֹ אוֹמֵר הַלּוֹמֵד עַל מְנָת לְלַמֵּד מַסְפִּיקִין בְּיָדוֹ לִלְמוֹד וּלְלַמֵּד וְהַלּוֹמֵד עַל מְנָת לַעֲשׂוֹת מַסְפִּיקִין בְּיָדוֹ לִלְמוֹד וּלְלַמֵּד לִשְׁמוֹר וְלַעֲשׂוֹת. רַבִּי צָדוֹק אוֹמֵר אַל תִּפְרוֹשׁ מִן הַצִּבּוּר וְאַל תַּעַשׂ עַצְמְךָ כְּעוֹרְכֵי הַדַּיָּנִין וְאַל תַּעֲשֶׂהָ עֲטָרָה לְהִתְגַּדֵּל בָּהּ וְלֹא קַרְדּוֹם לַחְפּוֹר בָּהּ וְכָךְ הָיָה הִלֵּל אוֹמֵר וּדְאִשְׁתַּמַּשׁ בְּתָגָא חֲלָף הָא לָמַדְתָּ כָּל הַנֶּהֱנֶה מִדִּבְרֵי תוֹרָה נוֹטֵל חַיָּיו מִן הָעוֹלָם:

Torah] as a crown to build yourself up, nor
as an adze to dig with, as Hillel said, 'The
one who would make use of the crown [of
the Torah] will pass away.' Thus you may
learn that whoever [improperly] uses the
word of Torah takes one's own life from
this world."

Rabbi Yishmael, his son [ben Yochanan ben Beroka]. A colleague of Rabban Shimon ben
Gamliel II and often quoted in agreement or disagreement with him, Rabbi Yishmael
lived in the middle of the second century.

One who studies in order to teach. Rashi suggests that the reason that one would study only
to teach would be to receive the title and honor of being a rabbi. He suggests an alternative
reading: Such a person would *not* be enabled to learn and teach.

Rabbi Tzadok. There were two rabbis named Tzadok, grandfather and grandson. It is difficult to determine which is referred to in this *mishnah*. If Rabbi Yishmael's presence in
this *mishnah* is any indication, the Tzadok here is the grandson. However, most scholars
ascribe the *mishnah* to the older Tzadok since the younger Tzadok was taken captive to
Rome. The older Tzadok lived in the late first century and early second century of the
common era. As one of priestly descent, he was known to have officiated in the Temple.
Later, Tzadok joined Yochanan ben Zakkai at Yavneh. Though a pupil of Shammai, he
often rendered decisions in accordance with the school of Hillel.

Do not separate yourself. This is a repetition of Hillel's saying from *Avot* 2:4.

Don't be like those who try to influence judges. This is a reiteration of Judah ben Tabbai in
Avot 1:8.

Don't use [the words of the Torah] as a crown. Maimonides notes that the scholars of the
talmudic period were not supported by their learning, whatever their rank. Rich and poor
were expected to study Torah. According to tradition, Hillel was a woodchopper, and
Chanina ben Dosa lived from week to week on a small measure of carob. Both were terri-
bly poor. Yet neither asked to be supported by their communities because of their great
learning. Moreover, we have never found that any of the scholars reproved those of their
own generations for not having made them rich. The scholars would not take money
because they did not want to imply to the masses that Torah was a profession. Maimonides
presents the case of Rabbi Tarfon who had once saved his own life by identifying himself.
From that day, Tarfon bewailed the fact that, in doing so, he had taken advantage of the
Torah. Maimonides also tells the story of Rabbi Yehudah who had opened his storehouses
to all in a time of famine. When, after a short time, he decided to provide food to only
the learned, he was told that his disciple Rabbi Yonatan was refusing any assistance because
he would then be taking advantage of the Torah. As a result, Rabbi Yehudah relented and
fed all the community.

Pirke Avot

Bartinoro states, "Let no one say that I will study so that I may be called Rabbi!"

An adze to dig with. The Hebrew word קַרְדֹּם *kardom* is often translated as "spade"; however, its use in many contexts suggests an implement that was swung down into the earth, hence it is translated here as "adze." Bartinoro adds that using the Torah as an implement to dig out a living demeans its sanctity. However, he does admit to an exception. Should a scholar be ill and suffering greatly, it would be proper for the community to bring the scholar gifts, and it would be proper for the scholar to accept them.

Heller notes that improper use of the Torah will remove a person from the life of the world to come.

4:6 Rabbi Yose used to say, "Whoever honors the Torah will be honored by others. Whoever dishonors the Torah will be dishonored by others."

ד:ו רַבִּי יוֹסֵי אוֹמֵר כָּל הַמְכַבֵּד אֶת הַתּוֹרָה גּוּפוֹ מְכֻבָּד עַל הַבְּרִיּוֹת וְכָל הַמְחַלֵּל אֶת הַתּוֹרָה גּוּפוֹ מְחֻלָּל עַל הַבְּרִיּוֹת:

Rabbi Yose [ben Chalafta]. A disciple of Rabbi Akiva, he supported himself by working in leather. Usually mentioned without his father's name, he lived in the middle of the second century of the common era. He was a leader of the post-Bar Kochba era.

Whoever honors the Torah. For Rashi, the honoring of the Torah relates directly to its treatment as a sacred object. One should not put a Torah scroll on a bench nor place one on top of another. One should not leave it open after it has been read, and one should pay close attention while it is being read.

4:7 Rabbi Yishmael, his son, would say, "Whoever restrains oneself from acting as judge removes from oneself enmity, robbery, and perjury. Whoever pompously renders decisions is a wicked and arrogant fool."

ד:ז רַבִּי יִשְׁמָעֵאל בְּנוֹ אוֹמֵר הַחֹשֵׂךְ עַצְמוֹ מִן הַדִּין פּוֹרֵק מִמֶּנּוּ אֵיבָה וְגָזֵל וּשְׁבוּעַת שָׁוְא וְהַגַּס לִבּוֹ בְּהוֹרָאָה שׁוֹטֶה רָשָׁע וְגַס רוּחַ:

Rabbi Yishmael. It is difficult to determine precisely which Rabbi Yishmael is the author of the *mishnah*. Some texts omit the word בְּנוֹ *beno*, "his son," after his name. Thus the author may be Rabbi Yishmael ben Elisha, known in this *mishnah* as Rabbi Yishmael, who was the colleague and opponent of Rabbi Akiva, or Rabbi Yishmael ben Yose ben Chalafta, who lived in the end of the second century of the common era and was apparently Yose ben Chalafta's oldest son, succeeding him as leader of the town of Sepphoris. (Cf. B. Talmud, *Eruvin* 86b.) Almost all the *halachah* he offers is taught in his father's name. While he is generally not mentioned by name in the *Mishnah* (apart from this passage) as a member of Yehudah Ha-Nasi's council, he influenced the editing of the *Mishnah* to a great extent.

Whoever restrains oneself. Rashi explains the judicial restraint here described as the attempt of the judge to get the litigants to settle and thereby avoid a trial. If the judge is successful, the judge will avoid the problems of a trial and its effects upon the litigants.

Whoever pompously renders decisions. For Maimonides, if pomposity moves a judge to render decisions, the judge lacks reverence for God.

4:8 He used to say, "Don't judge alone, for only the One [God] may do so. Don't say [to your fellow judges], 'Accept my view,' for it is up to them [to make that decision] and not up to you."

הוא הָיָה אוֹמֵר אַל תְּהִי דָן יְחִידִי שֶׁאֵין דָּן יְחִידִי אֶלָּא אֶחָד וְאַל תֹּאמַר קַבְּלוּ דַעְתִּי שֶׁהֵן רַשָּׁאִין וְלֹא אֶתָּה: ד:ח

Don't judge alone. Judging is too difficult and sensitive a process to be handled alone. Rashi, Maimonides, and Bartinoro all point out that, while an expert judge may indeed judge alone, it is an act of piety not to do so.

Accept my view. Bartinoro points out that, even if one is an expert and is judging along with nonexperts, the expert judge may not insist that they accept the expert view. Once in the role of judge, the individual judge has the right to render an individual decision.

4:9 Rabbi Yonatan would say, "Whoever may fulfill the Torah when poor will in the end fulfill it when rich. Whoever may neglect the Torah when rich will in the end neglect the Torah when poor."

רַבִּי יוֹנָתָן אוֹמֵר כָּל הַמְקַיֵּם אֶת הַתּוֹרָה מֵעֹנִי סוֹפוֹ לְקַיְּמָהּ מֵעֹשֶׁר וְכָל הַמְבַטֵּל אֶת הַתּוֹרָה מֵעֹשֶׁר סוֹפוֹ לְבַטְּלָהּ מֵעֹנִי: ד:ט

Rabbi Yonatan. He is not mentioned elsewhere in the *Mishnah.* According to ARN 30:1, this saying is attributed to Rabbi Yonatan ben Yosef, a disciple of Rabbi Akiva.

Whoever may fulfill the Torah when poor. Rashi explains that a wealthy person may claim that his possessions preclude his involvement in Torah study.

4:10 Rabbi Meir would say, "Do less business and do more Torah. Be humble in everyone's presence. If you have neglected the Torah, there are many who are like you. If you have labored in the Torah, God will give you a great reward."

רַבִּי מֵאִיר אוֹמֵר הֱוֵי מְמַעֵט בְּעֵסֶק וַעֲסוֹק בַּתּוֹרָה וֶהֱוֵי שְׁפַל רוּחַ בִּפְנֵי כָל אָדָם וְאִם בָּטַלְתָּ מִן הַתּוֹרָה יֶשׁ לְךָ בְּטֵלִים הַרְבֵּה כְּנֶגְדָּךְ וְאִם עָמַלְתָּ בַּתּוֹרָה יֶשׁ לוֹ שָׂכָר הַרְבֵּה לִתֶּן לָךְ: ד:י

Rabbi Meir. The greatest disciple of Rabbi Akiva, he was renowned as a scholar. His compilation of the Oral Law based on the teachings of his teacher Akiva served as the basis of the *Mishnah*, compiled by Rabbi Yehudah Ha-Nasi. (Cf. B. Talmud, *Sanhedrin* 86a.) Meir remained the friend of Elisha ben Abuyah, his teacher, even after Elisha had become a heretic. Rabbi Meir's wife, Beruriah, was a scholar in her own right.

Do more Torah. Bartinoro suggests that one should view Torah study as one's main occupation.

Be humble in everyone's presence. Maimonides suggests that one should be humble with any-one with whom one comes in contact. Only in this way will one be able to flee from self-aggrandizement.

If you have neglected the Torah. Rashi suggests that the person who turns away from the study of the Torah will be punished by distractions that will prevent one from gaining the rewards of Torah study.

4:11 Rabbi Eliezer ben Yaakov would say, "Whoever fulfills one commandment has acquired one advocate while whoever has committed one transgression has acquired one accuser. Repentance and good deeds may serve as a shield against punishment." Rabbi Yochanan Ha-Sandelar used to say, "Any gathering for the sake of Heaven will have permanence but that which is not for the sake of Heaven will not."

ד:יא רַבִּי אֱלִיעֶזֶר בֶּן יַעֲקֹב אוֹמֵר הָעוֹשֶׂה מִצְוָה אַחַת קוֹנֶה לוֹ פְּרַקְלִיט אֶחָד וְהָעוֹבֵר עֲבֵרָה אַחַת קוֹנֶה לוֹ קַטֵּגוֹר אֶחָד תְּשׁוּבָה וּמַעֲשִׂים טוֹבִים כִּתְרִיס בִּפְנֵי הַפֻּרְעָנוּת. רַבִּי יוֹחָנָן הַסַּנְדְּלָר אוֹמֵר כָּל כְּנֵסִיָּה שֶׁהִיא לְשֵׁם שָׁמַיִם סוֹפָהּ לְהִתְקַיֵּם וְשֶׁאֵינָהּ לְשֵׁם שָׁמַיִם אֵין סוֹפָהּ לְהִתְקַיֵּם:

Rabbi Eliezer. He was a disciple of Rabbi Akiva. While there are two *tannaim* by this name, the author of this *mishnah* was probably the one who lived during the second century and was among the sages who participated in the synod at Usha following the Hadrianic perse-cution. (Cf. *Shir Hashirim Rabbah* 2:5, No. 3.) Here a convention of surviving sages revived the Sanhedrin and all of its activities, including the offices of *nasi* and *av bet din.* This was part of the revival of spiritual and communal life that took place during the reign of Hadrian's successor, Antonius Pius (138-161).

Whoever fulfills one commandment. The words פְּרַקְלִיט *peraklit* and קַטֵּגוֹר *kategor*, here trans-lated as "advocate" and "accuser," are Greek loan words, which should be translated in contemporary usage as "defense attorney" and "prosecuting attorney." These words sug-gest some penetration of the outside world on Jewish usage. Borrowing from the Talmud (*Avodah Zarah* 2a), Rashi takes the advocate to refer to an angel who has been transformed from the deed itself and who will intercede on the individual's behalf before the throne of judgment. Evil deeds become accusing angels.

Rabbi Yochanan. Rabbi Yochanan's surname *Ha-Sandelar* may either indicate his trade as "sandalmaker" or his origin from the city of Alexandria. He lived in the first half of the second century and was one of Akiva's last pupils. Yochanan was included among the post-Bar Kochba scholars who tried to revive the study of Torah.

Any gathering for the sake of Heaven. Rashi contends that it is the outcome of such a gathering that will or will not endure rather than the gathering itself. This is really a measuring stick for all our activities. Time is precious, and we should use it to further the message of Torah.

4:12 Rabbi Elazar ben Shammua would say, "Let the honor of your student be as dear to you as your own. Let the honor of your associate be equal to the respect due to your teacher. Let the respect due to your teacher be equivalent to the reverence due to Heaven."

דיב רַבִּי אֶלְעָזָר בֶּן שַׁמּוּעַ אוֹמֵר יְהִי כְבוֹד תַּלְמִידְךָ חָבִיב עָלֶיךָ כְּשֶׁלָּךְ וּכְבוֹד חֲבֵרְךָ כְּמוֹרָא רַבָּךְ וּמוֹרָא רַבָּךְ כְּמוֹרָא שָׁמָיִם:

Rabbi Elazar. Among the last disciples of Rabbi Akiva, he lived in the middle of the second century of the common era and is generally referred to simply as Elazar.

The terms "student," "associate," and "teacher" suggest ranks in the academy. Thus, Rabbi Elazar's words are instructive for any teacher.

Let the honor of your student. Bartinoro finds biblical warrants for this *mishnah.* Moses said to Joshua his student, "Choose for *us* some men." (Exod. 17:9) Thus, Moses acted as if Joshua were his equal.

Let the honor of your associate. Although Aaron was older than Moses, he said, "Please, my lord...." (Num. 12:11) Thus, he treated Moses as his teacher.

Let the respect due to your teacher. Considering the prophesying of Eldad and Medad as rebellion against Moses, Joshua said, "My lord Moses, restrain them!" (Num. 11:28), as if to say that rebellion against Moses was equivalent to rebellion against God.

4:13 Rabbi Yehudah used to say, "Be very careful in [your] study for a mistake [by a scholar] will be considered as a deliberate sin." Rabbi Shimon said, "There are three crowns: the crown of Torah; the crown of priesthood; and the crown of royalty. However, the crown of a good name is greater than all of them."

דיג רַבִּי יְהוּדָה אוֹמֵר הֱוֵי זָהִיר בְּתַלְמוּד שֶׁשִּׁגְגַת תַּלְמוּד עוֹלָה זָדוֹן. רַבִּי שִׁמְעוֹן אוֹמֵר שְׁלֹשָׁה כְתָרִים הֵן כֶּתֶר תּוֹרָה וְכֶתֶר כְּהֻנָּה וְכֶתֶר מַלְכוּת וְכֶתֶר שֵׁם טוֹב עוֹלָה עַל גַּבֵּיהֶן:

Rabbi Yehudah and Rabbi Shimon, both disciples of Rabbi Akiva, disagreed in their evaluation of the Roman government. Rabbi Yehudah saw some positive elements in Roman rule. Rabbi Shimon was utterly opposed to that rule. As a result, Rabbi Shimon went into hiding for thirteen years.

Rabbi Yehudah. Rabbi Yehudah [bar Ilai] is the teacher most mentioned in the *Mishnah*. Rabbi Yehudah, mentioned without his father's name, lived in the middle of the second century of the common era. He came from Usha in the Galilee and studied under his own father, who was himself a pupil of Eliezer ben Horkenos. Rabbi Yehudah traveled to Lod to study with Rabbi Tarfon and later studied with Akiva. He was one of the five students ordained by Yehudah ben Bava (at the cost of his life) during the Hadrianic persecutions. (Cf. B. Talmud, *Sanhedrin* 14a.)

Be very careful in [your] study. Both Rashi and Bartinoro take Rabbi Yehudah's statement as a warning to scholars that care must be exercised in the analysis of the law lest decisions be made that could allow that which is prohibited. God will then treat indolence as insolence.

Rabbi Shimon. Rabbi Shimon [bar Yochai] lived in the middle of the second century of the common era. With only one exception, he is referred to throughout the *Mishnah* simply as Rabbi Shimon.

The crown of Torah. Rashi notes that the crown of Torah, a result of study, is open to all while the crown of priesthood and the crown of royalty require a certain lineage. The crown of a good name follows from the crown of Torah.

4:14 Rabbi Nehorai said, "Leave home and go to a place of Torah. Don't say that Torah will come to you or that your companions will make it yours. Don't depend on your own understanding."

ד:יד רַבִּי נְהוֹרַאי אוֹמֵר הֱוֵי גוֹלֶה לִמְקוֹם תּוֹרָה וְאַל תֹּאמַר שֶׁהִיא תָבוֹא אַחֲרֶיךָ שֶׁחֲבֵרֶיךָ יְקַיְּמוּהָ בְּיָדֶךָ וְאֶל בִּינָתְךָ אַל תִּשָּׁעֵן:

Rabbi Nehorai. The identity of Rabbi Nehorai is problematic. Since the name *Nehorai* suggests "enlightenment," some take it simply as another name for Rabbi Meir. Others maintain that both Rabbi Elazar ben Arach and Rabbi Meir enlightened their disciples. Thus, this name could refer to either one.

Leave home. Rashi suggests that this statement means that you should travel to a place where there is a scholar rather than (wait and) hope that a scholar will come to you. Bartinoro thinks that one should travel only if there is no scholar in one's hometown.

Your companions will make it yours. Both Rashi and Bartinoro warn against remaining home, expecting to learn from those who have made the trip and returned home.

Don't depend on your own understanding. Rashi, Maimonides, and Bartinoro stress the importance of the scholarly community in the understanding of Torah. One needs teachers, companions, and students to fully plumb the depths of Torah. One may not, therefore, depend merely on one's own understanding of the text. This sentiment is echoed in Proverbs 3:5, "Trust in *Adonai* with all your heart, and do not lean on your own understanding."

4:15 Rabbi Yannai said, "[The reason] why the guilty prosper or the innocent suffer is not within our grasp." Rabbi Matya ben Charash said, "Be the first to greet everyone; be a tail to lions rather than a head to foxes."

ד:טו רַבִּי יַנַּאי אוֹמֵר אֵין בְּיָדֵינוּ לֹא מִשַּׁלְוַת הָרְשָׁעִים וְאַף לֹא מִיִּסּוּרֵי הַצַּדִּיקִים. רַבִּי מַתְיָא בֶּן חָרָשׁ אוֹמֵר הֱוֵי מַקְדִּים בִּשְׁלוֹם כָּל אָדָם וֶהֱוֵי זָנָב לָאֲרָיוֹת וְאַל תְּהִי רֹאשׁ לַשׁוּעָלִים:

Rabbi Yannai. Not mentioned elsewhere in the *Mishnah*, he may have been the father of Rabbi Dostai. (Cf. *Avot* 3:8.) This is probably a reference to Yannai Rabbah (literally, the "great Yannai"), an *amora*, a rabbinic teacher of the talmudic period, who lived in Palestine in the second and third centuries as a student of Rabbi Yehudah Ha-Nasi. If he was indeed an early *amora* and a student of Yehudah Ha-Nasi, this would indicate that the final version of the *Mishnah* was not completed by 200 C.E., the commonly accepted date of completion.

Why the guilty prosper. Yannai's comment presents once again the difficult problem of theodicy: Why in a world created by a good God are wicked people at ease and good people in difficulty?

Rashi argues that we are dependent on human beings in this world to mete out rewards and punishments. Thus the system is by definition flawed. However, in the next life, which is solely in God's hands, virtue will be rewarded and vice will at last be punished.

Rabbi Matya. Rabbi Matya ben Charash, who lived in the middle of the second century, was a disciple of Rabbi Eliezer ben Horkenos. Following the Bar Kochba revolt and just prior to the Hadrianic persecution, he fled to Rome to found a school. (Cf. B. Talmud, *Sanhedrin* 32b.)

4:16 Rabbi Yaakov said, "This world is like a foyer before the world to come. Prepare yourself in the foyer so that you will be able to enter the banquet hall."

ד:טז רַבִּי יַעֲקֹב אוֹמֵר הָעוֹלָם הַזֶּה דּוֹמֶה לִפְרוֹזְדוֹר בִּפְנֵי הָעוֹלָם הַבָּא הַתְקֵן עַצְמְךָ בַּפְּרוֹזְדוֹר כְּדֵי שֶׁתִּכָּנֵס לַטְּרַקְלִין:

Rabbi Yaakov. The Rabbi Yaakov here is probably Yaakov ben Korshai, who lived in the second century and was a teacher of Yehudah Ha-Nasi. A disciple of Rabbi Meir, he is mentioned in disputes with Rabbi Akiva.

The word פְּרוֹזְדוֹר *perozdor*, "foyer," and טְרַקְלִין *teraklin*, "banquet hall," are loan words from the Greek. The assignment of Judaic notions to Greek terms indicates the level of intercultural penetration in Roman Palestine. The rooms in a Roman villa described in Greek terms are used to symbolize this world and the next as aspects of Jewish religion. Both Rashi and Maimonides contend that *teraklin* refers to the court of the king.

4:17 He would often say, "An hour spent in penitence and good deeds in this world is better than all of life in the world to come. An hour of contentment in the world to come is better than all of life in this world."

דיז הוּא הָיָה אוֹמֵר יָפָה שָׁעָה אַחַת בִּתְשׁוּבָה וּמַעֲשִׂים טוֹבִים בָּעוֹלָם הַזֶּה מִכֹּל חַיֵּי הָעוֹלָם הַבָּא וְיָפָה שָׁעָה אַחַת שֶׁל קוֹרַת רוּחַ בָּעוֹלָם הַבָּא מִכֹּל חַיֵּי הָעוֹלָם הַזֶּה:

Rashi, Maimonides, and Bartinoro all suggest that this world is the place of action and the next world the place of reward. As a result, if something is not achieved in this world, it will not be achieved in the next world.

4:18 Rabbi Shimon ben Elazar said, "When your friend becomes angry, don't try to calm him. When he is recently bereaved, don't try to comfort him. When he is about to make an oath, don't ask him questions. Just after he has been disgraced, don't try to see him."

דיח רַבִּי שִׁמְעוֹן בֶּן אֶלְעָזָר אוֹמֵר אַל תְּרַצֶּה אֶת חֲבֵרְךָ בִּשְׁעַת כַּעֲסוֹ וְאַל תְּנַחֲמֵהוּ בְּשָׁעָה שֶׁמֵּתוֹ מֻטָּל לְפָנָיו וְאַל תִּשְׁאַל לוֹ בִּשְׁעַת נִדְרוֹ וְאַל תִּשְׁתַּדֵּל לִרְאוֹתוֹ בִּשְׁעַת קַלְקָלָתוֹ:

Rabbi Shimon. A disciple of Rabbi Meir, he lived toward the end of the second century, was a contemporary of Rabbi Yehudah Ha-Nasi, and was probably the son of Elazar of Bartota. He lived in Tiberias and frequently accompanied Rabbi Meir in whose name he often taught.

Don't try to calm him. Rabbi Shimon advises the individual not to be among the "fools [who] rush in." One must allow time to effect a modicum of healing, whether one is angry or bereaved (literally, "when one's dead is lying before him").

Rashi points out that it is difficult to calm someone who has just become angry. Only after time, when the person has calmed down, can another help to calm him further. Bartinoro finds some biblical warrants for this *mishnah*. He recalls God's statement to Moses after the episode of the Golden Calf, "My Presence shall go and I will give you rest." (Exod. 33:14) This statement was made to tell Moses to wait until his anger passed. Even God waited before speaking to Adam and Eve after their sin. According to the text, "...they fashioned coverings for themselves and [then] they heard the voice of God...." (Gen. 3:7, 8)

Don't ask him questions. Rashi points out that people take oaths during moments of distress or out of anger. They seldom think through such oaths. To question such an oath might impel the one taking it to commit further to the vow.

Don't try to see him. Seeing someone in disgrace might embarrass the person even more.

4:19 Shmuel Ha-Katan said, "Rejoice not when your enemy falls. Let not your heart be glad when another stumbles. *Adonai* may see it, and [if] it displeases God, God may remove from him [the enemy] divine wrath." [Prov. 24:17, 18]

דיט שְׁמוּאֵל הַקָּטָן אוֹמֵר בִּנְפֹל אֽוֹיִבְךָ אַל תִּשְׂמָח וּבִכָּשְׁלוֹ אַל יָגֵל לִבֶּֽךָ פֶּן יִרְאֶה יְהֹוָה וְרַע בְּעֵינָיו וְהֵשִׁיב מֵעָלָיו אַפּוֹ:

Shmuel. He lived toward the end of the first century and was noted for his humility, hence his surname, *Ha-Katan*, "the little one." He is best known for his *Birkat Ha-Minim*, the blessing incorporated into the *Amidah*, which speaks out against Judeo-Christian heretics and informers.

Rashi explains that, because of Shmuel Ha-Katan's humility, this verse from Proverbs 24:17, 18 was Shmuel's favorite saying.

Divine wrath. Bartinoro understands the end of the verse to mean that God may turn away divine wrath from one's enemy and place it upon the person who rejoices at the fall of that enemy.

4:20 Elisha ben Abuyah said, "Regarding the one who studies when young, to what can that person be compared? To ink written on new paper. Regarding the one who studies when old, to what can that person be compared? To ink written on paper that has been erased." Rabbi Yose ben Yehudah of Kefar Ha-Bavli said, "Regarding the one who learns from the young, to what can this person be compared? To one eating unripe grapes and drinking wine from the winepress. Regarding the person who learns from the old, to what can this person be compared? To one eating ripe grapes and drinking old wine." Rabbi [however] said, "Don't look at the wine flask, but rather at what is in it. For there are new wine flasks filled with old wine, and there are old wine flasks that don't have even new wine."

דכ אֱלִישָׁע בֶּן אֲבוּיָה אוֹמֵר הַלּוֹמֵד יֶלֶד לְמָה הוּא דוֹמֶה לִדְיוֹ כְּתוּבָה עַל נְיָר חָדָשׁ וְהַלּוֹמֵד זָקֵן לְמָה הוּא דוֹמֶה לִדְיוֹ כְּתוּבָה עַל נְיָר מָחוּק. רַבִּי יוֹסֵי בַּר יְהוּדָה אִישׁ כְּפַר הַבַּבְלִי אוֹמֵר הַלּוֹמֵד מִן הַקְּטַנִּים לְמָה הוּא דוֹמֶה לְאוֹכֵל עֲנָבִים קֵהוֹת וְשׁוֹתֶה יַיִן מִגִּתּוֹ וְהַלּוֹמֵד מִן הַזְּקֵנִים לְמָה הוּא דוֹמֶה לְאוֹכֵל עֲנָבִים בְּשׁוּלוֹת וְשׁוֹתֶה יַיִן יָשָׁן. רַבִּי אוֹמֵר אַל תִּסְתַּכֵּל בַּקַּנְקַן אֶלָּא בְּמַה שֶּׁיֵּשׁ בּוֹ יֵשׁ קַנְקַן חָדָשׁ מָלֵא יָשָׁן וְיָשָׁן שֶׁאֲפִלּוּ חָדָשׁ אֵין בּוֹ:

The use of wine growing and wine making as symbols suggests how much viticulture was part of the ancient Jewish and general world.

Elisha ben Abuyah. As has been noted (cf. commentary on *Pirke Avot* 4:1), Elisha ben Abuyah was one of those who entered the Paradise of theosophical speculation. As a result, Elisha became a heretic. Although a heretic, Elisha was not forsaken by his disciple Rabbi Meir.

Regarding the one who studies when young. Maimonides suggest that what is learned in one's youth will not be easily forgotten. He adds that the wisdom of the young is filled with questions that have not been adequately examined or reflected upon. Time itself has improved the wisdom of the old.

Rabbi Yose ben Yehudah. He lived toward the end of the second century and was an older contemporary of Rabbi Yehudah Ha-Nasi, who is identified in this *mishnah* simply as "Rabbi." Yose ben Yehudah accompanied Rabbi Yehudah Ha-Nasi on tours of the country (cf. B. Talmud, *Nedarim* 62a) and held halachic discussions with him. (Cf. B. Talmud, *Pesachim* 112b.)

4:21 Rabbi Elazar Ha-Kappar said, "Envy, lust, and [the pursuit of] glory take a person out of this world."

ד:כא רַבִּי אֶלְעָזָר הַקַּפָּר אוֹמֵר הַקִּנְאָה וְהַתַּאֲוָה וְהַכָּבוֹד מוֹצִיאִין אֶת הָאָדָם מִן הָעוֹלָם:

Rabbi Elazar. He lived at the end of the second century and was a contemporary of Rabbi Yehudah Ha-Nasi.

Envy, lust, and [the pursuit of] glory. Rashi explains envy by quoting the verse, "Envy rots the bones." [Prov. 14:30] For Maimonides, any one of these three personal weaknesses will cause a person to forget one's knowledge of the Torah. Indeed, any of the three will negatively impact on a person's moral and intellectual virtues.

Bartinoro specifically identifies lust as the pursuit of eating, drinking, and sexual pleasure.

4:22 He used to say, "Those who are born will die. Those who die will live again. Those who [then] live are to be judged, to know, to make known, and to let it be known who is God, who is the Maker, who is the Creator, who is the One who understands, who is the Judge, who is the Witness, who is the Litigant. The Holy One of Blessing is the one who will judge [a judge] without iniquity, without forgetfulness, without partiality, without being bribed. Know that everything will be added up. Don't let your

ד:כב הוּא הָיָה אוֹמֵר הַיְלוֹדִים לָמוּת וְהַמֵּתִים לִחְיוֹת וְהַחַיִּים לָדוּן לֵידַע וּלְהוֹדִיעַ וּלְהִוָּדַע שֶׁהוּא אֵל הוּא הַיּוֹצֵר הוּא הַבּוֹרֵא הוּא הַמֵּבִין הוּא הַדַּיָּן הוּא הָעֵד הוּא בַּעַל דִּין הוּא עָתִיד לָדוּן. בָּרוּךְ הוּא שֶׁאֵין לְפָנָיו לֹא עַוְלָה וְלֹא שִׁכְחָה וְלֹא מַשּׂוֹא פָנִים וְלֹא מִקַּח שֹׁחַד וְדַע שֶׁהַכֹּל לְפִי הַחֶשְׁבּוֹן וְאַל יַבְטִיחֲךָ יִצְרֶךָ שֶׁהַשְּׁאוֹל בֵּית מָנוֹס לָךְ שֶׁעַל כָּרְחֲךָ אַתָּה נוֹצָר וְעַל כָּרְחֲךָ אַתָּה נוֹלָד וְעַל כָּרְחֲךָ אַתָּה חַי וְעַל כָּרְחֲךָ אַתָּה מֵת וְעַל כָּרְחֲךָ אַתָּה עָתִיד לִתֵּן דִּין וְחֶשְׁבּוֹן לִפְנֵי מֶלֶךְ מַלְכֵי הַמְּלָכִים הַקָּדוֹשׁ בָּרוּךְ הוּא:

inclination [to do evil] persuade you that you will be able to escape in the grave, for against your will were you formed. Against your will were you born. Against your will you live. Against your will you will die. Against your will you will make a reckoning before the Ruler of rulers, the Holy One of Blessing."

The notion of Torah as Law emanates from the notion of God as Lawgiver and Judge. The divine Judge is sure to give a just verdict. While we have not been born of our own volition, what we do with our lives is within our control. For Jewish tradition, this life and whatever comes next form a continuum. What we achieve here will be rewarded or punished in the hereafter.

Bartinoro comments that the final reckoning, which will take place at the judgment in the world to come, will be "penny by penny." Each and every act will be noted.

Transgression and Sin

A variety of words that denote sin are used in the Bible. The most common, *chet*, refers to a lack of perfection in completing an obligation. This failure to carry out one's duty can occur in relations between individuals or between an individual and God. In rabbinic literature, the term *averah* is usually used. In this regard, a sin is a rejection of God's will. Sins of commission are therefore more serious than are sins of omission. The rabbis consider most serious the sins of murder, idolatry, adultery, and incest. All other sins are considered light in comparison and in levels of gradation. According to the rabbis, all sin is caused by the *yetzer hara*, one's inclination to do evil. However, one should not view such a posture toward sin as if the rabbis believed that sin was inevitable or to be condoned. The *yetzer hara* entices the individual to sin, but one must rise above sin through the study of Torah and the observance of its precepts.

Pardes and Paradise

From the Persian, *pardes* comes to mean Paradise or pleasure garden. While *pardes* is often incorrectly used for the English loan word Paradise, it really means "orchard." Paradise is translated as *Gan Eden* (literally, the "Garden of Eden") and refers both to the primordial garden and the state of eternal bliss. Throughout rabbinic literature the word *pardes* operates on several levels. It acts as an acronym for the four major approaches to discovering the meaning of a text: P = *peshat*, the literal meaning; D = *derash*, the homiletic meaning; R = *remez*, the meaning that the text implies or hints at; and S = *sod*, the secret or mystical meaning of the text. *Pardes* also refers to theosophical speculation.

The Rabbinate

The rabbinate as an institution has changed greatly since it emerged over 2,000 years ago when it drew its authority from the notion of Oral Law. While it always distinguished itself through study (and not lineage as had the priesthood), the rabbinate has functioned differently in successive generations. In its early period, the rabbis were teachers and judges. Even after the Jewish people lost self-rule, the rabbis formed the semiautonomous judicial system that operated within the context of the law of the land. Rabbis had other vocations and professions. Controversy often erupted over the issue, but it was not really until the modern period that, borrowing from Christian models as well as other secular role models, the rabbinate became a profession in and of itself. Yet, throughout rabbinic literature there is a level of self-aggrandizement regarding study and those who possess the knowledge of Torah, namely the rabbis. Even within the context of the modern world, there are varieties to the rabbinic model. Judicial function in the liberal community is usually relegated to issues regarding personal status and life-cycle function. In the more traditional community, on a more or less voluntary basis, rabbis retain a broader judicial function.

To Study to Do

Judaism emphasizes action over belief; belief arises from action. Likewise one studies in order to practice and to teach, not simply to learn. In Judaism, knowledge of Torah (traditionally interpreted as God's law) is important only insofar as it affects the way of life of humankind. If knowledge is not translated into deed, it is useless. In Talmud, *Kiddushin* 40b, we read, "When Rabbi Tarfon and the sages were dining in the upper chamber in the house of Nitzah in Lydda, this question was asked of them, 'Which is greater, study or practice?' Rabbi Tarfon answered, 'Practice is greater.' Rabbi Akiva answered, 'Study is greater.' Then the sages responded, 'Study is greater because it leads to practice.'" Without learning, one cannot practice in accordance with the laws of Torah.

Rabbi Meir and Beruriah

Rabbi Meir was one of the leaders of the post-Bar Kochba period. He was essentially a halachist who played a pivotal part in the development of the *Mishnah*. According to the *aggadah*, Meir was descended from converts to Judaism (Jews-by-choice). His name means "the illuminator," and it is not clear whether that was the name with which he was born. He was a disciple of Rabbi Akiva but also came under the influence of Rabbi Yishmael and Elisha ben Abuyha (well known because he was considered a heretic). Ordained during the persecution that followed the Bar Kochba revolt, he fled from *Eretz Yisrael*. Later, he was among those assembled at Usha, where legislation was enacted leading to the renewal of the office of *nasi*, which had been abolished.

The *mishnah* (*Avot* 4:10) is referred to as the *mishnah* of Meir although it was edited by Yehudah Ha-Nasi. While there is a disagreement as to whether anonymous *mishnayot* are to be attributed to Yehudah Ha-Nasi, he certainly laid their foundation.

Meir's wife, Beruriah, is an example par excellence of the women in the talmudic period. The daughter of the martyred Chanina ben Teradyon, she is probably the only woman mentioned in talmudic literature whose views on legal matters are taken seriously. Stories abound about her great knowledge and her moral stature. Most well known is the story about the death of their two sons. Beruriah did not want to disturb Meir when he returned from the academy and force him to grieve on the Sabbath. She, therefore, related the news of their sons' deaths to him in a parable: "Sometime ago a man left me two jewels in trust. Shall I return them to him now that he is asking for them?" When Meir replied in the affirmative, she showed him their sons. (*Midrash* to Prov. 31:1)

Students and Teachers

There is a special relationship between students and teachers evidenced in rabbinic literature. This is an intimate relationship that colors the life of both scholar and student. The student speaks proudly of "my teacher" and, when repeating what has been learned, speaks in that teacher's name—humbly acknowledging the source of the student's own knowledge. While there is a level of mutual respect between student and teacher, the student expresses a reverence for the teacher, uniquely reserved for the relationship. For example, Rabbi Elazar suggests in the Talmud (*Kiddushin* 33b), "Sages who do not rise in the presence of their teachers are considered wicked and will not live long and will forget the Torah that they have learned."

Old Age and Learning

Jewish tradition approaches old age realistically with a great deal of reverence for those who have experienced the lessons in life and have grown in wisdom as a result of these experiences. As a result, the word chosen to represent old age and wisdom evolves from the same Hebrew root, *zaken*. And an elder represents a life of learning as well. Indeed, historically, Councils of Elders were established to guide the community. They remember what had happened in the past because they lived through it. Nevertheless, the sages understood the possibility for memory loss and physical malady in old age. And so, they were careful to overstate generalizations in regard to old age and learning. Yet, realizing the zest for youth and potential for the seizing of community authority and power among the youths, these rabbis articulated a position that held in high esteem the wisdom of lifetime learning through experience and study.

GLEANINGS

"everyone has one's moment" (4:3)

DEVELOPMENT OF SELF

The human self is not a gift; it is an achievement. It is not a static reality, sprung full-blown from the head of God. Rather it is a painfully earned progress past lions in the way–a triumph over ogres real and imaginary. The attainment of a self is a running battle, a continuing process, and a victory that is never fully consummated until the chambers of our heart flutter and fill for the last time.

At the beginning of the "saga of self" we face a booming, buzzing confusion. Our eyes awake to blurred lights and indistinct shapes. We hear soft voices that soothe us or loud noises that terrify us, and, as we gradually adjust ourselves to the rocking, uncertain earth, our restless minds begin to make a little pattern of order here, a little design of meaning there. Our emotions are without armor, defenseless and tender, and we feel the tensions that crackle like lightning through the atmosphere of the grown-up world. Gradually we adjust to the strange kingdom of childhood, but there are always dangers lurking in shaded corners, strange gusts of emotion that sweep through us like cold winds on an open prairie. Emotions of jealous possessiveness seize us when rivals threaten our primacy in the realm of our parents' love, new brothers and sisters awaken slumbering giants of jealousy and envy. Fear and anger, insecurity and pain blot out the sun of many a growing day.

As soon as we become masters of this little island of our earliest childhood, we find ourselves driven forth into a new and stranger world called "school," which fascinates and frightens us at the same time. Rivalry with our fellows, the awkward testing of our strength, the trials of puberty, the little failures and great losses that mar the beauty of adolescence tempt us to refuse the mixed blessings of growth. We yearn to regress to some earlier level, some older form of behavior where we were infinitely more shielded and protected.

The adolescent at moments wants to return to that well-loved country of his childhood where there was less competition, where everything was given to him. Every new stage of life is a shattering one emotionally and forces us to build some new adjustment out of broken fragments of our past, out of the precious shards of earlier molds.

Gradually, if we become well-adjusted adults, we learn how to accept the loss of our earlier privileges. We face the competition of our contemporaries and learn to share without too much bitterness our gifts and selves with others. We can stand punishment and immediate frustration without undue anxiety. We realize that for us the way lies ahead and that it is too late to turn back, that such a retreat will cause only unhappiness.

(Joshua Loth Liebman, *Peace of Mind*, New York: Simon and Schuster, 1946)

JOSHUA LOTH LIEBMAN (1907-1948). Reform rabbi, widely known as a radio preacher. His book *Peace of Mind* was phenomenally successful. It made an important contribution to the fields of religion and psychology, which were growing together at the time.

"Whoever dishonors the Torah" (4:6)

NOVELTY SEEKERS

Every age has its novelty seekers and its spasmodic hankering after the bizarre and the flamboyant. Every epoch has its false glitter and its cheap and easy cleverness. The young men and women of almost every age, except the excessively repressed ones, have sought after the sharp relish of the novel and the unconventional, whether in clothes or manners or amusements. Our own age is especially addicted to this idolatry of the novel. Our young people would break with conventions and restraints of the past and plunge into what they call the New Life. But this new life is, after all, no new life at all but an acceleration of the old rhythm–a swifter scansion of a hackneyed melody. The wild music and the wilder dances of today are as old as the jungle, and the late hours and loose talk, the irreverences, and the irresponsibilities of our day are no whit different from the stale bravados of every generation since the beginning of time–the same capers and the same totems. There is nothing new in novelty!

The New Life is not a new excitement but a new exultation–not a stimulant but a satisfaction. We renew ourselves, not by indulging our appetites, but by improving our tastes. As we acquire keener perceptions, finer discriminations, sounder judgments, new purposes, deeper loyalties, do we gain in newness and freshness and freedom.

The artist enters new worlds by way of his art, and by that token his life is renewed. As his art is perfected, his life is progressively renewed–like an endless drama of resurrection. The musician, the poet, the scholar traverse unexplored continents of beatitudes, untrod by the uninitiated, and to that degree their life is a perennial renewal. Every creative effort of heart of mind is a glorious hazardry into undiscovered worlds, bringing lilt and flame to the eager heart. The man who follows a beckoning ideal is assured of a constant refreshment of soul that will save him from the drab weariness of his advancing years.

Life should be an endless process of self-renewal, of spiritual growth and augmentation. Our business or profession should not be so mechanical as to restrict our development and confine us to repetition and monotony. We should, of course, attempt to advance to the very limits of our vocation, explore its every byway, marshall into play every talent we possess, but we must continue our self-fulfillment beyond it and outside of it. No occupation, however large its scope, is large enough to enclave our whole personality. Like a jewel radiating through numerous facets, our spirit should adventure along manifold ways.

(Abba Hillel Silver, "Renewal," Cleveland: The Temple, Tifereth Israel, n.d.)

ABBA HILLEL SILVER (1893-1963). One of the leading rabbis of his time. Together with Stephen S. Wise, he was among the confidants of Franklin D. Roosevelt, trying to make him aware of the Nazi "Final Solution." A great orator and great thinker, a leader of the Zionist movement, he was rabbi of The Temple, Tifereth Israel, Cleveland, Ohio.

"God will give you a great reward" (4:10)

BETWEEN GOD AND MAN

The religion of the pagan world was a religion concerned with only the present. According to the ideas of the Babylonians, the Greeks, and the Romans, man could not change his fate. His destiny was prescribed by the circle of the planets, the stars, the sun, and the moon. Their religion consisted of a machinery capable of changing the constellation of the stars to suit the purposes of man. The religion of the pagans, therefore, was a religion of technique. They needed experts who were able to influence the stars and to make the gods willing to oblige man's wishes. The pagan religion, therefore, was a priest's religion. The priests were religious experts, magicians, sorcerers, and holy technicians who, with their sacrifices and incantations, had the key to the mystery of the world. They were so preoccupied with the transformation of the destiny of man for the immediate purposes of the day that the idea of how the world would look in the future escaped them entirely. The result was that the messianic idea was alien to them. Their religion was static, the product of a frozen mind, dedicated to magic and mystery.

For the Jew, history always was the meeting ground between God and man. Everybody had a chance to meet God and to live up to God's laws and commandments. Man could fail in this endeavor. He could fail to meet the requirements of the ethical precepts of the Bible. But he could return from his error and push forward the course of history by dedicating himself to its eternal demands.

In the Jewish religion the all-embracing force of the priest was broken. On Mount Sinai the whole people of Israel was consecrated as a people of priests. Each member of the congregation was called upon to exercise the function of the priest in his family. The idea as the elevation of animal man to a spiritual being was born. The course of history from then on was not anymore determined by the constellations of the stars. It was not manipulated by secret techniques of a special priest caste. The course of history was given into the hand of each individual who had to decide for himself whether he wanted to work for the ethical progress of mankind or for its downfall.

(Hugo Hahn, *Gleanings*, New York: Congregation Habonim, 1974)

HUGO HAHN (1893-1967). A rabbi in Essen and a leader of one of the largest congregations in Germany. He was ordained by the rabbinical seminary in Breslau and received a Ph.D. from the University of Erlangen in Germany. He came to America and founded Congregation Habonim, a congregation of refugees, in New York City.

"An hour spent in penitence and good deeds" (4:17)

CAN WE ATONE?

We believe that we cannot atone by the mere repetition of formulae, however inspiring they may be; we cannot atone by external offerings; we cannot atone by a mere "excuse me" or "I beg your pardon," even if these be spoken to God. If by atonement we understand only a ritual conformity rather than a spiritual, ethical transformation—then is there no such thing, idea, or experience as "atonement"! But there *is* atonement, if by it we understand a firm resolution to lead a better life—in the immediate present and in the future. Atonement, then, means for us a conscious self-regeneration–in the present and for the future. It means, then, a spiritual rebirth of the sinner–in the present and for the future. Atonement means a reintegration, a reconstruction of life, a reconsecration to higher purposes and greater ideals–in the present and for the future. As to the past–that which is once done cannot be undone. The wrong omitted cannot be eradicated. What is past cannot be recalled. "Of the power of making things that are past never to have been, even God is deprived," said Aristotle, and Jewish philosophers concur. "What's past is prologue," said Shakespeare. We cannot undo the past, but we can assure a better future.

(Abraham J. Feldman, *Lights and Shadows*, W. Hartford, Connecticut: Congregation Beth Israel, 1928)

ABRAHAM J. FELDMAN (1893-1977). The longtime rabbi at Congregation Beth Israel in W. Hartford, Connecticut. An ardent Zionist and former president of the CCAR, he was a classical reformer who exercised a great deal of influence on the Reform rabbinate of his generation.

"An hour of contentment in the world to come" (4:17)

WHY I BELIEVE IN THE ETERNAL

We can by no effort of ours bring ourselves to deny that something exists somehow, somewhere. Even if we think that all things outside ourselves are unreal appearances, that this fair world, the heavens, and the earth are merely a dream of our mind, yet we doubters and dreamers still exist. You can not think of a time when there was absolutely nothing in existence, nor are you able to think of a time when existence itself shall be annihilated. Take the wings of imagination and fly from star-system to star-system to the uttermost bounds of all known galaxies, beyond the region of the faintest and remotest cosmic cloud; even in the heart of eternal night and silence and cold you are still floating on the waves of being and are unable to break away from your soul's inseparable companion, from the idea of omnipresent existence. Should you fancy space beyond all stellar regions to be absolutely empty, still space is left, space exists. You can put no bound to space in thought. Beyond the uttermost reach of imagination infinitude stretches, one, indivisible, eternal, pregnant with the seeds of star-births, heaving with the throbs of universal force. You cannot conceive a limit set to force. You cannot say, only to a certain point in space does it go and cannot dart beyond a certain fixed boundary line. Where force is, there dwells being; there are beating the pulses of all-pervading energy. Being, then, has no limits in space or time. Existence is infinite and eternal. Well may the idea of infinite and eternal existence thrill us with religious awe and cause us to observe towards it an attitude of speechless wonder. It is the simplest and surest and most universal fact. It is the taproot of all truths. It underlies all thoughts.

(Adolph Moses, *Yahvism*, Louisville: National Council of Jewish Women, 1903)

ADOLPH MOSES (1840-1902). Born in Poland and ordained at the Breslau Seminary, where he left for a short time to enlist in Garibaldi's fight for Italian freedom. Following study at the University of Vienna and a prison term for joining the Polish insurrection against Russia, he was called to a pulpit in Montgomery, Alabama, in 1870. After also serving in Mobile, Alabama, he served a pulpit in Louisville, Kentucky, until his death. An exceptional scholar, he was coeditor of *Zeitgeist* and greatly influenced Reform Judaism.

CHAPTER FIVE

The World Was Created by Ten Statements

5:1 The world was created by ten statements. Why does the Torah teach [us] that? Indeed, the world could have been created by one statement! That teaching was [offered] to punish the wicked who would destroy the world that was created by ten statements and to reward the righteous who maintain the world created by [these] ten statements.

ה:א בַּעֲשָׂרָה מַאֲמָרוֹת נִבְרָא הָעוֹלָם וּמַה תַּלְמוּד לוֹמַר וַהֲלֹא בְּמַאֲמָר אֶחָד יָכוֹל לְהִבָּרְאוֹת אֶלָּא לְהִפָּרַע מִן הָרְשָׁעִים שֶׁמְּאַבְּדִין אֶת הָעוֹלָם שֶׁנִּבְרָא בַּעֲשָׂרָה מַאֲמָרוֹת וְלִתֵּן שָׂכָר טוֹב לַצַּדִּיקִים שֶׁמְּקַיְּמִין אֶת הָעוֹלָם שֶׁנִּבְרָא בַּעֲשָׂרָה מַאֲמָרוֹת:

Most of the sayings in this chapter are anonymous and are related to numbers.

By ten statements. Ten times is the phrase "and God said" found in the first and second chapters of Genesis. Our commentators count nine statements in the first chapter of Genesis and find the tenth statement in Psalms 33:6, "By the word of *Adonai* were the heavens made."

Rashi suggests that the ten statements indicate God's labor in the creative process. Maimonides argues that each statement was given to indicate the majesty of the created world.

5:2 There were ten generations from Adam to Noah to prove the patience of God. Although all those generations provoked God, only then [after ten generations] did God bring the Flood upon them. There were ten generations from Noah to Abraham to prove the patience of God. Although all those generations provoked God, only then [after ten generations] did Abraham come to receive the reward [that might have been intended] for all of them.

ה:ב עֲשָׂרָה דוֹרוֹת מֵאָדָם וְעַד נֹחַ לְהוֹדִיעַ כַּמָּה אֶרֶךְ אַפַּיִם לְפָנָיו שֶׁכָּל הַדּוֹרוֹת הָיוּ מַכְעִיסִין וּבָאִין עַד שֶׁהֵבִיא עֲלֵיהֶם אֶת מֵי הַמַּבּוּל. עֲשָׂרָה דוֹרוֹת מִנֹּחַ וְעַד אַבְרָהָם לְהוֹדִיעַ כַּמָּה אֶרֶךְ אַפַּיִם לְפָנָיו שֶׁכָּל הַדּוֹרוֹת הָיוּ מַכְעִיסִין וּבָאִין עַד שֶׁבָּא אַבְרָהָם אָבִינוּ וְקִבֵּל שָׂכָר כֻּלָּם:

Ten generations. Maimonides sees in the ten generations, as with the ten statements in the previous *mishnah* and the ten trials in the following *mishnah*, opportunities for the progressive improvement of one's moral and intellectual qualities. Bartinoro argues that Abraham's merit preserved those generations.

The patience of God. Rashi explains that God was patient, hoping that each generation might repent. Bartinoro draws a more modern moral from this *mishnah*: Let the reader not be amazed by God's patience with those nations that presently subjugate Israel.

5:3 Abraham was tested ten times. He withstood every test to show [how] great was his love [for God].

הוּג עֲשָׂרָה נִסְיוֹנוֹת נִתְנַסָּה אַבְרָהָם אָבִינוּ וְעָמַד בְּכֻלָּם לְהוֹדִיעַ כַּמָּה חִבָּתוֹ שֶׁל אַבְרָהָם אָבִינוּ׃

Abraham was tested ten times. According to Maimonides, the ten trials were (1) his exile from his home in response to God's command of לֶךְ־לְךָ *lech-lecha* (Gen. 12:1); (2) the famine in the land of Canaan, which seemed to belie God's promise, "I will make you into a great nation, and I will bless you" (Gen. 12:2); (3) the violence done to Abraham in the taking of Sarah into Pharaoh's house (Gen. 12:10-20); (4) his battle with the four kings (Gen. 14); (5) his need to take Hagar as a wife after his despair over not having children with Sarah (Gen. 16:1ff.); (6) the command to circumcise himself although he was an old man (Gen. 17:11); (7) the violence of having his wife taken into the house of the king of Gerar (Gen. 20:1-18); (8) Abraham's compulsion to send away Hagar although she had borne him a son (Gen. 21:9-21); (9) the difficulty of sending away his son Yishmael (Gen. 21:12); and (10) the binding of Isaac (Gen. 22).

5:4 Ten miracles were performed for our ancestors in Egypt. Ten occurred at the sea. Ten plagues were brought by the Holy One of Blessing against the Egyptians in Egypt and ten at the sea. Ten times did our ancestors test the Holy One of Blessing, as it says, "And they tested Me these ten times and would not hearken to My voice." [Num. 14:22]

הוּד עֲשָׂרָה נִסִּים נַעֲשׂוּ לַאֲבוֹתֵינוּ בְּמִצְרַיִם וַעֲשָׂרָה עַל הַיָּם. עֶשֶׂר מַכּוֹת הֵבִיא הַקָּדוֹשׁ בָּרוּךְ הוּא עַל הַמִּצְרִיִּים בְּמִצְרַיִם וְעֶשֶׂר עַל הַיָּם. עֲשָׂרָה נִסְיוֹנוֹת נִסּוּ אֲבוֹתֵינוּ אֶת הַקָּדוֹשׁ בָּרוּךְ הוּא בַּמִּדְבָּר שֶׁנֶּאֱמַר וַיְנַסּוּ אֹתִי זֶה עֶשֶׂר פְּעָמִים וְלֹא שָׁמְעוּ בְּקוֹלִי׃

Ten miracles. Rashi's comment contains an old *midrash* outlining the ten miracles that were performed at the Sea of Reeds. Moses asked the people to arise and cross over. They would not do so until the sea could be formed into channels. Moses lifted up his staff, and the sea became channels: the first miracle occurred. Again, he asked that the people cross, but they demurred. Only if the sea were formed into heaps would they cross. Moses lifted up his staff, and the sea was so formed: the second miracle. Again, he asked the people to cross over; again, they held back. Only if the sea became fissures would they cross. Moses lifted up his staff, and the third miracle occurred. Again, Moses asked the people to cross. Again, they refused. Only if the sea could be plastered over would they cross. This miracle was performed: the fourth. "Cross over," Moses pleaded. "Only if the sea becomes a desert," they answered. That was the fifth miracle. He then asked that they cross over, and again they would not. The people asked that the sea be changed into crumbs, which was done, that the sea be changed into boulders, which was also done, and that the sea be changed into dry land. This, too, was done. Thus were performed the sixth, seventh, and eighth miracles. They asked then that the sea become walls, and it became walls: the ninth miracle. Finally, they asked that the sea become skin bottles, and this became the tenth miracle.

This *midrash* considers the miracles at the sea as a kind of test of God as well as a test of Moses. The *midrash* is a rabbinic elaboration of the biblical evaluation of the Jewish people: עַם קְשֵׁה עֹרֶף *am kesheh oref*, a "stiff-necked people."

5:5 Ten miracles were performed for our ancestors in the Temple. The odor of the meat of the sacrifice never caused a woman to miscarry. That meat never became putrid. No fly was ever seen in the slaughterhouse. No [disqualifying] pollution ever befell the High Priest on the Day of Atonement. Rain never put out the fire of the wood arranged [on the altar]. The wind did not disturb the smoke column [from the altar]. No defect was ever found in the *omer*, or in the two loaves, or in the showbread. Although the people were tightly pressed together, there was plenty of room when they prostrated themselves. No one was ever hurt by snake or scorpion in Jerusalem. No one ever said, "There is no room for me to spend the night in Jerusalem."

ה:ה עֲשָׂרָה נִסִּים נַעֲשׂוּ לַאֲבוֹתֵינוּ בְּבֵית הַמִּקְדָּשׁ לֹא הִפִּילָה אִשָּׁה מֵרֵיחַ בְּשַׂר הַקֹּדֶשׁ וְלֹא הִסְרִיחַ בְּשַׂר הַקֹּדֶשׁ מֵעוֹלָם וְלֹא נִרְאָה זְבוּב בְּבֵית הַמִּטְבָּחַיִם וְלֹא אִירַע קֶרִי לְכֹהֵן גָּדוֹל בְּיוֹם הַכִּפּוּרִים וְלֹא כִבּוּ הַגְּשָׁמִים אֵשׁ שֶׁל עֲצֵי הַמַּעֲרָכָה וְלֹא נִצְּחָה הָרוּחַ אֶת עַמּוּד הֶעָשָׁן וְלֹא נִמְצָא פְסוּל בָּעֹמֶר וּבִשְׁתֵּי הַלֶּחֶם וּבְלֶחֶם הַפָּנִים. עוֹמְדִים צְפוּפִים וּמִשְׁתַּחֲוִים רְוָוחִים וְלֹא הִזִּיק נָחָשׁ וְעַקְרָב בִּירוּשָׁלַיִם מֵעוֹלָם וְלֹא אָמַר אָדָם לַחֲבֵרוֹ צַר לִי הַמָּקוֹם שֶׁאָלִין בִּירוּשָׁלָיִם:

The odor of the meat. According to Rashi, the odor of the sacrifices was neither attractive enough nor repellent enough to cause a miscarriage.

Rain never put out the fire. Maimonides notes that the altar was in the middle of the court-yard of the Temple and open to the air. It was open as well to the effects of rain and wind.

In the omer, or in the two loaves, or in the showbread. The עוֹמֶר *omer*, a "sheaf of barley," refers to the new barley offered on the second day of Passover. The two loaves were those baked from the wheat of the first-fruit offering of the Feast of Weeks (Shavuot). The showbread was the twelve loaves of unleavened bread placed by the priests in the sanctuary.

(Cf. Exod. 25:30.) Had there been any defect in any of these three, there would have been no opportunity for their replacement.

There is no room for me. Bartinoro notes that the phrase צַר לִי הַמָּקוֹם *tzar li hamakom*, here translated as "there is no room for me," is a quotation from Isaiah 49:20.

5:6 Ten things were created on the eve of the [first] Shabbat at twilight. They are: the mouth of the earth; the mouth of the well; the mouth of the ass; the rainbow; the manna; the staff [of Moses]; the *shamir*; the writing; the writing instrument; and the tablets. Some say: destructive spirits; the grave of Moses; and the ram of our patriarch Abraham. Some even say the first tongs [which are] made by tongs.

הו עֲשָׂרָה דְבָרִים נִבְרְאוּ בְּעֶרֶב שַׁבָּת בֵּין הַשְּׁמָשׁוֹת וְאֵלּוּ הֵן פִּי הָאָרֶץ פִּי הַבְּאֵר פִּי הָאָתוֹן הַקֶּשֶׁת וְהַמָּן וְהַמַּטֶּה וְהַשָּׁמִיר הַכְּתָב וְהַמִּכְתָּב וְהַלֻּחוֹת. וְיֵשׁ אוֹמְרִים אַף הַמַּזִּיקִין וּקְבֻרָתוֹ שֶׁל מֹשֶׁה וְאֵילוֹ שֶׁל אַבְרָהָם אָבִינוּ וְיֵשׁ אוֹמְרִים אַף צְבָת בִּצְבָת עֲשׂוּיָה:

Ten things. This list contains things that were deemed miraculous and that seemed outside the natural order developed within the Six Days of Creation. The first three refer to three wondrous events: the earth opening its mouth to swallow Korach and his company (Num. 16:32); the well accompanying and supplying the Israelites in their wanderings in the wilderness (Num. 21:16-18); and the speaking of Balaam's ass. (Num. 22:28-30) The miracle of the rainbow was that it was given as a sign that there would never again be a flood. (Gen. 9:12-17) The manna fed the Israelites for forty years in the wilderness. (Exod. 16:15) With his staff, Moses performed wonders and brought plagues. (Exod. 4:17) Although the word שָׁמִיר *shamir* in Jeremiah 17:1 refers to a "flint," in the rabbinic mind, the word referred to a miraculous "worm" that when placed on the hardest stone could split it. (*Mishnah Sotah* 9:12) This worm, now extinct, was so hard that it was purported to cleave large stones as it crawled over them. Solomon was said to have used it to cut the stones for the building of the Temple. It was also to have been used to engrave the names of the tribes on the two stones for the shoulders of the *ephod* worn by the High Priest. (Cf. Exod. 28:9ff.; *Sotah* 48b; *Gittin* 68a; and Jer. 17:1.) It is significant because the use of iron tools in the building of an altar to God is forbidden. (Exod. 20:22)

Rashi understands "the writing" as the letters of the Ten Commandments written on the two tablets and "the writing instrument" as the instrument used to write them.

Some say. Having presented the ten wonders, the *mishnah* adds four more after the words "Some say." Bartinoro gives a clear explanation of the origin of the destructive spirits. It seems that, after having created Adam and Eve, God was occupied in creating these spirits. Alas, with the onset of the Sabbath, God did not have time to complete bodies for them, and so these poor spirits had to exist without a body. (No wonder they are destructive!)

The grave of Moses and the ram of Abraham are examples of things that met a specific need at a specific time. The first is wondrous because it is known only to God.

(Deut. 34:6) The second is wondrous because it saved Isaac and with him the future Jewish people. (Gen. 22:13)

The last wonder is an attempt to answer the question that must have occurred to anyone using tongs. If one needs tongs to hold material to make tongs, who made the first ones?

5:7 Seven things distinguish a fool and seven things distinguish a wise person. The wise person does not speak in the presence of one who is wiser. The wise person does not interrupt when another is speaking. The wise person is not in a hurry to answer. The wise person asks according to the subject and answers according to the Law. The wise person speaks about the first matter first and the last matter last. If there is something the wise person has not heard [and therefore does not know], the wise person says, "I have never heard [of it]." The wise person acknowledges what is true. The opposite of all these qualities is found in a fool.

ה:ז שִׁבְעָה דְבָרִים בַּגֹּלֶם וְשִׁבְעָה בֶּחָכָם. חָכָם אֵינוֹ מְדַבֵּר לִפְנֵי מִי שֶׁגָּדוֹל מִמֶּנּוּ בְּחָכְמָה וּבְמִנְיָן וְאֵינוֹ נִכְנָס לְתוֹךְ דִּבְרֵי חֲבֵרוֹ וְאֵינוֹ נִבְהָל לְהָשִׁיב שׁוֹאֵל כָּעִנְיָן וּמֵשִׁיב כַּהֲלָכָה וְאוֹמֵר עַל רִאשׁוֹן רִאשׁוֹן וְעַל אַחֲרוֹן אַחֲרוֹן וְעַל מַה שֶׁלֹּא שָׁמַע אוֹמֵר לֹא שָׁמַעְתִּי וּמוֹדֶה עַל הָאֱמֶת וְחִלּוּפֵיהֶן בַּגֹּלֶם:

A fool...a wise person. The word גֹּלֶם *golem*, here translated as "fool," comes from biblical Hebrew meaning a shapeless mass or an embryo. (Ps. 139:16) Rabbinic Hebrew carries the notion further. It understands the word to denote something unfinished or, as it is used here, the kind of person contrasted with the wise.

Golem gives Maimonides the opportunity to give differential definitions of five terms found in rabbinic literature that deal with folly and wisdom. They are בּוּר *bur*, עַם הָאָרֶץ *am haaretz*, גֹּלֶם *golem*, חָכָם *chacham*, and חָסִיד *chasid*. The first, for Maimonides, has neither intellectual nor ethical virtues nor the ability to acquire them. Maimonides takes the word *bur* from the phrase שָׂדֶה בּוּר *sedeh bur*, an "uncultivated field." (We might translate the term as "boor.") *Am haaretz*, for Maimonides, is a person who has ethical virtues but lacks intellectual virtues. Such a person is useful in and for society. (We might translate the term as "ignoramus.") *Golem*, for Maimonides, is a person who possesses both intellectual and ethical virtues, but they are in a confused and scattered fashion within that person. Like the word *golem*, meaning that which is unfashioned and unformed, so is such a person. (We have translated the term as "fool.") *Chacham* refers to a person whose intellectual and ethical virtues have reached their proper stage of perfection. (We might translate the term as "wise.") *Chasid* refers to a person who, having achieved perfection in both ethical and intellectual virtues, now prefers to stress the ethical virtues. (We might translate the term as "pious.")

5:8 Seven kinds of punishment come into the world for seven categories of transgression. If some give tithes while some do not, a famine resulting from drought ensues. Thus, some will be sated, and others will starve. If all have decided not to tithe, then a famine resulting from anxiety and drought ensues. If all resolve not to give the *challah*, then a totally destructive famine will ensue. Pestilence comes to the world because of crimes that the Torah declares deserving of death but that could not be judged by any [human] court and for [transgressions involving] the seventh-year produce. The sword comes into the world because of justice delayed and justice denied and because of those who misinterpret the Torah.

הָּח שִׁבְעָה מִינֵי פֻּרְעָנִיּוֹת בָּאִין לָעוֹלָם עַל שִׁבְעָה גוּפֵי עֲבֵרָה מִקְצָתָן מְעַשְּׂרִין וּמִקְצָתָן אֵינָן מְעַשְּׂרִין רָעָב שֶׁל בַּצֹּרֶת בָּא מִקְצָתָן רְעֵבִים וּמִקְצָתָן שְׂבֵעִים. גָּמְרוּ שֶׁלֹּא לְעַשֵּׂר רָעָב שֶׁל מְהוּמָה וְשֶׁל בַּצֹּרֶת בָּא. וְשֶׁלֹּא לִטּוֹל אֶת הַחַלָּה רָעָב שֶׁל כְּלָיָה בָּא. דֶּבֶר בָּא לָעוֹלָם עַל מִיתוֹת הָאֲמוּרוֹת בַּתּוֹרָה שֶׁלֹּא נִמְסְרוּ לְבֵית דִּין וְעַל פֵּרוֹת שְׁבִיעִית. חֶרֶב בָּאָה לָעוֹלָם עַל עִנּוּי הַדִּין וְעַל עִוּוּת הַדִּין וְעַל הַמּוֹרִים בַּתּוֹרָה שֶׁלֹּא כַהֲלָכָה:

Drought. Rashi suggests there are two kinds of drought. One merely forces up the market price, causing deprivation for only a portion of the people. The other causes deprivation to the entire populace. The latter occurs when all have decided not to tithe and is associated with an anxiety that prevents the enjoyment of any kind of food.

Anxiety. Maimonides directly relates anxiety to the alarms of war. He explains that utterly destructive famine is due to the complete absence of any rain, fulfilling the biblical curse "The heavens above your head will be brass." (Deut. 28:23)

Challah. This thick-loaf offering is referred to in the Torah. (Num. 15:20) The special bread eaten on Shabbat and the festivals gets its name from this reference.

Who misinterpret the Torah. Rashi and Bartinoro take the phrase literally and explain that such persons permit what is forbidden and forbid what is permitted.

5:9 Wild animals come to the world [to attack people] because of false swearing and the profaning of God's name. Exile comes to the world because of idolatry, sexual impropriety, bloodshed, and the [neglect of the sabbatical] release of the land. Pestilence increases during four periods: in the fourth year, in the seventh year, in the year follow-

הָּט חַיָּה רָעָה בָּאָה לָעוֹלָם עַל שְׁבוּעַת שָׁוְא וְעַל חִלּוּל הַשֵּׁם. גָּלוּת בָּאָה לָעוֹלָם עַל עֲבוֹדַת כּוֹכָבִים וְעַל גִּלּוּי עֲרָיוֹת וְעַל שְׁפִיכוּת דָּמִים וְעַל שְׁמִטַּת הָאָרֶץ. בְּאַרְבָּעָה פְרָקִים הַדֶּבֶר מִתְרַבֶּה. בָּרְבִיעִית וּבַשְּׁבִיעִית וּבְמוֹצָאֵי שְׁבִיעִית וּבְמוֹצָאֵי הֶחָג שֶׁבְּכָל שָׁנָה וְשָׁנָה. בָּרְבִיעִית מִפְּנֵי מַעֲשַׂר עָנִי שֶׁבַּשְּׁלִישִׁית. בַּשְּׁבִיעִית מִפְּנֵי מַעֲשַׂר עָנִי שֶׁבַּשִּׁשִּׁית. בְּמוֹצָאֵי

ing that year, and each year at the end of the Festival [of Sukot]. The fourth year [increase] is because of [the failure to give] the tithe for the poor due in the sixth year. [The increase] in the year following is because of [transgressing the laws of] the seventh-year produce. [The increase] following each Festival [of Sukot] is because of the theft of what is due to the poor.

שְׁבִיעִית מִפְּנֵי פֵּרוֹת שְׁבִיעִית. בְּמוֹצָאֵי הֶחָג שֶׁבְּכָל שָׁנָה וְשָׁנָה מִפְּנֵי גֶזֶל מַתְּנוֹת עֲנִיִּים:

False swearing. Bartinoro understands שְׁבוּעַת שָׁוְא *shevuat shav*, here translated as "false swearing," as "vain swearing," i.e., for no useful purpose. He explains the profanation of the name of God as a public transgression done in a manner so that others may copy this illicit act.

[Neglect of the sabbatical] release of the land. This *mishnah* places the neglect of the sabbatical year on the same plane as the three cardinal sins of Judaism: idolatry, bloodshed, and sexual impropriety. גִּלּוּי עֲרָיוֹת *gilui arayot* is here translated as "sexual impropriety" because the term embraces adultery, incest, and those sexual behaviors described in Leviticus 18 and 20.

Pestilence. The *mishnah* ascribes the increase of pestilence to the lack of concern for the poor.

5:10 There are four kinds of human beings. One says, "What is mine is mine and what is yours is yours." That is the usual kind, although some say that is the Sodom kind. [The one who says,] "What is mine is yours and what is yours is mine" is an ignoramus. [The one who says,] "What is mine is yours and what is yours is yours" is a saint. [And the one who says,] "What is mine is mine and what is yours is mine" is a sinner.

הּ אַרְבַּע מִדּוֹת בָּאָדָם. הָאוֹמֵר שֶׁלִּי שֶׁלִּי וְשֶׁלְּךָ שֶׁלָּךְ זוֹ מִדָּה בֵּינוֹנִית וְיֵשׁ אוֹמְרִים זוֹ מִדַּת סְדוֹם. שֶׁלִּי שֶׁלָּךְ וְשֶׁלְּךָ שֶׁלִּי עַם הָאָרֶץ. שֶׁלִּי שֶׁלָּךְ וְשֶׁלְּךָ שֶׁלָּךְ חָסִיד. שֶׁלָּךְ שֶׁלִּי וְשֶׁלִּי שֶׁלִּי רָשָׁע:

The Sodom kind. Bartinoro explains the reference to Sodom as the person who is unwilling to help another. This person would have been a fit inhabitant of that infamous city.

An ignoramus. The *am haaretz,* here translated as "ignoramus," was, in the rabbinic mind, a rustic boor, lacking education, and hence to be contrasted with the תַּלְמִיד חָכָם *talmid chacham,* the "disciple of the wise."

5:11 There are four kinds of dispositions: [One is] easy to anger and easy to calm. That one's gain is nullified by the loss. [One is] hard to anger and hard to calm. That one's loss is nullified by the gain. [One is] hard to anger and easy to calm. That one is a saint. [The last is] easy to anger and hard to calm. That one is a sinner.

Gain...loss. Rashi explains that whatever benefit results from being easy to pacify is lost by being easy to provoke. Likewise, whatever benefit is gained by being hard to anger is lost by being hard to assuage.

Bartinoro finds a particular fault in being easy to anger. He contends that one's activities will be harmed by one's irascible personality.

הּ:יא אַרְבַּע מִדּוֹת בְּדֵעוֹת. נוֹחַ לִכְעוֹס וְנוֹחַ לִרְצוֹת יָצָא הֶפְסֵדוֹ בִּשְׂכָרוֹ. קָשֶׁה לִכְעוֹס וְקָשֶׁה לִרְצוֹת יָצָא שְׂכָרוֹ בְּהֶפְסֵדוֹ. קָשֶׁה לִכְעוֹס וְנוֹחַ לִרְצוֹת חָסִיד. נוֹחַ לִכְעוֹס וְקָשֶׁה לִרְצוֹת רָשָׁע:

5:12 There are four kinds of students. One is quick to learn and quick to forget. What that one gains, that one loses. One is slow to learn but slow to forget. What that one loses, that one gains. One learns quickly and is slow to forget. [Such a person will be] a scholar. Regarding the one who is slow to learn and quick to forget, that one will have a bad portion.

A scholar. Bartinoro's text for the third kind of student read זֶה חֵלֶק טוֹב *zeh chelek tov*, "this is a good portion," in place of חָכָם *chacham*, "scholar." Maimonides' text, which did have *chacham*, moves him to note that the text did not use the term חָסִיד *chasid*, "saint," since what is being described in the text is intellectual rather than moral virtue.

That one will have a bad portion. Heller suggests that the last student has a bad portion because it might have been possible for a pious student with Heaven's help to retain what had been learned slowly.

הּ:יב אַרְבַּע מִדּוֹת בְּתַלְמִידִים מָהִיר לִשְׁמוֹעַ וּמָהִיר לְאַבֵּד יָצָא שְׂכָרוֹ בְּהֶפְסֵדוֹ. קָשֶׁה לִשְׁמוֹעַ וְקָשֶׁה לְאַבֵּד יָצָא הֶפְסֵדוֹ בִּשְׂכָרוֹ. מָהִיר לִשְׁמוֹעַ וְקָשֶׁה לְאַבֵּד זֶה חֵלֶק טוֹב. קָשֶׁה לִשְׁמוֹעַ וּמָהִיר לְאַבֵּד זֶה חֵלֶק רָע:

5:13 There are four kinds of people who would give to charity. One wishes to give but [believes] that others should not. That one's eye is evil to those others. One [wishes that] others give and that he should not. His eye is evil toward himself. One [wishes that] he should give and so should others. That one is a saint. [The] one [who believes that he] should not give nor should others is a sinner.

הּ:יג אַרְבַּע מִדּוֹת בְּנוֹתְנֵי צְדָקָה. הָרוֹצֶה שֶׁיִּתֵּן וְלֹא יִתְּנוּ אֲחֵרִים עֵינוֹ רָעָה בְּשֶׁל אֲחֵרִים. יִתְּנוּ אֲחֵרִים וְהוּא לֹא יִתֵּן עֵינוֹ רָעָה בְּשֶׁלּוֹ. יִתֵּן וְיִתְּנוּ אֲחֵרִים חָסִיד. לֹא יִתֵּן וְלֹא יִתְּנוּ אֲחֵרִים רָשָׁע:

Give to charity. There is the implicit assumption that giving charity is a מִצְוָה *mitzvah*, an "obligation" that conveys merit. When one engages in that *mitzvah* and concurrently wishes that others do not implies a desire that other individuals not gain that merit attendant to giving צְדָקָה *tzedakah*. If one thinks that others should give but one should not give one's own, that individual rejects the obligation and its merit for oneself. When one reaches the level of belief that all should give, that individual is accepting the obligation of charity. When one contends that none should give, that individual totally rejects the obligation in principle.

5:14 There are four kinds of persons who would go to the house of study. One goes but does not practice. [This one] has the reward for going. One practices but does not go. [This one] gets the reward for practice. The one who goes and practices is a saint. The one who neither goes nor practices is a sinner.

הּיד אַרְבַּע מִדּוֹת בְּהוֹלְכֵי בֵית הַמִּדְרָשׁ. הוֹלֵךְ וְאֵינוֹ עוֹשֶׂה שְׂכַר הֲלִיכָה בְּיָדוֹ. עוֹשֶׂה וְאֵינוֹ הוֹלֵךְ שְׂכַר מַעֲשֶׂה בְּיָדוֹ. הוֹלֵךְ וְעוֹשֶׂה חָסִיד. לֹא הוֹלֵךְ וְלֹא עוֹשֶׂה רָשָׁע:

Study...practice. Rabbinic Judaism saw a connection between study and practice. In the fullness of its meaning, Torah stood for doctrine and behavior.

Rashi explains why the first does not practice. That person did not study. Instead, the individual merely listened to the studies of others. Rashi, therefore, feels that, had the first individual studied, he would also have practiced.

Maimonides, as a philosopher, presents a lesson on intellectual and ethical virtues. The person who has mastered both wisdom and practice will know that the mean is the goal to be followed. The person who moves beyond the mean to the good is called a saint. The person who moves beyond the mean toward evil is called a sinner. The person who has intellectual virtues but has moved from the mean toward evil is called a cunning sinner. If such a person has gone beyond the mere predisposition to do evil and has actually done something injurious to others, that individual is called an evil sinner. The person who has intellectual virtues but also has some ethical deficiencies will be called חָכָם לְהָרַע *chacham lehara*, a "wise man who does evil." The person who embodies all possible positive intellectual and ethical virtues is rarely found. As a matter of fact, philosophers think that the existence of such a person, while possible, is improbable. Maimonides would call such a person a "person of God" or an "angel of God."

Bartinoro suggests that the reason one might go to the *bet midrash* to study and still not practice is a result of the inability to understand what is being taught.

5:15 There are four kinds [of disciples] who sit before the sages: the sponge, the funnel, the strainer, and the sieve. The sponge soaks up everything. The funnel takes in at one end and pours out at the other. The strainer lets out the wine and keeps the dregs. The sieve lets out the flour [dust] and keeps the fine flour.

הּטו אַרְבַּע מִדּוֹת בְּיוֹשְׁבִים לִפְנֵי חֲכָמִים. סְפוֹג וּמַשְׁפֵּךְ מְשַׁמֶּרֶת וְנָפָה. סְפוֹג שֶׁהוּא סוֹפֵג אֶת הַכֹּל. וּמַשְׁפֵּךְ שֶׁמַּכְנִיס בְּזוֹ וּמוֹצִיא בְזוֹ. מְשַׁמֶּרֶת שֶׁמּוֹצִיאָה אֶת הַיַּיִן וְקוֹלֶטֶת אֶת הַשְּׁמָרִים וְנָפָה שֶׁמּוֹצִיאָה אֶת הַקֶּמַח וְקוֹלֶטֶת אֶת הַסֹּלֶת:

Four kinds. Anyone who has been a student or a teacher has encountered all four kinds of students.

Flour. Maimonides explains the somewhat problematic last line. While קֶמַח *kemach* is usually translated as "flour," following Maimonides, we translate it as "flour dust." Thus, it becomes clear as to how a sieve operates: It lets out the finer material while retaining what is coarse.

5:16 When love depends on something [beyond itself], when that something [beyond itself] disappears, that love disappears. However, when love does not depend on something [beyond itself], that love will never disappear. Which love depended on something [beyond itself]? The love between Amnon and Tamar. Which love did not depend on something [beyond itself]? The love of David and Jonathan.

יו כָּל אַהֲבָה שֶׁהִיא תְלוּיָה בְדָבָר בָּטֵל דָּבָר בְּטֵלָה אַהֲבָה. וְשֶׁאֵינָהּ תְּלוּיָה בְדָבָר אֵינָהּ בְּטֵלָה לְעוֹלָם. אֵיזוֹ הִיא אַהֲבָה שֶׁהִיא תְלוּיָה בְדָבָר זוֹ אַהֲבַת אַמְנוֹן וְתָמָר. וְשֶׁאֵינָהּ תְּלוּיָה בְדָבָר זוֹ אַהֲבַת דָּוִד וִיהוֹנָתָן:

The love between Amnon and Tamar. Amnon's love for his half-sister, Tamar, ended as soon as he had raped her. (Cf. II Sam. 13:14ff.)
For Bartinoro the love that Amnon had for Tamar was because of her beauty.

The love of David and Jonathan. For Bartinoro, this love was a fulfillment of God's design for the world since David was to become king of Israel. (Cf. I Sam. 18:1: "Jonathan loved David as his own soul.")

5:17 Any controversy that is for the sake of Heaven shall in the end be resolved. A controversy that is not for the sake of Heaven shall not be resolved. Which controversy was for the sake of Heaven? [The controversy] between Hillel and Shammai. Which controversy was not for the sake of Heaven? [The controversy] of Korach and his band.

יז כָּל מַחֲלֹקֶת שֶׁהִיא לְשֵׁם שָׁמַיִם סוֹפָהּ לְהִתְקַיֵּם וְשֶׁאֵינָהּ לְשֵׁם שָׁמַיִם אֵין סוֹפָהּ לְהִתְקַיֵּם. אֵיזוֹ הִיא מַחֲלֹקֶת שֶׁהִיא לְשֵׁם שָׁמַיִם זוֹ מַחֲלֹקֶת הִלֵּל וְשַׁמַּאי. וְשֶׁאֵינָהּ לְשֵׁם שָׁמַיִם זוֹ מַחֲלֹקֶת קֹרַח וְכָל עֲדָתוֹ:

Any controversy that is for the sake of Heaven. Maimonides believes that the difference in the outcomes of the controversies reflects the intent of those involved. Those who wish to instruct others, although they may differ, will be rewarded. Those who wish to cause others to sin will be punished.

Pirke Avot

Shall...be resolved. Bartinoro understands the term לְהִתְקַיֵּם *lehitkayem,* "to be established," which we have translated as "to be resolved," to refer to the participants rather than to the controversy. Hence Hillel and Shammai were granted long life while the lives of Korach and his band were snuffed out.

[The controversy] between Hillel and Shammai. Of the controversy between Hillel and Shammai, rabbinic tradition would say, "These and these are the words of the living God." (B. Talmud, *Eruvin* 13b)

5:18 No sin will occur through any individual who would bring people to righteousness. No repentance will be possible to any person who would cause the multitude to sin. Moses was meritorious and made the multitude meritorious. Their merit was attributed to him, as it says, "He executed the righteousness of *Adonai* and divine ordinances with Israel." [Deut. 33:21] Yaravam, the son of Nevat, sinned and caused the multitude to sin. The sin of the multitude is attributed to him, as it says, "For the sins of Yaravam that he sinned and caused Israel to sin." (I Kings 15:30)

הָיֶּח כָּל הַמְזַכֶּה אֶת הָרַבִּים אֵין חֵטְא בָּא עַל יָדוֹ וְכָל הַמַּחֲטִיא אֶת הָרַבִּים אֵין מַסְפִּיקִין בְּיָדוֹ לַעֲשׂוֹת תְּשׁוּבָה. מֹשֶׁה זָכָה וְזִכָּה אֶת הָרַבִּים זְכוּת הָרַבִּים תָּלוּי בּוֹ שֶׁנֶּאֱמַר צִדְקַת יְהֹוָה עָשָׂה וּמִשְׁפָּטָיו עִם יִשְׂרָאֵל. יָרְבְעָם בֶּן נְבָט חָטָא וְהֶחֱטִיא אֶת הָרַבִּים חֵטְא הָרַבִּים תָּלוּי בּוֹ שֶׁנֶּאֱמַר עַל חַטֹּאות יָרְבְעָם אֲשֶׁר חָטָא וַאֲשֶׁר הֶחֱטִיא אֶת יִשְׂרָאֵל:

Bring people to righteousness. Rashi reads the first line of this *mishnah* to underscore the relationship between student and teacher. It would be improper to forgive a sinner who repents but has led his students into sin.

Cause the multitude to sin. Again, Rashi focuses on the relationship between student and teacher. Protecting this relationship, Rashi argues that this arrangement might find the teacher in *Gan Eden* while the students are in *Gehinnom.* This teacher would not be given opportunity to repent. This does not make future study possible.

5:19 Whoever possesses the following three qualities is a disciple of Abraham our patriarch. Whoever possesses the following three [opposite] qualities is a disciple of Balaam the wicked. A good eye, a humble spirit, a restricted desire, [these belong] to the disciples of Abraham. An evil eye, a proud spirit, and an unrestricted desire [belong to] the disciples of Balaam the

הָיֶּט כָּל מִי שֶׁיֵּשׁ בּוֹ שְׁלֹשָׁה דְבָרִים הַלָּלוּ הוּא מִתַּלְמִידָיו שֶׁל אַבְרָהָם אָבִינוּ וּשְׁלֹשָׁה דְבָרִים אֲחֵרִים הוּא מִתַּלְמִידָיו שֶׁל בִּלְעָם הָרָשָׁע. עַיִן טוֹבָה וְרוּחַ נְמוּכָה וְנֶפֶשׁ שְׁפָלָה תַּלְמִידָיו שֶׁל אַבְרָהָם אָבִינוּ. עַיִן רָעָה וְרוּחַ גְּבוֹהָה וְנֶפֶשׁ רְחָבָה תַּלְמִידָיו שֶׁל בִּלְעָם הָרָשָׁע. מַה בֵּין תַּלְמִידָיו שֶׁל אַבְרָהָם אָבִינוּ לְתַלְמִידָיו שֶׁל בִּלְעָם הָרָשָׁע. תַּלְמִידָיו שֶׁל אַבְרָהָם אָבִינוּ אוֹכְלִין בָּעוֹלָם הַזֶּה וְנוֹחֲלִין הָעוֹלָם הַבָּא

86

wicked. What is the difference between the disciples of Abraham and the disciples of Balaam? The disciples of Abraham enjoy this world and will inherit the world to come, as it says, "That I may cause those who love Me to inherit substance and that I may fill their treasures." [Prov. 8:21] The disciples of Balaam the wicked will inherit *Gehinnom* and will go down into the pit of destruction, as it says, "But You, O God, will bring them down into the pit of destruction; bloodthirsty and deceitful people will not live out half their days." [Ps. 55:24]

שֶׁנֶּאֱמַר לְהַנְחִיל אֹהֲבַי יֵשׁ וְאוֹצְרוֹתֵיהֶם אֲמַלֵּא. אֲבָל תַּלְמִידָיו שֶׁל בִּלְעָם הָרָשָׁע יוֹרְשִׁין גֵּיהִנֹּם וְיוֹרְדִין לִבְאֵר שַׁחַת שֶׁנֶּאֱמַר וְאַתָּה אֱלֹהִים תּוֹרִדֵם לִבְאֵר שַׁחַת אַנְשֵׁי דָמִים וּמִרְמָה לֹא יֶחֱצוּ יְמֵיהֶם:

This *mishnah* may reflect a polemic against Christianity. Balaam is considered to be the leader of heathens, who, according to the rabbis, is equated with immorality and viciousness. (Cf. Num. 25:1-9; 31:16) For the rabbis, Balaam epitomizes evil and idolatry. In the Bible, when Balaam is asked by King Balak of Moab to issue curses against Israel, he instead delivers four prophecies. Balaam is unaware that his intention to curse Israel has been thwarted. While Balaam is mentioned by name in B. Talmud, *Sanhedrin* 106a, b, it is, most likely, Jesus whom the rabbis really meant. It was a common technique of the rabbis to set two kinds of masters and two kinds of disciples in opposition. One group represented the Jewish people; the other group reflected the emerging Judeo-Christians. Thus, by indicating the outcome of both groups, they warn against Judeo-Christianity.

A good eye. Rashi explains a "good eye" as one who lives without jealousy.

A restricted desire. Rashi takes נֶפֶשׁ שְׁפָלָה *nefesh shefalah*, here translated as "restricted desire," as a soul that monitors or humbles itself.

The disciples of Abraham. Maimonides finds biblical warrants in Abraham's life for the three virtues assumed of his disciples. (Gen. 14:23 ["restricted desire"]; 18:27 ["a humble spirit"]; 12:11 ["a good eye"]) In a like manner, Maimonides finds biblical warrants for the three vices in Balaam's life. (Deut. 23:5; Num. 31:16; 24:16)

5:20 Yehudah ben Tema used to say, "Be as strong as a leopard, as quick as an eagle, as fast as a deer, and as brave as a lion to do the will of your Parent in heaven." He used to say, "The shameless [will go] to *Gehinnom* and the shamefaced [will go] to *Gan Eden. Adonai* our God, may it be Your will that Your city will be speedily built in our days. Grant our portion in Your Torah."

ה:כ יְהוּדָה בֶן תֵּימָא אוֹמֵר הֱוֵי עַז כַּנָּמֵר וְקַל כַּנֶּשֶׁר רָץ כַּצְּבִי וְגִבּוֹר כָּאֲרִי לַעֲשׂוֹת רְצוֹן אָבִיךָ שֶׁבַּשָּׁמָיִם. הוּא הָיָה אוֹמֵר עַז פָּנִים לְגֵיהִנֹּם וּבֹשֶׁת פָּנִים לְגַן עֵדֶן. יְהִי רָצוֹן מִלְפָנֶיךָ יְהוָה אֱלֹהֵינוּ וֵאלֹהֵי אֲבוֹתֵינוּ שֶׁיִּבָּנֶה בֵּית הַמִּקְדָּשׁ בִּמְהֵרָה בְיָמֵינוּ וְתֵן חֶלְקֵנוּ בְּתוֹרָתֶךָ:

87

Yehudah ben Tema. Not mentioned elsewhere in the *Mishnah*, he is thought to have lived around the middle of the second century. He and his colleagues are mentioned in B. Talmud, *Hagigah* 4a as "masters of the *Mishnah*."

Adonai our God. It is possible that the prayer that ends ben Tema's *mishnah* is misplaced and should be at the end of this entire chapter. Instead, it was placed here next to ben Tema's teaching.

5:21   He used to say, "At five [one begins the study of] the Bible. At ten the *Mishnah*. At thirteen [one takes on] the [responsibility for] the *mitzvot*. At fifteen [one begins the study of] the Talmud. At eighteen [one is ready for] marriage. At twenty to pursue [a livelihood]. At thirty [one attains full] strength. At forty [one gains] understanding. At fifty [one gives] counsel. At sixty [one reaches] old age. At seventy [one reaches] the fullness of age. At eighty [one reaches] strong old age. At ninety [one is] bent. And, at one hundred, it is as if one had already died and passed from the world."

הכא הוּא הָיָה אוֹמֵר בֶּן חָמֵשׁ שָׁנִים לַמִּקְרָא בֶּן עֶשֶׂר שָׁנִים לַמִּשְׁנָה בֶּן שְׁלֹשׁ עֶשְׂרֵה לַמִּצְוֹת בֶּן חֲמֵשׁ עֶשְׂרֵה לַגְּמָרָא בֶּן שְׁמוֹנָה עֶשְׂרֵה לַחֻפָּה בֶּן עֶשְׂרִים לִרְדּוֹף בֶּן שְׁלֹשִׁים לַכֹּחַ בֶּן אַרְבָּעִים לַבִּינָה בֶּן חֲמִשִּׁים לְעֵצָה בֶּן שִׁשִּׁים לְזִקְנָה בֶּן שִׁבְעִים לְשֵׂיבָה בֶּן שְׁמוֹנִים לִגְבוּרָה בֶּן תִּשְׁעִים לָשׁוּחַ בֶּן מֵאָה כְּאִלּוּ מֵת וְעָבַר וּבָטֵל מִן הָעוֹלָם:

The numbers in this list have been determined in different ways. On the basis of Leviticus 19:23-25, Rashi and Bartinoro deduce the age when the child learns the *alef-bet* and begins the study of Torah. For Rashi, the age to begin the study of the *Mishnah* seems to result from the doubling of the age for the beginning of the study of the Bible. Thirteen is established according to Rashi's calculations from Levi's age when he and his brother Shimon prepared to avenge their sister's honor. (Cf. Gen. 34:25) Rashi tells us that the age of marriage at eighteen was deduced from the word אָדָם *adam*, primordial "man." It is used eighteen times from the beginning of the Torah until the creation of woman. (Cf. Gen. 2:23.)

Twenty as the age to begin pursuing a livelihood is suggested by the age of enlistment in the ancient army of Israel, as indicated in Numbers 1:3. Since the Levites began their service in the Tabernacle at the age of thirty, this must be the age of full strength. The Levites were responsible for carrying the sacred instruments of the Tabernacle. (Num. 4:47) They ceased their work at the age of fifty but still served in some capacity. (Num. 8:25-26) Thus, their service must have been counsel. Hence fifty is the age for such counsel.

Job 12:12 contains the uncommon word יְשִׁישִׁים *yeshishim*, "old people." The word could creatively be read יֵשׁ שִׁשִׁים *yesh shishim*, "there is sixty." Hence sixty is the demarcation of old age.

Psalms 90:10 contains the words "The days of our years are three-score years and ten, / Or even by reason of strength four-score years." From this we learn that the fullness of age comes at seventy and the strength of age at eighty.

5:22   Ben Bag Bag used to say, "Turn it, and turn it, for everything is in it. Reflect on it and grow old and gray with it. Don't turn from it, for nothing is better than it."

הּ:כב   בֶּן בַּג בַּג אוֹמֵר הֲפָךְ בָּהּ וַהֲפָךְ בָּהּ דְּכֹלָּא בָהּ וּבָהּ תֶּחֱזֵי וְסִיב וּבְלַה בָהּ וּמִנַּהּ לָא תָזוּעַ שֶׁאֵין לְךְ מִדָּה טוֹבָה הֵימֶנָּה:

[Yochanan] ben Bag Bag. Said to have been a disciple of Hillel, he apparently lived in the first century. His surname may be symbolic and really an acronym/abbreviation for *ben ger* ("son of a proselyte") and *bat ger* ("daughter of a proselyte"). A few other statements are reported in his name (e.g., B. Talmud, *Eruvin* 27b). Some identify ben Bag Bag as Yochanan ben Bag Bag, who was considered to be an expert in Torah. (Cf. *Tosefta Ketuvim* 5:1.) One tradition holds that both ben Bag Bag and ben Hei Hei (*Pirke Avot* 5:23) refer to the same person, the potential convert to Judaism who came to Hillel and asked our teacher to teach him the Torah on one foot.

According to Heller, since the comment is so important, it is given in Aramaic, a language widely understood at the time.

Turn it. The Torah.

Reflect on it. Unlike other reading, Torah is to be studied slowly. We read it over and over again, each time looking for new meaning in its nuances. This is a lifelong endeavor for as our life experiences change so does our perception of sacred text.

5:23   Ben Hei Hei said, "According to the difficulty is the reward."

הּ:כג   בֶּן הֵא הֵא אוֹמֵר לְפוּם צַעֲרָא אַגְרָא:

Ben Hei Hei is also said to have been a disciple of Hillel since questions addressed to Hillel are attributed to him. He would have lived in the first century. His name may also be symbolic. He was a proselyte, the son (בֶּן *ben*) of Abraham and Sarah to whose names the letter ה *hei* was added. As in the previous *mishnah*, his statement is also in Aramaic. ARN attributes both statements to Hillel.

Maimonides contends that this *mishnah* refers to study. He suggests that what is learned with ease is forgotten with ease. However, what is learned with difficulty is forgotten with difficulty.

Bartinoro expands on Maimonides' view. Bartinoro maintains that not only will the difficulty of Torah study be rewarded but so will the difficulty of the performance of the *mitzvot*.

The Generations of Adam to Noah

Many peoples have both creation and flood stories. While scholars cite Babylonian parallels for our own early biblical narratives, it is clear that the Torah versions include a different and significantly more profound moral ideal–one that is consistent with the ethical monotheism eventually identified as Judaism. While it is not important to know what specifically took place between the generations of Adam and Noah nor how many generations took their turn on earth, it is clear that the Torah comes to teach us that we have the potential to create or corrupt the earth through our lives and actions. Thus, God as Creator realized the divine responsibility of cleansing the earth, washing it free of the corruption that had polluted it. For us, it represents the positive possibility of human potential to begin anew. However, it also reminds us through the ever-present rainbow that such destruction will no longer be wrought by God–but we may indeed bring such destruction on ourselves.

At the Twilight of Creation

Since the rabbis accepted past miracles and the possibility of future ones, they sought to explain those things in the Torah that appeared to deviate from the natural order. Thus, according to Maimonides, they suggested that these things were part of original creation, yet with a kind of timer that would go off (and put the "miracle" into motion) at the time specified by the Torah text. These things that appear to the uninformed reader as "miracles," said the rabbis, were really all created at the twilight of creation, just as the sun began to set on the sixth day and God was prepared to rest on Shabbat. The rabbis viewed the account of creation, *maaseh bereshit*, as belonging to esoteric lore and encouraged their constituents to refrain from speculation.

The Sword Came into the World

While it is true that Judaism places a strong emphasis on the pursuit of peace, it is also true that, although there are Jews who preach pacifism, war is considered a just (if distasteful) option in some cases. The choice to go to war will always be difficult and limited by moral parameters, but it is considered a legitimate option and not only one of last resort. The tradition speaks of an obligatory war (*milchemet mitzvah* or *milchemet chovah*), which may be waged for one of three reasons: first, against the "seven nations" that inhabited Canaan; second, against Amalek, who attacked the weak and defenseless Israelites without provocation; and third, against an aggressor as an act of self-defense. Some rabbinic authorities even view a preemptive war as obligatory.

Idolatry, Sexual Impropriety, and Bloodshed

While Judaism stands firm on the attention an individual must pay toward the fulfillment of the *mitzvot*, Jewish law allows for the nonobservance of *mitzvot* when one's life is in danger, except in three cases: idolatry, sexual impropriety, and murder (literally, bloodshed). According to Jewish law, one must be prepared to die (and suffer martyrdom) rather than transgress any of the three. (Cf. B. Talmud, *Sanhedrin* 74a.)

Nor can one do any of these things to save another person's life. Neither can there be any justification for these acts on medical grounds. (Cf. Jerusalem Talmud, 14:4.) However, in the area of incest, there is some disagreement regarding whether the same law holds true for a woman (under duress) as for a man. In some cases, the rabbis even used the term idolatry as a metaphor for sexual impropriety (e.g., adultery).

Gehinnom or Gan Eden?

The Jewish version of "hell," *Gehinnom*, literally refers to a valley south of Jerusalem on one of the borders between the territories of Judah and Benjamin. (Cf. Josh. 15:8; 18:16.) During the time of the monarchy it was a site associated with a cult that burned children. Jeremiah condemned the practice. In the rabbinic period, the name is used to refer to the place of torment reserved for the wicked after death. It stand in contradistinction to *Gan Eden*, the "Garden of Eden," which, in rabbinic literature, became known as the place of reward for the righteous. In the Bible, these two names never connote the abode of souls after death. Yet, in rabbinic literature, such references abound: in *Pesachim* 54a, *Gehinnom* and *Gan Eden* existed even before the world was created; *Gehinnon* is at the left hand of God and *Gan Eden* at God's right in the *midrash* to Psalms 50:12.

The Importance of Debate in Judaism

All learning takes place in dialogue. While solitary study also has its place, the soul of rabbinic Judaism is found in the debate–typically associated with the academy. All opinions are given serious thought for everyone adds to the living notion of sacred literature. The give and take in the Talmud, generally referred to as *pilpul* (literally, "pepper"), actually gives flavor to rabbinic texts. Such struggle is necessary to ascertain the true meaning of any text.

GLEANINGS

"He withstood every test" (5:3)

THE MORAL GAP

We need a crash program of research in human moral learning. We need to find out a great deal more about how a human being can be taught to understand ethical truths, accept them, profit from one's own errors, and most important to learn from the accumulated moral wisdom of the race. If in two hundred years we can progress from a steam engine to an atomic engine, why in two thousand years can we not move from biblical literature to biblical living? The commercial world uses research extensively, how to package, how to market, etc. If subliminal suggestion can persuade people to buy more popcorn during the intermission, why in the name of Heaven can we not find ways of persuading them to seek the kingdom of God?

Now this does not mean communicating just the vocabulary of moral values. Too many of us suffer from the illusion that, if one knows what is right, he will do the right, that moral knowledge will result in moral action. But it is not so. In an examination on the Bible, a child will copy from his neighbor the commandment "You shall not steal." Repeating the Lord's Prayer every morning in public schools does not mean that the children will live by it all day. It is not moral knowledge we need so much as moral will.

We have plenty of moral know-how. We are like the farmer described in a story popular a decade ago. A country farm agent came to see a local farmer one day to urge his attendance at some lectures on better farming, better use of soil, fertilizer, seed, etc. The farmer said he was not coming and, when he was asked why, replied, "I'm not farming as good as I know how now!"

We aren't living as good as we know how now. The moral gap is not only a gap between principle and practice. As the Bible puts it, "These people draw near Me with their mouth, but their heart is far away."

(Robert I. Kahn, *May the Words of My Mouth*, Houston: Temple Emanu-El, 1984)

ROBERT I. KAHN (1910-   ). Rabbi emeritus of Temple Emanu-El in Houston and former president of the CCAR. An advocate of Reform Judaism, he is recognized as an outstanding orator and spokesperson.

"There are four kinds of [disciples]" (5:15)

SEAL THE TORAH IN THEIR HEARTS

It is not sufficient to immerse ourselves thoroughly in Torah and then share our insights and understanding with our students and congregants. The only way we can "seal the Torah in their hearts" is to be secure enough to involve our students in the process. We cannot allow them to sit passively at their desks or in the pews as they listen to our interpretations and analyses. We have to ask them to grapple actively with the sacred texts of our tradition in order to shape their sense of priorities and their direction in life. We, like Moses, cannot stand at the peak of the mountain and dispense the secrets of Torah to our followers, but rather we, like him, must struggle with our disciples to internalize the words of Torah, to imbibe its waters, thereby making the slow, arduous trek through the arid desert to the Promised Land.

If we succeed in this sacred task, if we fulfill Isaiah's charge to us to "bind the Torah to the hearts and minds of our followers," our students and our congregants, then we become, as Isaiah says, signs and models to be emulated by other Jews and other human beings. By internalizing the words of Torah, our actions will have an ultimate, redemptive effect upon the world and as the prophet subsequently emphasizes:

> The people that walked in darkness will have seen a great light; they that dwelt in the land of the shadow of death, upon them has the light shone.   (Isa. 9:1)

Restoration and triumph will be assured. Though we live in a context of violence and pain, and things look so hopeless, by seeing and understanding "the shining light (of Torah)," we will eventually experience the messianic.

(Norman J. Cohen, "Seal the Torah among His Disciples," New York: Hebrew Union College-Jewish Institute
of Religion, 1984)

NORMAN J. COHEN (1943-   ). Dean and professor of Midrash at HUC-JIR, New York. Known for his uncanny abilities as a teacher of text, he is able to communicate the profundity of sacred literature through the prism of his own soul.

"A good eye, a humble spirit" (5:19)

MY FAITH

My faith is supported by personal experience. I have learned to pray, and when I pray I can make an effort to adjust my life in harmony with the spirit of goodness. I *can* feel the revelation of God, even as my forebears could. I see the wonders of creation and the uniformity of the laws by which they hang together. I recognize the one mind of the God Creator. I see the marvels of harmony in natural colors and the harmony of sound in the songs of the birds. Again, I bring homage to God the Creator. I see goodness in my fellow human beings. I experience love; I recognize discoveries based upon the law of truth. I see works of art. I listen to sublime music–God, God everywhere! I hear within myself the voice of conscience bidding me seek to be good and just and merciful. I feel the stings of remorse when I lack courage, when I fail in obedience. My God remains within me when I would ignore God. I experience pain. But all this is so difficult. The existence of the perfect God, revealed in the Bible, and in the world, in the lives of others, and in my own soul, makes my own imperfections so overwhelming. I find it so hard to live up to my religion. Can it not be all a mistake, seeing it is so often beyond our attainment?

But how about love? Do you doubt its existence between parents and children, husband and wife, and friends, because it is sometimes absent when it should never fail? How about light? Do you doubt the existence of the sun because it is often hidden? Is there no truth in the world because falsehood is so inclined to vaunt itself? Have you never seen beauty? Ugliness exists, but beauty *must* prevail.

No, friends, I don't think we can be mistaken in the absolute and eternal God idea. When we have failed and uttered such incalculable absurdities, and acted with such unfathomable stupidity, our eyes and hearts were not sufficiently trained. We had not got far enough on the mountain of life to get the right perspective. The light was still shaded; our eyes were still weak. And, even today, this is our state–weak, imperfect, in definite and unquestionable need of guidance. It is through our mistakes that we can attain to God. But we must *dare* to struggle if we would attain. We must *use* our mistakes if we would climb nearer to truth. In God's light we see light, and away from God there is darkness now and evermore. God's light must grow more and more until we can reach the Perfect Day.

(Lily Montagu, "Can We Possibly Be Mistaken?" in Ellen M. Umansky, *Lily Montagu: Sermons, Addresses, Letters, and Prayers*, New York: Mellen Press, 1985)

LILY MONTAGU (1873-1963). A social worker and magistrate who pioneered Liberal Judaism in Britain. She conducted worship services and wrote on religious subjects. With Claude Montefiore, she established the Jewish Religious Union, which sponsored the Liberal Jewish Synagogue (in London), and the World Union for Progressive Judaism.

"Turn it, and turn it" (5:22)

ETHICS AND REVELATION

That man is free and moral is presupposed by all systems of law, human and divine, for law would be ineffective if subjects were not credited with moral freedom.

It is maintained in Scripture that this moral freedom is not acquired; it is innate, for Adam and Eve obeyed and disobeyed commands of God.

Reward or punishment as the consequence of obedience or disobedience is just only when the individual is addressed as a free moral agent. From the very beginning all nations considered it just to reward the obedient and to punish the disobedient. Scripture records a like attitude by God toward man himself. Man's moral freedom is recognized in all law, divine and human. Compulsory agencies coercing men to act contrary to law, divine or human, are contrary to the facts of human nature–therefore, without validity.

Responsibility is the necessary consequence of this freedom. Man is responsible for his commissions and omissions toward himself, toward his fellowmen, and toward God.

Conscience is undeliberate reason; it has the intuitive discernment that the right and the good are the right and the good and ought to be done and that the opposite of these ought to be shunned because they are wrong and evil. Conscious reason defines the right and good and their opposites. Conscience comprises the sense of duty, the satisfaction in its performance, and the regret in its violation. It is man's own tribunal, which calls him to account, approves or disapproves. The first fratricide in Scripture exclaimed, "My iniquity is too great to bear," and iniquity implies the effort to commit wrong and also the consciousness of wrong as a crime.

Man is a member of society; his doings and omissions concern society as much and more than they concern himself; he is accountable to society. The human family is part of God's creation; the individual and society are equally accountable to the Creator. God's laws preserve this world, and every violation of these laws of society is an attempt to destroy it. The right and good preserve whatever wrong and evil destroy.

That which is right and good in commission or omission may be called moral, and the opposite of these is immoral. All men, however, are moral by nature.

The immoral by nature is an abnormality, or it is the product of corruption. This is scriptural doctrine. Adam and Eve did not violate God's commandment of their own free will; it was the persuasion of the serpent beguiling Eve that led Adam to transgression.

Morality is a system of definitions as to the right and the good and their opposites. They are the product of reason and are, therefore, capable of instruction. The child, although moral by birth, is unconscious of morality, and it becomes consciously moral in the same progressive manner as it becomes intelligent. Morality conditions the existence of society and the life of the individual within it; it must accordingly be taught effectually. Consisting of rules of action, it ought to be taught by practice till each rule or law becomes lodged in the consciousness and becomes a habit. This, however, is impossible for the teacher in a limited sphere of influence, and it is the office of the religious educator to establish what is the moral duty of man.

It is the duty of everyone to get to know himself, for self-consciousness is the supreme fact of life; to know what are his relations and his duties to his fellowman and to his Maker. This self-knowledge embraces the recognition of our faults and shortcomings and the desire to overcome them. This is moral self-training. An earnest person must strive to become wiser and better with every passing day. The daily improvements shall grow virtuous habit. This is self-culture.

He that knows himself, his relations and duties to his fellowman and to his Maker, and has overcome the faults and shortcomings of his nature is, in the language of Scripture, holy. Holiness is the highest degree of moral life. In a holy person virtue has become constant.

The contents of the science of morality consist in definitions of what is right and good and what is otherwise. Morality will always have to be inculcated for the majority in every generation is immature, and their reason is not adequately developed.

When a definition of a moral fact has obtained the consent of the best of men, it becomes a moral law; and, when it has obtained the consent of a community, it becomes public law. Such moral laws and public laws constitute the foundation of ethics.

But this is the weak feature of ethics. There exists no fixed and final authority for moral or public law. "The consent of the best class of men" or "the consent of a community or of the majority in it" are indefinite conceptions. In the early days of humanity, definitions of morality were accepted as facts of superhuman reason, as revelations, as messages of inspired men. This gave them recognizable authority. Revelation is the only authority of ethics now, as it was then; every other basis is inadequate for the superstructure.

We acknowledge but one revelation as genuine: the Torah. It is the paramount duty of conscientious Israelites to learn from the Torah to know ourselves, our relations and duties to our fellowmen and to our Maker, and to teach these constantly and diligently. If, understanding our own, and comparing it impartially with ethics constructed upon another basis, we should find ours inferior, we are obligated to learn the better from others. But, if ours is proven to be superior, the duty would devolve upon us to teach that. This is the plan of the investigation that we would urge.

(Isaac Mayer Wise, *Life and Selected Writings*, Cincinnati: Robert Clarke Co., 1900)

ISAAC MAYER WISE (1819-1900). Architect of the Reform movement in America. He founded the UAHC, HUC-JIR, and the CCAR to support the establishment of a Judaism that would meet the needs of modernity while still being faithful to the traditions of Judaism.

"According to the difficulty" (5:23)

THE COVENANT: ITS PURPOSE

What is the purpose of the covenant? Many fragmentary answers have been given in the trimillennial and variegated history of Judaism, and perhaps only this much of a generalization is possible–that, located between Creation and Redemption, a Jew testifies to the reality of the first and the hope for the second. This testimony has a positive and a negative aspect. The positive is the possibility, unheard of prior to the advent of Judaism, of a mutual relation between a God beyond the heaven of heavens and man on earth. The negative is against all the false gods–against idolatry.

Of the two the second testimony is the more urgent. The *Tanach* belittles atheism for only "the fool has said in his heart, there is no God." (Ps. 14:1; 53:1) The fear of idolatry, however, is so pervasive that the Book cannot be understood without it. The most fearful case of idolatry mentioned is that of Mesha, the king of Moab, who "took his oldest son that should have reigned in his stead and offered him for a burnt-offering upon the wall." (II Kings 3:27) Idolatrous child sacrifice is condemned with horror throughout the *Tanach*, most eloquently so by the prophet Micah, who goes on to declare that the true service of the true God consists of doing justly, loving mercy, and walking humbly with God. (Mic. 6:6-8) A seemingly strange *midrash* asserts that Micah's reference to child sacrifice is only apparently a condemnation of what such as Mesha did, and it is in reality a praise of what Abraham was prepared to do but, at the last moment, was stopped from doing–sacrifice Isaac as God had commanded. But how can the intention be praiseworthy when the execution must be shrunk from with horror? Another *midrash* supplies the answer. When Abraham ascended Mount Moriah, intending to follow God's command, all the nations of the world watched. And, when they saw what Abraham was prepared to do, they abandoned all their idols. But, alas, they soon forgot their great resolve and returned to their former ways.

The first part of the last cited *midrash* indicates the rock-bottom purpose of the divine-Jewish covenant; its last part, that this purpose is not accomplished and over and done with but rather remains indispensable until the end of days. What is that rock-bottom purpose? "Who is a Jew?" a *midrash* asks. "One who testifies against the idols."

(Emil Fackenheim, *What Is Judaism?* New York: Simon and Schuster, Inc., 1987)

EMIL FACKENHEIM (1916-   ). A religious existentialist. This rabbi and theologian grapples with the notion of revelation, stating that a religious concern for living presupposes the assertion that revelation actually happened. Israel's relationship with God is central to his thinking. His philosophical concerns include the dilemmas of liberal Judaism and authority and religious responsibility to the social order.

CHAPTER SIX

Whoever Studies the Torah for Its Own Sake Merits Many Things

The sages taught [the following] in the style of the *Mishnah*. Blessed be the One who chose them and their teaching.

שָׁנוּ חֲכָמִים בִּלְשׁוֹן הַמִּשְׁנָה בָּרוּךְ שֶׁבָּחַר בָּהֶם וּבְמִשְׁנָתָם:

6:1 Rabbi Meir said, "Whoever studies the Torah for its own sake merits many things. Indeed the entire world is rendered worthy for this one's sake. This one is called friend, beloved, one who loves God, one who loves humankind, one who pleases God, and one who pleases humankind. [The Torah] clothes this person in humility and reverence and prepares the person to be righteous and pious, upright, and trustworthy. It keeps the individual far from sin and brings this person near to merit. From this person others gain counsel and wisdom, understanding and strength, as it says, 'Counsel and wisdom are mine [the Torah's]. I am understanding. Strength is mine.' [Prov. 8:14] It gives the individual sovereignty and dominion and the ability to judge. To this person the secrets of the Torah are revealed so that this person becomes like an ever-flowing spring, like a river that never dries up. This person becomes modest and patient and forgiving of insults. [The Torah] makes this person great and raises this person above all things."

א:ו רַבִּי מֵאִיר אוֹמֵר כָּל הָעוֹסֵק בַּתּוֹרָה לִשְׁמָהּ זוֹכֶה לִדְבָרִים הַרְבֵּה וְלֹא עוֹד אֶלָּא שֶׁכָּל הָעוֹלָם כֻּלּוֹ כְּדַאי הוּא לוֹ נִקְרָא רֵעַ אָהוּב אוֹהֵב אֶת הַמָּקוֹם אוֹהֵב אֶת הַבְּרִיּוֹת מְשַׂמֵּחַ אֶת הַמָּקוֹם מְשַׂמֵּחַ אֶת הַבְּרִיּוֹת וּמַלְבַּשְׁתּוֹ עֲנָוָה וְיִרְאָה וּמַכְשַׁרְתּוֹ לִהְיוֹת צַדִּיק חָסִיד יָשָׁר וְנֶאֱמָן וּמְרַחַקְתּוֹ מִן הַחֵטְא וּמְקָרַבְתּוֹ לִידֵי זְכוּת וְנֶהֱנִין מִמֶּנּוּ עֵצָה וְתוּשִׁיָּה בִּינָה וּגְבוּרָה שֶׁנֶּאֱמַר לִי עֵצָה וְתוּשִׁיָּה אֲנִי בִינָה לִי גְבוּרָה. וְנוֹתֶנֶת לוֹ מַלְכוּת וּמֶמְשָׁלָה וְחִקּוּר דִּין וּמְגַלִּין לוֹ רָזֵי תוֹרָה וְנַעֲשָׂה כְּמַעְיָן הַמִּתְגַּבֵּר וּכְנָהָר שֶׁאֵינוֹ פוֹסֵק וְהֹוֶה צָנוּעַ וְאֶרֶךְ רוּחַ וּמוֹחֵל עַל עֶלְבּוֹנוֹ וּמְגַדַּלְתּוֹ וּמְרוֹמַמְתּוֹ עַל כָּל הַמַּעֲשִׂים:

Chapter Six is really a part of neither the *Mishnah* in general nor of the Tractate *Pirke Avot* in particular. It is called a *baraita*: a collection of sayings not included in the *Mishnah*. The word *baraita* means "external," "outside," or "extraneous matter." It is sometimes called *tosefta* (literally, an "addition" to the *Mishnah*). The introductory remark indicates that, while this is not part of the *Mishnah*, it is taught in mishnaic style and is offered in praise of God, who selected the sages as teachers of the *Mishnah*.

When the custom developed of reading a chapter of *Pirke Avot* on the Sabbaths between Pesach and Shavuot, the rabbis wanted to provide readings for the sixth Sabbath. This chapter was compiled to meet that need. As a result, it has its own name; in reality, it has two names. Since the subject matter of the chapter praises Torah, it is called קִנְיַן תּוֹרָה *Kinyan Torah*, the "Acquisition of the Torah." And, since the first teacher cited in this chapter is Rabbi Meir, it is also called *Perek de-Rabbi Meir*, the "Chapter of Rabbi Meir" (or the "*Baraita* of Rabbi Meir"). Maimonides and Bartinoro did not comment on this chapter since it was not included in the *Mishnah*. However, Rashi did comment on this chapter.

Blessed be the One. While it is generally assumed to refer to God, some suggest that "the one" refers either to the individual who studies or the person who chose this particular chapter to study.

6:2 Rabbi Yehoshua ben Levi would say, "Every day a heavenly voice proceeds from Mount Chorev and proclaims, 'Woe to all humans because of their contempt for the Torah!' One who does not occupy oneself with the Torah is called a reprobate, as it says, 'As a gold ring in a swine's snout, so is a beautiful woman without sense.' [Prov. 11:22] Another verse says, 'And the tablets were the work of God and the writing was the writing of God, which was engraved on the tablets.' [Exod. 32:16] Don't read 'engraved' [*charut*] but rather [read] 'freedom' [*cherut*], for only the individual who is engaged in the study of the Torah is [truly] free. That person who is engaged in the regular study of Torah is exalted as it says, 'And from Mattanah to Nachaliel and from Nachaliel to Bamot.'" [Num. 21:19]

וב אָמַר רַבִּי יְהוֹשֻׁעַ בֶּן לֵוִי בְּכָל יוֹם וָיוֹם בַּת קוֹל יוֹצֵאת מֵהַר חוֹרֵב וּמַכְרֶזֶת וְאוֹמֶרֶת אוֹי לָהֶם לַבְּרִיּוֹת מֵעֶלְבּוֹנָהּ שֶׁל תּוֹרָה. שֶׁכָּל מִי שֶׁאֵינוֹ עוֹסֵק בַּתּוֹרָה נִקְרָא נָזוּף שֶׁנֶּאֱמַר נֶזֶם זָהָב בְּאַף חֲזִיר אִשָּׁה יָפָה וְסָרַת טָעַם. וְאוֹמֵר וְהַלֻּחֹת מַעֲשֵׂה אֱלֹהִים הֵמָּה וְהַמִּכְתָּב מִכְתַּב אֱלֹהִים הוּא חָרוּת עַל הַלֻּחֹת. אַל תִּקְרָא חָרוּת אֶלָּא חֵרוּת שֶׁאֵין לְךָ בֶּן חוֹרִין אֶלָּא מִי שֶׁעוֹסֵק בְּתַלְמוּד תּוֹרָה וְכָל מִי שֶׁעוֹסֵק בְּתַלְמוּד תּוֹרָה הֲרֵי זֶה מִתְעַלֶּה שֶׁנֶּאֱמַר וּמִמַּתָּנָה נַחֲלִיאֵל וּמִנַּחֲלִיאֵל בָּמוֹת:

This passage demonstrates three techniques of wordplay in rabbinic interpretation: *notarikon* (generally translated as a kind of shorthand), which is the use of the letters of a verse to convey a meaning not indicated by the words; the use of the consonants of words with different vowels to suggest something not originally conveyed by the words; and the reading of meaning into proper nouns.

The first technique is utilized in defining a נָזוּף *nazuf*, here translated as "reprobate," the one who will not study the Torah. On the basis of the first letters of two words and the last letter of one of the verse in Proverbs 11:22: נֶזֶם זָהָב בְּאַף *Nezem Zahav beaF* [N,Z,F], the rabbis built this word. The second technique is presented in the reading of חֵרוּת *cherut*, "freedom," for חָרוּת *charut*, "engraved." In the third example, the rabbis took the word "Mattanah," a place name, to stand for the word מַתָּנָה *mattanah*, "gift"; "Nachaliel," another place name, to be a compound of נַחֲלָה *nachalah*, "inheritance," and אֵל *El*, "God"; and the place name "Bamot" to stand for בָּמוֹת *bamot*, "high places." It is clear that such methods of interpretation move far beyond the literal meaning of the text. In many such cases, the biblical text has simply become a springboard for the interpreter's message. Even as rabbinic Judaism followed such methods of interpretation, it also taught that אֵין מִקְרָא יוֹצֵא מִידֵי פְּשׁוּטוֹ *ein mikra yotzei midei peshuto*, "no biblical text loses its literal meaning." (B. Talmud, *Shabbat* 63a)

Rabbi Yehoshua ben Levi. Rabbi Yehoshua was of the first generation of the *amoraim*, those scholars whose comments on the *Mishnah* form the *Gemara* (literally, "completion"). (The *Mishnah* and *Gemara* together form the Talmud.) Rabbi Yehoshua lived in Palestine in the middle of the third century. He was a leading exponent of *aggadah*.

A heavenly voice. בַּת קוֹל [*bat kol*]. In the rabbinic mind, this was a kind of substitute for prophecy. (Cf. B. Talmud, *Yoma* 9b.) Mount Chorev is another name for Mount Sinai. It may refer to the still small voice heard by Elijah in the wilderness of Mount Chorev. (Cf. I Kings 19:12.)

Contempt for the Torah. This contempt is shown by a lack of study.

Reprobate. Rashi explains the *nazuf* as one who has been punished in the first stage in a series of stages of being banned. For the rabbis, the beautiful woman without discretion and the swine with a golden ring are images of incongruency. So, too, is a scholar who will not study.

6:3 Whoever learns from another, one chapter or one law or one verse or one word or even one letter, is bound to accord the teacher honor. We learn this from King David who learned only two things from Achitophel but called him teacher, companion, and friend, as it says, "You are my equal, my companion, and my familiar friend." [Ps. 55:14] There is certainly an inference to be drawn. If David, king of

ו:ג הַלּוֹמֵד מֵחֲבֵרוֹ פֶּרֶק אֶחָד אוֹ הֲלָכָה אַחַת אוֹ פָּסוּק אֶחָד אוֹ דִבּוּר אֶחָד אוֹ אֲפִלּוּ אוֹת אַחַת צָרִיךְ לִנְהָג בּוֹ כָּבוֹד שֶׁכֵּן מָצִינוּ בְּדָוִד מֶלֶךְ יִשְׂרָאֵל שֶׁלֹּא לָמַד מֵאֲחִיתֹפֶל אֶלָּא שְׁנֵי דְבָרִים בִּלְבָד קְרָאוֹ רַבּוֹ אַלּוּפוֹ וּמְיֻדָּעוֹ שֶׁנֶּאֱמַר וְאַתָּה אֱנוֹשׁ כְּעֶרְכִּי אַלּוּפִי וּמְיֻדָּעִי. וַהֲלֹא דְבָרִים קַל וָחֹמֶר וּמַה דָּוִד מֶלֶךְ יִשְׂרָאֵל שֶׁלֹּא לָמַד מֵאֲחִיתֹפֶל אֶלָּא שְׁנֵי דְבָרִים בִּלְבָד קְרָאוֹ רַבּוֹ אַלּוּפוֹ וּמְיֻדָּעוֹ הַלּוֹמֵד מֵחֲבֵרוֹ פֶּרֶק אֶחָד אוֹ הֲלָכָה אַחַת אוֹ פָּסוּק אֶחָד אוֹ דִבּוּר אֶחָד אוֹ אֲפִלּוּ אוֹת

Israel, learned only two things from Achitophel and regarded him as his teacher, companion, and friend, how much the more should one who learns a chapter, a law, a verse, a word, or even a letter from another accord that other [person such] honor. Honor can only mean Torah as it says, "The wise shall inherit honor" [Prov. 3:35] [and] "The perfect shall inherit good." [Prov. 28:10] *Good* means *Torah* as it says, "I give you good doctrine, do not forsake My Torah." [Prov. 4:2]

אַחַת עַל אַחַת כַּמָּה וְכַמָּה שֶׁצָּרִיךְ לִנְהֹג בּוֹ כָּבוֹד וְאֵין כָּבוֹד אֶלָּא תוֹרָה שֶׁנֶּאֱמַר כָּבוֹד חֲכָמִים יִנְחָלוּ וּתְמִימִים יִנְחֲלוּ טוֹב וְאֵין טוֹב אֶלָּא תוֹרָה שֶׁנֶּאֱמַר כִּי לֶקַח טוֹב נָתַתִּי לָכֶם תּוֹרָתִי אַל תַּעֲזֹבוּ׃

One chapter. This is a reference to a single subject rather than to chapters in which the Bible is currently divided.

Achitophel. Achitophel of the Judean town of Gilah was an "advisor" to King David. (Cf. II Sam. 15:12; I Chron. 27:33-34.) He was the only one of David's inner circle who joined Avshalom in his revolt against his father. (Cf. II Sam. 15:12.) According to B. Talmud, *Kallah Rabbati* 8:100, David learned two things from Achitophel: to study with a companion and to go to prayer with humility.

A letter. The learning of a letter refers to the question of spelling a particular word with an *alef* or an *ayin*, both "soundless" letters. It is possible through a simple emendation that שְׁנֵי דְבָרִים *shenei devarim*, "two things," becomes שֶׁנִּדְבָּרִים *shenidevarim*, "who conversed together." This reasoning suggests an alternative interpretation: If King David showed honor to one from whom he had learned nothing but with whom he had merely conversed, how much more is it one's obligation to show honor to a colleague from whom one has learned Torah.

Good means Torah. The last part of this *baraita* includes a kind of rabbinic logic where a=b, b=c, and a=c. Since the wise equal the perfect and honor equals good, it will follow that the wise who inherit the honor, which is equivalent to the good, will also inherit the Torah, which is equivalent to the good.

6:4 This is the way of the [study] of the Torah: you will eat bread with salt. You will drink water by measure, you will endure a life of privation. [All] while you labor in the Torah. If you do this, "Happy shall you be and good will be yours." [Ps. 128:2] Happy shall you be in this world and good will be yours in the world to come. Don't seek greatness for yourself and don't covet glory. More than you've learned, do! Don't han-

ו:ד כַּךְ הִיא דַרְכָּהּ שֶׁל תּוֹרָה פַּת בְּמֶלַח תֹּאכַל וּמַיִם בִּמְשׂוּרָה תִּשְׁתֶּה וְעַל הָאָרֶץ תִּישָׁן וְחַיֵּי צַעַר תִּחְיֶה וּבַתּוֹרָה אַתָּה עָמֵל אִם אַתָּה עֹשֶׂה כֵּן אַשְׁרֶיךָ וְטוֹב לָךְ אַשְׁרֶיךָ בָּעוֹלָם הַזֶּה וְטוֹב לָךְ לָעוֹלָם הַבָּא. אַל תְּבַקֵּשׁ גְּדֻלָּה לְעַצְמְךָ וְאַל תַּחְמֹד כָּבוֹד יוֹתֵר מִלִּמּוּדֶךָ עֲשֵׂה וְאַל תִּתְאַוֶּה לְשֻׁלְחָנָם שֶׁל שָׂרִים שֶׁשֻּׁלְחָנְךָ גָּדוֹל מִשֻּׁלְחָנָם וְכִתְרְךָ גָּדוֹל מִכִּתְרָם וְנֶאֱמָן הוּא בַּעַל מְלַאכְתְּךָ שֶׁיְּשַׁלֶּם לָךְ שְׂכַר פְּעֻלָּתֶךָ׃

ker after the tables of kings for your table
is greater than theirs. Your crown is grander
than theirs. [Only] your Employer can be
depended on to pay you the reward of your
labor.

Rashi understands this *baraita* as an injunction for the poor not to forsake the study of
Torah by using poverty as an excuse. He does not see it as advice for the wealthy to give
up their wealth as a condition for study.

You will drink. A quotation from Ezekiel 4:11.

6:5 [The requirements for] the Torah are
greater than those for the priesthood or for
royalty. Royalty is acquired by thirty qualities and the priesthood by twenty-four. The
Torah [on the other hand] is acquired by
forty-eight: study; careful listening; vocal
repetition; insight; mental acuity; awe; reverence; humility; joy; service to the sages;
association with fellow students; arguing
with the disciples; self-control; [the knowledge of] the Bible and the *Mishnah*; moderation in business, in sleep, in speech, in
pleasure, in laughter, in worldly affairs; by
being patient; by having a good heart; by
having trust in the sages; and by the acceptance of suffering.

ו:ה גְּדוֹלָה תוֹרָה יוֹתֵר מִן הַכְּהֻנָּה וּמִן הַמַּלְכוּת
שֶׁהַמַּלְכוּת נִקְנֵית בִּשְׁלֹשִׁים מַעֲלוֹת וְהַכְּהֻנָּה נִקְנֵית
בְּעֶשְׂרִים וְאַרְבַּע וְהַתּוֹרָה נִקְנֵית בְּאַרְבָּעִים וּשְׁמוֹנָה
דְבָרִים. וְאֵלּוּ הֵן בְּתַלְמוּד בִּשְׁמִיעַת הָאֹזֶן בַּעֲרִיכַת
שְׂפָתַיִם בְּבִינַת הַלֵּב בְּאֵימָה בְּיִרְאָה בַּעֲנָוָה בְּשִׂמְחָה
בְּטָהֳרָה בְּשִׁמּוּשׁ חֲכָמִים בְּדִקְדּוּק חֲבֵרִים בְּפִלְפּוּל
הַתַּלְמִידִים בְּיִשּׁוּב בְּמִקְרָא בְּמִשְׁנָה בְּמִעוּט סְחוֹרָה
בְּמִעוּט דֶּרֶךְ אֶרֶץ בְּמִעוּט תַּעֲנוּג בְּמִעוּט שֵׁנָה
בְּמִעוּט שִׂיחָה בְּמִעוּט שְׂחוֹק בְּאֶרֶךְ אַפַּיִם בְּלֵב טוֹב
בֶּאֱמוּנַת חֲכָמִים בְּקַבָּלַת הַיִּסּוּרִין:

Variant texts of this *baraita* contain the list of required items in different order. This is a
comparison between status that is hereditary (i.e., priesthood and royalty) and status that
is earned. The status of a scholar (based on learning alone) promotes the notion that the
crown of the Torah is greater than the crown of either the priest or the king. At the time
this text was written, there was neither a functioning priesthood nor a functioning king-
ship in the Jewish community. Nevertheless, Torah study became a means of democratiza-
tion. Only a certain lineage could aspire to be king of Israel and only the individual of a
particular group lineage could be a priest, but anyone could become a scholar.

Rashi refers the reader to I Samuel 8 for a list of the qualities required of a king. He
directly relates twenty-four qualities of the priest to the twenty-four kinds of offerings to
which a priest is entitled.

Service to the sages. Rabbi Yochanan said in the name of Rabbi Shimon bar Yochai, "It is
even better to minister to the teacher of the Law than to study it." (B. Talmud, *Berachot* 7b)

A *baraita* states, "Others say, 'If one has studied Torah and *Mishnah* but has not served the sages, that one is [still] an *am haaretz*.'" (*Berachot* 47b)

6:6 [Knowledge of Torah is acquired by] the one who knows one's place, who rejoices in one's portion, who sets a limit to one's words, who claims no credit for oneself, who is beloved, who loves God, who loves people, who loves justice, who loves reproof, who loves equity, who distances oneself from glory, who does not arrogantly show off learning, who does not enjoy judging, who bears the yoke with one's colleague, who judges the colleague favorably, [even while] directing that person to truth and peace, the one whose study has calmed the mind, who asks and answers, who listens and adds, who studies in order to teach and who studies in order to practice, who makes one's teacher wiser, who reports exactly what has been learned, and who quotes a teaching in the name of the one who said it. Behold you have learned that who reports something in the name of the one who said it brings redemption into the world as it says, "And Esther said in the name of Mordecai." [Esther 2:22]

ו:ו הַמַּכִּיר אֶת מְקוֹמוֹ וְהַשָּׂמֵחַ בְּחֶלְקוֹ וְהָעוֹשֶׂה סְיָג לִדְבָרָיו וְאֵינוֹ מַחֲזִיק טוֹבָה לְעַצְמוֹ אָהוּב אוֹהֵב אֶת הַמָּקוֹם אוֹהֵב אֶת הַבְּרִיּוֹת אוֹהֵב אֶת הַצְּדָקוֹת אוֹהֵב אֶת הַמֵּישָׁרִים אוֹהֵב אֶת הַתּוֹכָחוֹת וּמִתְרַחֵק מִן הַכָּבוֹד וְלֹא מֵגִיס לִבּוֹ בְּתַלְמוּדוֹ וְאֵינוֹ שָׂמֵחַ בְּהוֹרָאָה נוֹשֵׂא בְעוֹל עִם חֲבֵרוֹ וּמַכְרִיעוֹ לְכַף זְכוּת וּמַעֲמִידוֹ עַל הָאֱמֶת וּמַעֲמִידוֹ עַל הַשָּׁלוֹם וּמִתְיַשֵּׁב לִבּוֹ בְּתַלְמוּדוֹ שׁוֹאֵל וּמֵשִׁיב שׁוֹמֵעַ וּמוֹסִיף הַלּוֹמֵד עַל מְנָת לְלַמֵּד וְהַלּוֹמֵד עַל מְנָת לַעֲשׂוֹת הַמַּחְכִּים אֶת רַבּוֹ וְהַמְכַוֵּן אֶת שְׁמוּעָתוֹ וְהָאוֹמֵר דָּבָר בְּשֵׁם אוֹמְרוֹ הָא לָמַדְתָּ כָּל הָאוֹמֵר דָּבָר בְּשֵׁם אוֹמְרוֹ מֵבִיא גְאֻלָּה לָעוֹלָם שֶׁנֶּאֱמַר וַתֹּאמֶר אֶסְתֵּר לַמֶּלֶךְ בְּשֵׁם מָרְדֳּכָי:

Some texts join this *baraita* to the previous one. Other texts have a slight variation in the enumeration of the items under consideration. If one reflects on this passage, it should be clear that Jewish learning previously depended on the memorization of material transmitted orally and received aurally.

Who makes one's teacher wiser. That the teacher might say as did Rabbi Chanina, "I have learned much from my teachers. I have learned more from my colleagues than from my teachers. But I have learned more from my students than from all of them." (B. Talmud, *Taanit*, 7a)

6:7 Great is the Torah because it gives life to those who perform it in this world and in the next as it says, "For they are life to them that find them, and healing to all their flesh." [Prov. 4:22] And it says, "It shall be health to your navel and marrow to your

ו:ז גְּדוֹלָה תוֹרָה שֶׁהִיא נוֹתֶנֶת חַיִּים לְעוֹשֶׂיהָ בָּעוֹלָם הַזֶּה וּבָעוֹלָם הַבָּא שֶׁנֶּאֱמַר כִּי חַיִּים הֵם לְמוֹצְאֵיהֶם וּלְכָל בְּשָׂרוֹ מַרְפֵּא: וְאוֹמֵר רִפְאוּת תְּהִי לְשָׁרֶּךָ וְשִׁקּוּי לְעַצְמוֹתֶיךָ: וְאוֹמֵר עֵץ חַיִּים הִיא לַמַּחֲזִיקִים בָּהּ וְתוֹמְכֶיהָ מְאֻשָּׁר: וְאוֹמֵר כִּי לִוְיַת חֵן הֵם לְרֹאשֶׁךָ

bones." [Prov. 3:8] And it says, "It is a tree of life to all who hold fast to it and all its supporters are happy." [Prov. 3:18] And it also says, "They are a chaplet of grace for your head and chains around your neck." [Prov. 1:9] And it says, "It shall give you a chaplet of grace; a crown of glory shall it give you." [Prov. 4:9] And it says, "By me your days will be multiplied and the years of your life increased." [Prov. 9:11] And it says, "Length of days is in her right hand; riches and honor are in her left hand." [Prov. 3:16] And it says, "For length of days and years of life and peace shall be added to you." [Prov. 3:2]

וַעֲנָקִים לְגַרְגְּרֹתֶיךָ: וְאוֹמֵר תִּתֵּן לְרֹאשְׁךָ לִוְיַת חֵן עֲטֶרֶת תִּפְאֶרֶת תְּמַגְּנֶךָּ: וְאוֹמֵר כִּי בִי יִרְבּוּ יָמֶיךָ וְיוֹסִיפוּ לְךָ שְׁנוֹת חַיִּים: וְאוֹמֵר אֹרֶךְ יָמִים בִּימִינָהּ בִּשְׂמֹאולָהּ עֹשֶׁר וְכָבוֹד: וְאוֹמֵר כִּי אֹרֶךְ יָמִים וּשְׁנוֹת חַיִּים וְשָׁלוֹם יוֹסִיפוּ לָךְ: וְאוֹמֵר דְּרָכֶיהָ דַרְכֵי נֹעַם וְכָל נְתִיבוֹתֶיהָ שָׁלוֹם:

The texts from Proverbs are in praise of wisdom; the rabbis interpret wisdom as referring to Torah. The piling up of verses from Proverbs in praise of wisdom is thus converted to a praise of Torah.

For the rabbis, as we have seen, the study of Torah promised providence in this life and eternity in the next.

6:8 Rabbi Shimon ben Menasya said in the name of Rabbi Shimon bar Yochai, "Beauty, strength, wealth, honor, wisdom, old age, gray hair [advanced age], and children befit the righteous and befit the world, as it says, 'Gray hair is a crown of glory; in the way of righteousness, it may be found.'" [Prov. 16:31] Another verse says, "Wealth is the crown of the wise." [Prov. 14:24] Still another verse says, "Grandchildren are the crown of the old while their parents are the glory of children." [Prov. 17:6] Yet another verse says, "Strength is the glory of the young while gray hair is the beauty of the old." [Prov. 20:29] A final verse says, "The moon will be confounded and the sun ashamed, for *Adonai Tzevaot* will reign on Mount Zion and in Jerusalem. And before God's elders will be glory." [Isa. 24:23] Rabbi Shimon ben Menasya said, "These seven qualities that the sages attributed to the righteous were all realized in Rabbi [Yehudah Ha-Nasi] and his sons."

ו:ח רַבִּי שִׁמְעוֹן בֶּן מְנַסְיָא מִשּׁוּם רַבִּי שִׁמְעוֹן בֶּן יוֹחָאִי אוֹמֵר הַנּוֹי וְהַכֹּחַ וְהָעֹשֶׁר וְהַכָּבוֹד וְהַחָכְמָה וְהַזִּקְנָה וְהַשֵּׂיבָה וְהַבָּנִים נָאֶה לַצַּדִּיקִים וְנָאֶה לָעוֹלָם שֶׁנֶּאֱמַר עֲטֶרֶת תִּפְאֶרֶת שֵׂיבָה בְּדֶרֶךְ צְדָקָה תִּמָּצֵא: וְאוֹמֵר עֲטֶרֶת זְקֵנִים בְּנֵי בָנִים וְתִפְאֶרֶת בָּנִים אֲבוֹתָם: וְאוֹמֵר תִּפְאֶרֶת בַּחוּרִים כֹּחָם וַהֲדַר זְקֵנִים שֵׂיבָה: וְאוֹמֵר וְחָפְרָה הַלְּבָנָה וּבוֹשָׁה הַחַמָּה כִּי מָלַךְ יְהוָה צְבָאוֹת בְּהַר צִיּוֹן וּבִירוּשָׁלַ‍ִם וְנֶגֶד זְקֵנָיו כָּבוֹד: רַבִּי שִׁמְעוֹן בֶּן מְנַסְיָא אוֹמֵר אֵלּוּ שֶׁבַע מִדּוֹת שֶׁמָּנוּ חֲכָמִים לַצַּדִּיקִים כֻּלָּם נִתְקַיְּמוּ בְּרַבִּי וּבְבָנָיו:

Some texts name the first Rabbi Shimon of this *mishnah* as Shimon ben Yehudah, a disciple of Rabbi Shimon bar Yochai, who lived toward the end of the second century.

Rabbi Shimon ben Menasya. A contemporary of Rabbi Yehudah Ha-Nasi, he lived at the end of the second century and in the early third century. His statements are usually found in the *baraitot*, often disagreeing with the *mishnah* or supplementing it. A student of Rabbi Meir, he fixed the *halachah* according to a view more strict than that of the rabbis who preceded him.

Rabbi Shimon bar Yochai. A disciple of Rabbi Akiva, he lived in the middle of the second century. He fled Roman persecution to live in a cave, where he is said to have composed the *Zohar*.

Wisdom. The Vilna Gaon does not include wisdom on the list because it is not included in the biblical quotation. Later in this text only seven are listed; adding wisdom would make it eight. Likewise, the Palestinian Talmud does not include old age.

Adonai Tzevaot. Often translated as "Lord of hosts," it reflects a notion that God is my Army. As a result, the Israelites carried the tablets in the front of the processional that led them to war–part of the portable מִשְׁכָּן *mishkan*. In the rabbinic period, the notion that God's spirit provides strength to the Jewish people was introduced in this context.

And his sons. Rabbi Yehudah Ha-Nasi appointed his son Gamliel as patriarch and his other son Shimon to be *chacham*. (B. Talmud, *Ketubot* 103b)

6:9 Rabbi Yose ben Kisma said, "Once I was traveling and a man met me and greeted me. When I returned his greeting, he said to me, 'Rabbi, where do you come from?' I replied, 'From a great city of sages and scholars.' He then said, 'Rabbi, would you be willing to live with us in our place? [If you would] I would give you a million golden dinars along with precious stones and pearls!' I said to him, 'Were you to give me all the silver and gold and precious stones and pearls in the world, I would live only in a place of Torah!' Thus it is written in the Book of Psalms by the hand of David, king of Israel, 'The Torah of your mouth is better to me than thousands of gold and silver.' [Ps. 119:72] Not only that, but, at the moment of a person's departure

ט: אָמַר רַבִּי יוֹסֵי בֶּן קִסְמָא פַּעַם אַחַת הָיִיתִי מְהַלֵּךְ בַּדֶּרֶךְ וּפָגַע בִּי אָדָם אֶחָד וְנָתַן לִי שָׁלוֹם וְהֶחֱזַרְתִּי לוֹ שָׁלוֹם. אָמַר לִי רַבִּי מֵאֵיזֶה מָקוֹם אָתָּה. אָמַרְתִּי לוֹ מֵעִיר גְּדוֹלָה שֶׁל חֲכָמִים וְשֶׁל סוֹפְרִים אֲנִי. אָמַר לִי רַבִּי רְצוֹנְךָ שֶׁתָּדוּר עִמָּנוּ בִּמְקוֹמֵנוּ וַאֲנִי אֶתֵּן לְךָ אֶלֶף אֲלָפִים דִּינְרֵי זָהָב וַאֲבָנִים טוֹבוֹת וּמַרְגָּלִיּוֹת. אָמַרְתִּי לוֹ אִם אַתָּה נוֹתֵן לִי כָּל כֶּסֶף וְזָהָב וַאֲבָנִים טוֹבוֹת וּמַרְגָּלִיּוֹת שֶׁבָּעוֹלָם אֵינִי דָר אֶלָּא בִּמְקוֹם תּוֹרָה וְכֵן כָּתוּב בְּסֵפֶר תְּהִלִּים עַל יְדֵי דָוִד מֶלֶךְ יִשְׂרָאֵל טוֹב לִי תוֹרַת פִּיךָ מֵאַלְפֵי זָהָב וָכָסֶף. וְלֹא עוֹד אֶלָּא שֶׁבִּשְׁעַת פְּטִירָתוֹ שֶׁל אָדָם אֵין מְלַוִּין לוֹ לְאָדָם לֹא כֶסֶף וְלֹא זָהָב וְלֹא אֲבָנִים טוֹבוֹת וּמַרְגָּלִיּוֹת אֶלָּא תוֹרָה וּמַעֲשִׂים טוֹבִים בִּלְבָד. שֶׁנֶּאֱמַר בְּהִתְהַלֶּכְךָ תַּנְחֶה אֹתָךְ בְּשָׁכְבְּךָ תִּשְׁמֹר עָלֶיךָ וַהֲקִיצוֹתָ הִיא תְשִׂיחֶךָ. בְּהִתְהַלֶּכְךָ תַּנְחֶה אֹתָךְ

[from this world], neither silver nor gold nor precious stones nor pearls accompany the individual, only Torah and good deeds, as it says, 'When you walk, it will guide you; when you lie down, it will watch over you; and when you awake, it will speak to you.' [Prov. 6:22] 'When you walk, it will guide you'-in this world. 'When you lie down, it will watch over you'-in the grave. 'And when you awake, it will speak to you'-in the world to come. Moreover, it [another verse] says, 'Silver and gold are Mine, says *Adonai Tzevaot*.'" [*Hag.* 2:8]

בָּעוֹלָם הַזֶּה. בְּשָׁכְבְּךָ תִּשְׁמוֹר עָלֶיךָ בַּקֶּבֶר. וַהֲקִיצוֹתָ הִיא תְשִׂיחֶךָ לָעוֹלָם הַבָּא: וְאוֹמֵר לִי הַכֶּסֶף וְלִי הַזָּהָב נְאֻם יְהֹוָה צְבָאוֹת:

Rabbi Yose ben Kisma. A contemporary of Rabbi Chananya ben Teradyon, Rabbi Yose lived at the beginning of the second century. Because he counseled against the Bar Kochba revolt, he remained undisturbed during the Roman persecution. This is the only personal experience related in all of *Pirke Avot* except perhaps 1:17.

6:10 The Holy One of Blessing marked out five things as divine possessions. They are: the Torah, heaven and earth, Abraham, Israel, and the Temple. How do we know this about the Torah? Because it says, "*Adonai* possessed me in the beginning of the way, before the works of old." [Prov. 8:22] How do we know this about the heaven and earth? Because it says, "The heaven is My throne and the earth is My footstool; what kind of house will you build for Me and what place will be My rest?" [Isa. 66:1] And it says, "*Adonai*, how numerous are Your works! In wisdom You have made them all. The earth is full of Your riches." [Ps. 104:24] How do we know this about Abraham? Because it says, "And God blessed him and said, 'Blessed be Abram of God most high, Possessor of heaven and earth.'" [Gen. 14:19] How do we know this of Israel? Because it says, "Until Your people pass over, *Adonai*, until the people pass over what You have acquired." [Exod. 15:16] And another verse says, "Unto the saints,

וֹ: חֲמִשָּׁה קִנְיָנִים קָנָה הַקָּדוֹשׁ בָּרוּךְ הוּא בְּעוֹלָמוֹ וְאֵלּוּ הֵן. תּוֹרָה קִנְיָן אֶחָד. שָׁמַיִם וָאָרֶץ קִנְיָן אֶחָד. אַבְרָהָם קִנְיָן אֶחָד. יִשְׂרָאֵל קִנְיָן אֶחָד. בֵּית הַמִּקְדָּשׁ קִנְיָן אֶחָד: תּוֹרָה מִנַּיִן דִּכְתִיב יְהֹוָה קָנָנִי רֵאשִׁית דַּרְכּוֹ קֶדֶם מִפְעָלָיו מֵאָז: שָׁמַיִם וָאָרֶץ מִנַּיִן דִּכְתִיב כֹּה אָמַר יְהֹוָה הַשָּׁמַיִם כִּסְאִי וְהָאָרֶץ הֲדֹם רַגְלָי אֵי זֶה בַיִת אֲשֶׁר תִּבְנוּ לִי וְאֵי זֶה מָקוֹם מְנוּחָתִי: וְאוֹמֵר מָה רַבּוּ מַעֲשֶׂיךָ יְהֹוָה כֻּלָּם בְּחָכְמָה עָשִׂיתָ מָלְאָה הָאָרֶץ קִנְיָנֶךָ: אַבְרָהָם מִנַּיִן דִּכְתִיב וַיְבָרְכֵהוּ וַיֹּאמַר בָּרוּךְ אַבְרָם לְאֵל עֶלְיוֹן קוֹנֵה שָׁמַיִם וָאָרֶץ: יִשְׂרָאֵל מִנַּיִן דִּכְתִיב עַד יַעֲבוֹר עַמְּךָ יְהֹוָה עַד יַעֲבוֹר עַם זוּ קָנִיתָ: וְאוֹמֵר לִקְדוֹשִׁים אֲשֶׁר בָּאָרֶץ הֵמָּה וְאַדִּירֵי כָּל חֶפְצִי בָם: בֵּית הַמִּקְדָּשׁ מִנַּיִן דִּכְתִיב מָכוֹן לְשִׁבְתְּךָ פָּעַלְתָּ יְהֹוָה מִקְּדָשׁ יְהֹוָה כּוֹנְנוּ יָדֶיךָ: וְאוֹמֵר וַיְבִיאֵם אֶל גְּבוּל קָדְשׁוֹ הַר זֶה קָנְתָה יְמִינוֹ:

which are on the earth, and the excellent
in whom is My delight." [Ps. 16:3] How do
we know this of the Temple? Because it
says, "The place, *Adonai*, which You have
made for You to dwell in. The sanctuary,
Adonai, which Your hands have established." [Exod. 15:17] Another verse says,
"And God brought them to the border of
the sanctuary, to this mountain, which
God's right hand had acquired." [Ps. 78:54]

In this brief text, the rabbis present the essential claims of rabbinic Judaism. The world
was created by God. The Torah is the plan of creation. The people of Israel are the students of the Torah. Abraham is the progenitor of the Jewish people. The Temple is the
focus of Jewish piety. These are all special concerns and the possessions of God.

One might think that, since this *baraita* begins with a kind of numerical formula, it
belongs in chapter five. It is included here because Torah is considered one of the special
possessions.

Saints [literally, holy ones]. This refers to Israelites who have become sanctified by receiving
Torah.

6:11 Whatever the Holy One of Blessing created
in the world, God did only for God's own
glory, as it says, "Everything that is created
for My name, I have created for My glory.
I have formed it; indeed, I have made it."
[Isa. 43:7] And another verse says, "*Adonai*
will reign forever and ever." [Exod. 15:18]

וּיא כָּל מַה שֶּׁבָּרָא הַקָּדוֹשׁ בָּרוּךְ הוּא בְּעוֹלָמוֹ לֹא בְרָאוֹ
אֶלָּא לִכְבוֹדוֹ שֶׁנֶּאֱמַר כֹּל הַנִּקְרָא בִשְׁמִי וְלִכְבוֹדִי
בְּרָאתִיו יְצַרְתִּיו אַף עֲשִׂיתִיו: וְאוֹמֵר יְהֹוָה יִמְלֹךְ
לְעוֹלָם וָעֶד:

This statement is a fitting coda on a chapter in praise of those who study Torah. Through
this act of study, they praise God. It reflects the conclusion of the worship service at the
end of the עָלֵינוּ *Alenu* (before *Kaddish*), which the reading of *Pirke Avot* directly precedes
(in a traditional milieu). In some manuscripts, as well as in early editions of *Pirke Avot*,
there are other endings (either here or at the end of chapter five). (Cf. 1:18.) A fitting
alternative, often used, opens with a saying of Meir, "When Rabbi Meir concluded the
reading of the Book of Job, he said, 'It is the destiny of human beings to die and of cattle
to be slaughtered [for food], and all are doomed to death. Happy is the individual who
was raised on Torah and who works at Torah, who by his life causes spiritual joy to our
Maker, who advances with a good reputation and leaves this world with a good name.'"

Wisdom Literature

This term applies to specific biblical books (Proverbs, Job, Ecclesiastes, and specific verses in Psalms) and some apocryphal works (Ben Sira, Wisdom of Solomon, IV Maccabees). Wisdom is a central feature of this literature, but it also refers to wisdom learned through a fear of God and a knowledge of the *mitzvot* rather than a philosophically abstract concept of wisdom. The application of this wisdom leads to a good life. On the other hand, "the wisdom of God" is described as the sum total of divine characteristics on which rest both moral and physical world order.

The Divine Voice

The heavenly or divine voice that revealed the will of God to humankind is referred to as the *bat kol*. (*Avot* 6:2) According to the rabbis, the *bat kol* (literally, daughter of the voice or a feminine sound of some sort) was already heard in the biblical period. (Cf. B. Talmud, *Makkot* 23b.) In this reference to the classic story of Solomon's wisdom and the dispute of two women who claim to be the mother of a particular child (cf. I Kings 3:27), a *bat kol* determined the outcome.

When the period of prophecy ended, the *bat kol* served as the means of communication between God and human beings. Usually, the *bat kol* was considered an external voice, but the rabbis report that it was sometimes heard in dreams. (Cf. B. Talmud, *Hagigah* 14b.) It was cited in two places in Talmud, *Eruvin* 13b: disputing whether the *halachah* is according to Bet (the house of) Shammai or according to Bet (the house of) Hillel; and disputing whether a certain kind of oven can be considered clean or unclean. However, the authority of the *bat kol* was rejected by Rabbi Yehoshua who claimed that Torah is not in heaven. (*Baba Metzia* 59b) This is a remarkable assertion of independence of human reasoning. Later, the rabbis accepted Rabbi Yehoshua's view (*Baba Metzia* 59b) and allowed the *bat kol* to function only in controversies between Hillel and Shammai. (*Eruvin* 13b)

Mount Sinai

Mount Sinai, on which the Torah was revealed, referred to by various names in the Bible, is also called Mount Chorev, derived from the root (חרב *ch r v*) for "dryness." Some contend that these two terms refer to different mountains or perhaps to a peak (*chorev*) in the (Sinai) mountain range. Both terms are used interchangeably in Jewish tradition. It has become the central place of theophany in Jewish historical experience.

GLEANINGS

"That person who is engaged in the regular study of Torah is exalted" (6:2)

THE FUNCTION OF EDUCATION

The first function of education, therefore, is to teach man to think intensively, to think critically, and to think imaginatively; to endow his mental life as far as possible with the power of concentration, with canons of judgment, and with the urge to adventure in the undiscovered continents of truth. But this is not the whole of education. Education for efficiency is only one-half of education. Education that stops with efficiency may prove the greatest menace to man and to society. The most dangerous criminal may be the man who is plentifully endowed with the gifts of concentration, reason, and imagination but with no morals. Perhaps the most dangerous epochs in civilization are those in which the mind of the race has outdistanced its spirit, in which the increased power of the race, made available through new discoveries and inventions, is not harnessed and guided by an equally increased ethical purpose and by higher consecrations.

Intelligence is not enough. Intelligence plus character—that is the goal of true education. To integrate human life around central, focusing ideals and to supply the motive power as well as the technique for attaining these ideals—that is the highest effort of education. The complete education gives us not only power of concentration but worthy objectives upon which to concentrate; not only a critical faculty for precise judgment but also profound sympathies with which to temper the asperity of our judgments; not only a quickened imagination but also an enkindling enthusiasm for the objects of our imagination. It is not enough to know truth. We must love truth and sacrifice for it. It is not enough to be quick of perception. We must be quick to respond to the appeal of human loyalties. Our lives need much more than a precise, eager, and powerful intellect. They need not only knowledge, which is power, but wisdom, which is control. They need not only truth, which is light, but goodness, which is warmth. They need love and loyalties and the lift of aspirations. They need charm and dignity and a splendid restraint. They need quietness and peace and kindly human contacts. The broad education will, therefore, transmit to us, not only the accumulated knowledge of the race, but also the accumulated experience of social living. It will translate truth into a way of life. It will educate us for the good life.

(Abba Hillel Silver, *Religion in a Changing World*, New York: Richard R. Smith, 1930)

ABBA HILLEL SILVER (1893-1963). One of the leading rabbis of his time. Together with Stephen S. Wise, he was among the confidants of Franklin D. Roosevelt, trying to make him aware of the Nazi "Final Solution." A great orator and great thinker, a leader of the Zionist movement, he was rabbi of The Temple, Tifereth Israel, Cleveland, Ohio.

"The Torah [on the other hand] is acquired by forty-eight [qualities]" (6:5)

MEMORY

The other main pillar of the Jewish religion is remembering. It is the telling and retelling each year of stories of the past. The history of the Jews is kept alive in its religious forms, the Exodus from Egypt, the stay in Babylon, the giving of the commandments at Sinai, the destruction of the Temples. Jewish religious schools all teach Jewish history and in doing so create Jewish nationhood. Jewish children know the story of the Spanish Inquisition and the condition of the Jews in modern Russia. Jewish schools tell the tale of the sufferings of the Wandering Jew, who, according to Christian myth, is wandering because he mocked Christ and, according to the historical fact, because Christians have not truly accepted the teachings of their Christ. "Remember this"; "Remember that." The past is a part of every Jewish child's experience, not for just the holidays but all through the year. "It is done as it was done," and "It is said as it was said." Jewish secular law and Jewish religious practices are all based on referrals to tractates and commentaries of other centuries. This makes Jews continually the witnesses of their own past and gives the odd flavor to their reasonings–as if history were happening in both the vertical and the horizontal time line, as if things moved forward and stayed still at the same time.

(Anne Roiphe, *Generation without Memory*, New York: Simon and Schuster, 1981)

ANNE ROIPHE (1935-   ). A contemporary novelist who has written several provocative and profound fictional and nonfictional pieces that challenge the very foundation of American Judaism.

"Great is the Torah because it gives life to those who perform it" (6:7)

THE SPIRITUAL JOURNEY

Judaism has many legends of people who go on spiritual journeys, who through accident or by design are blessed or cursed to look upon the Garden. And all of the stories, in one way or another, have a surprising conclusion. The visitor is given a choice. The searcher who has just arrived is rewarded with the final question: "And now that you have survived and beheld these wonders, do you choose to remain here with 'us' or will you return to your spouse and children?" Whereupon, the visitor is invariably devastated. "Oh, my God! I forgot all about them! They must be worried sick! Are they all right?" So you must make a choice. Which will it be: those ordinary people who did not understand and perhaps may never understand, yet by whose nurture and struggle you have lived to attain this blessed moment; or worldless bliss here with spiritual beings who are beyond such humanity?

And here is the twist: If the searcher chooses to remain with eternity, the searcher loses eternity! If the searcher chooses this finite world, the searcher is rewarded with eternity! This is expressed in a slightly different way by the saying that the pious are not in Paradise, Paradise is in the pious.

(Lawrence Kushner, *The River of Light: Spirituality, Judaism, and Consciousness*, Woodstock, Vermont: Jewish Lights Publishing, 1990)

LAWRENCE KUSHNER (1943-   ). Reform rabbi at Temple Beth El in Sudbury, Massachusetts. He is a driving force behind mystical spiritual renewal in Reform Judaism.

"I would live only in a place of Torah" (6:9)

THE REPAIR OF THE WORLD

As we start where we are, addressing ourselves to particular constituencies and particular needs for healing or repair, we slowly build the institutions and communities that can begin to bring the future into being. As we create communities that can nourish and sustain us; as we work to transform the institutions that most deeply affect us; as we enact and celebrate together moments of commitment, clarity, and vision, we generate energy for further change that is rooted in what we have already envisioned and accomplished. Remembering women's history, writing new *midrashim*, empowers us to create more inclusive communities and prods us to challenge all the institutions of the Jewish community to perpetuate and live out of a richer Jewish memory. Creating new, diverse, and egalitarian communities leads us to a new understanding of divinity, which in turn calls us to draw the circle of community ever wider and wider. Expanding the circle of community vivifies the erotic bonds of community, which in turn leads us to reclaim a suppressed part of Jewish history and also reminds us of our responsibilities toward others. Just as structures of domination support one another, so do our efforts at justice. The sum of the changes that we seek eludes us as a total system because those working for change have less power than the complex and entrenched institutions of hierarchical power that dominate our world. But lured on by the ground already attained and by the Ground of that ground that empowers us, we remember the words of *Mishnah Avot* 2:16: "It is not incumbent upon us to finish the task, but neither are we free to desist from it altogether." As we work toward the creation of a feminist Judaism as part of a larger struggle toward a more just world, we place our small piece in a mosaic that will finally provide a new pattern–a new religious and social order.

(Judith Plaskow, *Standing Again at Sinai*, New York: Harper and Row, 1990)

JUDITH PLASKOW. Contemporary feminist theologian and associate professor of Religious Studies at Manhattan College. She has presented a feminist reconstruction of Judaism.

Index

Authors of the Gleanings

Baeck, Leo 17, 53
Bamberger, Bernard 33
Borowitz, Eugene B. 33

Cohen, Norman J. 92

Eisendrath, Maurice 32

Fackenheim, Emil 96
Feldman, Abraham J. 74
Freehof, Solomon 16

Geiger, Abraham 16, 54
Guttmann, Alexander 35

Hahn, Hugo 74

Kahn, Robert I. 92
Kushner, Lawrence 53, 109

Leibman, Joshua Loth 34, 72

Montagu, Lily 93
Moses, Adolph 75

Plaskow, Judith 15, 54, 110

Rivkin, Ellis 15
Roiphe, Anne 108

Silver, Abba Hillel 73, 108

Wise, Isaac Mayer 94

General Subjects and Themes

Accountability 36, 46, 47, 68
Afterlife (world to come) 13, 22, 29, 30, 43, 56, 65, 66, 68, 100, 102, 103, 105
Age, and youth 44, 67, 68, 71, 88, 103
Anger 26, 66, 83
Apikoros (nonbeliever) 29

Bat kol (a heavenly voice) 98, 99, 107

Cardinal sins: idolatry, sexual impropriety, bloodshed 81, 91
Charity 22, 30, 83
Community, 19, 20, 21, 58
Controversy, Hillel vs. Shammai; Korach vs. his men 85, 86

Deeds, good 3, 42, 47, 105
Derech eretz (path or way of life) 18, 19, 47
Destiny, human 68, 69

Disciples, 1, 23, 84, 86, 87

Ethics 33, 34, 35, 92, 94
Evil 5, 34

Fear, of God 3, 85
Fear, of sin 42
Fence against sin (fence around the Torah) 1, 12, 44
Foreknowledge, divine 46
Forgetfulness 41
Freedom of Choice 46, 52

Gan Eden 69, 87, 91
Gehinnom 4, 87, 91
God, human beings in image of 45
God, synonyms for 38, 49
Goodness vs. evil, Abraham vs. Balaam 86, 87

Index

Honor 18, 26, 56, 60, 63, 99, 100, 103
Hospitality 4
Humility 36, 58, 61, 97

Inclinations, good and evil 25, 26, 27, 31, 56, 68, 86

Judgment 1, 5, 6, 12, 14, 20, 21, 46, 60, 61, 68
Justice, divine 46, 68, 69

Kindness 2
Knowledge 47

Life stages 88
Love, divine 63, 77, 102, 105, 106
        human 45, 85
        of Torah 45, 102, 105

Mitzvot 10, 49, 57, 62, 88

Name, good 22, 63
Neglect of Torah 61
Numbers, use and significance of 37, 38, 39, 40, 50, pp. 76-88, 105

Peace 8, 9, 12, 22, 90
Pestilence 81
Prayer 28, 32
Profanation of God's name 58, 81
Punishment 18, 62, 65, 76, 81

Repentance 26, 27, 31, 62, 86

Responsibility 29, 30
Retribution 5, 6
Reverence, for God 3, 61, 63, 97
Reverence, for Torah 60
Reward 18, 19, 37, 57, 76, 89, 65

Self-denial 18, 19
Selfishness 68, 82
Service of God 3
Sin 18, 19, 57, 69, 81, 86, 62
Solitude 38, 39
Study 5, 9, 16, 18, 19, 29, 40, 54, 58, 67, 70, 83, 84, 97, 98, 100

Temple worship 2, 13, 78, 105, 106
Temptation 21
Tithing 11, 44, 81, 82
Torah (*passim,* and) 2, 8, 9, 10, 15, 16, 54, 59, 60, 61, 62, 64, 89, 92, 97, 98, 100, 101, 102, 103, 104, 105, 106, 107
Tradition 3, 4, 5, 6, 7, 8, 44
Truth 12

Universalism 8
Utterance, divine 76

Wisdom 22, 42, 44, 47, 56, 80, 103, 107
Work 7, 19

Yoke 39, 50
Youth, and age 67, 68, 103
Zugot 4, 5, 6, 7, 8

The Sages of Pirke Avot
Pre-Tannaitic (ca. 200 B.C.E. – 10 C.E.)

Akavya b. Mahalalel 36
Antigonos of Socho 3
Avtalyon 7, 8
Ben Bag Bag, Yochanan 89
Ben Hei Hei 89
Hillel the Elder 8, 9, 10, 20, 21, 22, 23, 58, 59

Joshua b. Perachyah 5
Judah b. Tabbai 6
Nittai of Arbel 5
Shammai the Elder 8, 10, 23
Shemayah 7
Shimon b. Shetach 6
Simon the Righteous (Simeon the Just) 2, 3

112

Yose b. Yochanan of Jerusalem 4
Yose b. Yoezer of Zeredah 4

First Generation (ca. 10-80 c.e.)

Chanina, deputy of the priests 36
Gamliel the Elder (Gamliel I), Rabban 11
School of Hillel 59, 86
School of Shammai 59, 86

Shimon b. Gamliel (I), Rabban 11, 12
Yochanan b. Zakkai 23, 24, 25, 31

Second Generation (ca. 80-120 c.e.)

Chalafta b. Dosa of Kefar Chananya 39
Chanina b. Dosa 42
Dosa b. Harkinas 42
Elazar b. Arach 23, 24, 25, 29
Elazar b. Azaryah 47
Eliezer b. Horkenos 23, 24, 25, 26

Nechunya b. Hakanah 39
Shimon b. Netanel 23, 24, 25, 28
Shmuel Ha-Katan 67
Tzadok 58
Yehoshua b. Chananya 23, 24, 25, 27
Yose Ha-Kohen 23, 24, 25

Third Generation (ca. 120-140 c.e.)

Akiva 44, 45, 46, 47, 51
Ben Azzai, Shimon 57
Ben Zoma, Shimon 56
Chananya b. Akashya XIV
Chananya b. Teradyon 36
Chanina b. Chachinai 38
Elazar b. Chisma 48
Elazar b. Yehudah of Bartota 40

Elazar of Modin 43
Elisha b. Abuyah 67
Levitas of Yavneh 58
Matya b. Charash 65
Tarfon 29, 30
Yishmael b. Elisha 44, 60, 61
Yochanan b. Beroka 58
Yose b. Kisma 104

Fourth Generation (c.a. 140-165 c.e.)

Abba Shaul 24
Chalafta b. Dosa of Kefar Chananyah 39
Elazar b. Shammua 63
Eliezer b. Yaakov II 62
Meir 41, 61, 64, 70, 97
Shimon b. Yochai 37, 63, 64, 103

Yaakov b. Korshai 40, 65, 66
Yehudah b. Ilai 63, 64
Yishmael b. Yochanan b. Beroka 58, 59
Yochanan Ha-Sandelar 62
Yonatan 61
Yose b. Chalafta 27, 60

Fifth Generation (c.a. 165 – 200 c.e.)

Dostai b. Yannai 41
Elazar Ha-Kappar 68
Nehorai 64
Shimon b. Elazar 66
Shimon b. Menasya 103

Yehudah b. Tema 87, 88
Yehudah Ha-Nasi 18, 67
Yishmael b. Yose b. Chalafta 60, 61
Yose b. Yehudah of Kefar Ha-Bavli 67

Sixth Generation (c.a. 200 – 220 c.e.)

Gamliel III, Rabban 19, 20

Post-Tannaitic Generation (c.a. 240 c.e.)

Yannai 65
Yehoshua b. Levi 98